TOWARDS ETHICAL POLICING

KEY THEMES IN POLICING

Series summary: This textbook series is designed to fill a growing need for titles which reflect the importance of incorporating 'evidence-based policing' within Higher Education curriculums. It will reflect upon the changing landscape of contemporary policing as it becomes more politicised, professionalised and scrutinised, and draw out both changes and continuities in its themes.

Series Editors: Megan O'Neill, University of Dundee, Marisa Silvestri, University of Kent and Stephen Tong, Canterbury Christ Church University

Forthcoming
Practical Psychology for Policing – Jason Roach, January 2021

Published
Critical Perspectives on Police Leadership – Claire Davis and Marisa Silvestri, March 2020

Police Occupational Culture: Research and Practice – Tom Cockcroft, March 2020

Policing the Police: Challenges of Democracy and Accountability – Michael Rowe, February 2020

Miscarriages of Justice: Causes, Consequences and Remedies – Sam Poyser, Angus Nurse and Rebecca Milne, May 2018

Key Challenges in Criminal Investigation – Martin O'Neill, February 2018

Plural Policing: Theory and Practice – Colin Rogers, November 2016

Understanding Police Intelligence Work – Adrian James, April 2016

Editorial advisory board
Paul Quinton, College of Policing
Nick Fyfe, University of Dundee
Jennifer Brown, London School of Economics
Charlotte E. Gill, George Mason University

TOWARDS ETHICAL POLICING

Dominic A. Wood

First published in Great Britain in 2020 by

Policy Press
University of Bristol
1-9 Old Park Hill
Bristol
BS2 8BB
UK
t: +44 (0)117 954 5940
pp-info@bristol.ac.uk
www.policypress.co.uk

North America office:
Policy Press
c/o The University of Chicago Press
1427 East 60th Street
Chicago, IL 60637, USA
t: +1 773 702 7700
f: +1 773-702-9756
sales@press.uchicago.edu
www.press.uchicago.edu

British Library Cataloguing in Publication Data
A catalogue record for this book is available from the British Library

Library of Congress Cataloging-in-Publication Data
A catalog record for this book has been requested

978-1-4473-4558-9 hardback
978-1-4473-4559-6 paperback
978-1-4473-4561-9 ePub
978-1-4473-4560-2 ePDF

Cover design by Andrew Corbett
Front cover image: istock
Printed and bound in Great Britain by CMP, Poole
Policy Press uses environmentally responsible print partners

Contents

List of abbreviations   viii
Series preface   ix

Introduction   1
    Critical friends   2
    Aims of the book   4
    The importance of reasoning within ethical policing 6
    Outline of the chapters   8

1   **Establishing the parameters of ethical policing**   13
    Introduction   13
    An emphasis on moral obligation in understanding   14
    ethical policing
    Ethical policing is competent policing   18
    Ethical policing requires reflective practice   18
    A normative approach to understanding ethical policing 19
    The contested nature of policing within liberal democratic 20
    contexts
    Philosophical but not unnecessarily abstract   22
    Embedding ethical reasoning in routine police work 25
    Conclusion   26

2   **From ethical neutrality to principled policing**   29
    Introduction   29
    Are principles necessary to achieve ethical policing? 30
    The classical liberal perspective and the role of ethical 31
    neutrality within liberal individualism
    The limitations of ethical neutrality   38
    A distinction within moral philosophy between amorality 41
    and immorality
    Moral obligations, Immanuel Kant and a deontological ethic 43
    Conclusion   47

3   **The role of human rights in providing the basis for** 49
   good policing
    Introduction   49
    The emergence of rights: a brief overview   50
    Challenges of embedding human rights in policing   54
    Do human rights provide a moral basis for policing? 57

The universalism and international character of human
rights versus national self-interest 61

Human rights do not necessarily achieve what they are
supposed to achieve 66

Conclusion 70

4   **Justice as fairness, procedural justice and police**   73
     legitimacy
     Introduction 73
     Philosophical and empirical accounts of legitimacy 74
     Procedural justice, consensual legitimacy and policing 75
     by consent
     The liberal democratic understanding of legitimacy related 79
     to ethical policing
     The dual characteristics of legitimacy as a defining feature 84
     of liberal democratic societies
     Rawls' liberal democratic thinking as it applies to 87
     ethical policing
     Conclusion 92

5   **Ethical policing in practice: consequences matter**   95
     Introduction 95
     Utilitarian ethics as a form of consequentialism 96
     Noble cause corruption 98
     The declining influence of *harm to others* 100
     The *dirty hands* doctrine 103
     Lesser evil ethics 108
     The problematic nature of obligation with contexts of 109
     police ethics: consequences matter!
     Moral aspirations as opposed to morally binding 111
     obligations
     Conclusion 114

6   **Embedding ethics within police practice**   117
     Introduction 117
     An officer's responsibilities within ethical policing 118
     Aristotle's virtue ethics 121
     The re-emergence of virtue ethics in the 20th century 125
     Context, particularism and the linking of ethics to a practice 128
     Understanding virtue as it relates to the will 133
     Police discretion and the idea of reflective police practice 134
     Conclusion 138

Contents

Concluding remarks   **141**
    Looking forward   144

References   147
Index   165

List of abbreviations

ASBO	Antisocial Behaviour Order
ECHR	European Convention on Human Rights
HRA	Human Rights Act 1998
IOPC	Independent Office for Police Conduct
IPC	Independent Police Commission
JCHR	Joint Committee on Human Rights
JIT	Joint Investigative Team
NDM	National Decision Model
PCC	Police and Crime Commissioners
PEQF	Policing Education Qualifications Framework
RUC	Royal Ulster Constabulary
SEBP	Society of Evidence Based Policing
UDHR	Universal Declaration of Human Rights
UNCAT	United Nations Convention against Torture and Other Cruel, Inhuman or Degrading Treatment or Punishment

Series preface

Megan O'Neill, Marisa Silvestri and Stephen Tong

The *Key Themes in Policing* series aims to provide relevant and useful books to support the growing number of policing modules on both undergraduate and postgraduate programmes. The series also aims to support all those interested in policing; from criminology, law and policing students to policing professionals to those who wish to join policing services. It also seeks to respond to the call for evidence-based policing led by organisations such as the College of Policing in England and Wales. By producing a range of high-quality, research-informed texts on important areas in policing, contributions to the series support and inform both professional and academic policing curriculums.

Towards Ethical Policing by Dominic A. Wood is the eighth publication in the series. The book offers a rich insight and appreciation of how ethical policing can be understood within and through police practices. Despite the inherently contested nature of police work, policing is not normally discussed in such terms. In this way, the book challenges traditional approaches to understandings of ethics and policing and argues that if we are to take the idea of ethical policing seriously, then we need to recognise the importance of seeing police officers as moral agents with a considerable degree of moral responsibility attached to their role as public officials. For Wood, ethical policing is not found within policies or legislation, or even within a code of police ethics, but rather, ethical policing is located and realised through police interactions with other human beings. The book requires readers to be reflective in engaging with key concepts and ideas within moral philosophy, but the book is not about moral philosophy per se: it is first and foremost about policing. Ethical policing is not established in the abstract, but rather in the real-life contexts within which it is practised. This book makes a significant contribution to police scholarship and provides a challenging read for students of policing and criminal justice.

Dominic Wood is Head of the School of Law, Criminal Justice and Policing at Canterbury Christ Church University. He has published extensively on different political aspects of policing and is particularly interested in the shifting philosophical underpinnings of policing from liberal to democratic principles. He has been a policing scholar for over 25 years and has been leading contributions in the development of police curriculums in higher education and debates concerning police professionalisation.

Introduction

From the experiences I have had working with the police I am invariably overwhelmed by the heroic nature of the job performed by officers, and even more amazed by the level of patience and toleration most demonstrate in the face of hostile and violent provocation. Above all else, the 'nobility' (Waddington, 2013, p.12) or 'romance' (Delattre, 2011, p.1) of the police calling is apparent, such that police officers demonstrate levels of resilience, and a willingness to endure many a sling and arrow, beyond my own capacity to do so. In saying this, I am not blind to the fact that there is a negative flipside to the positive aspects of what Bacon (2014, p.111) refers to as the police's 'heightened sense of mission', which, as he rightly suggests, can also manifest itself as 'an inflated sense of authority' and self-importance.

A book on policing will always incite the passions of its supporters and detractors alike. My intention is to be balanced on such matters, but above all else, it is not the purpose of this book to be judgemental or critical of the police and, if it is read as such, then I have fallen short of my goal. Police are confronted with increasingly difficult and complex demands under circumstances that make, as Delattre (2011, p.355) puts it, 'the possibility of fulfilling the police mission' ever more challenging. Moreover, as Delattre (2011) notes, we expect increasingly higher levels of ethical behaviour from police officers despite the arguably diminishing levels of civic virtue tolerated across society at large (Delattre, 2004). Despite the rhetoric of presenting the police as *ordinary citizens*, our expectations require police to do quite remarkable things. Our idea of the police officer is an exceptional, extraordinary individual, and as Fleming (2015, p.1) says: 'Police officers hold a unique role in liberal democracies.' No doubt many officers fall short of this ideal and some will even fail to meet the most basic ethical criteria required of a citizen. Nonetheless, my experience of collaborating with the police for 25 years has impressed upon me the dedication and integrity of those officers I have had the privilege to work with. This is particularly so given the political hostilities towards the police, and what Waddington (2013, p.12) portrays as the constant 'chorus of civil libertarian critics'. It is not my intention to add to the arsenal of critical voices that lambast the police for this or that shortcoming. Quite the opposite, my motivation is to lend support to the police.

I should also stress that I have never been a police officer. I explain this to each new group of police officers I teach. Indeed, I point out that I fit very well O'Hear's (1988) defence of academics as individuals engaged in useless activities, in many respects the antithesis of the police officer. I sleep better at night knowing that people like me, who will gladly spend hour after hour discussing whatever there is to be discussed, are not patrolling the streets. Given this, I understand that police officers might ask on what authority I profess to have any insights into ethical policing. I am conscious that I do not have the experience of policing that gives unique insights into human behaviour. I am conscious that this is missing from the book; it does not possess direct policing insights that can only come from those engaged in policing. What I have found though over the years of teaching police officers is that creative energies are formed through the interactions I have shared with the police and I hope that similar energies will be produced when officers read the book and add their own practical and reflective insights in making sense of my arguments.

I have also sought to avoid the plethora of mnemonics and decision-making models that are found in books on police ethics (MacVean and Neyroud, 2012). I appreciate that officers might find these comforting, although many officers I speak to do not, but overall I suggest such techniques very quickly become a replacement for ethical reasoning. My approach is more in line with the approach adopted by Paul Feyerabend (1975) in *Against Method*. Feyerabend is a scientist who challenges the hegemony of scientific method in scientific practice. In a similar vein to Feyerabend's (1975) intentions within science, my purpose is to get police officers thinking for themselves. I see this as the way towards ethical policing. Following step-by-step guides to how a police officer should reason will not achieve this aim.

Critical friends

In academia we have a concept of the critical friend. This is someone who is trusted not only to support and encourage, but also to point out errors in our thinking and to ask insightful questions that help us to see things with greater clarity. I consider myself a friend of the police in this sense. As this implies, I do not think the police are perfect, but they face difficult challenges that require the support of critical friends. As MacVean and Spindler (2015, p.110) note, a Committee on Standards in Public Life report published in 2013 showed that police officers shared bottom place with MPs in having 'the worst ethical standards in public life' as perceived by the general public. There have simply been far too many high-profile examples of police wrongdoing in recent years that highlight serious police failings (MacVean and

Spindler, 2015). Stephen Lawrence, Hillsborough and the Rotherham abuse scandal, to name but a few, are all examples that demonstrate a range of failings from, at the very least, policing inadequacies, to criminal negligence and worse. Such failings cause suffering to the victims of police wrongdoing, in addition to their friends and families. Moreover, we cannot underestimate the social harm that follows from corrupt, inept, lazy, inadequate or generally bad policing, nor indeed the harm this causes to policing as a profession and to the officers performing their respective policing duties heroically.

However, while acknowledging the significance of such failings, I will argue that a focus on unethical policing is rather limited as a means of establishing what we understand to be ethical policing. Studies on police corruption (Sherman, 1974; Newburn, 1999; Punch, 1985, 2003, 2009) are of value in highlighting incidents of bad policing and in suggesting remedies. However, the journey from police corruption to ethical policing is not straightforward or simple. There are pitfalls we need to avoid here. First, incidents of bad policing can have a disproportionate impact on how we view the police. This is understandable given the harm caused by such incidents, but we need to remember that they are not representative of most policing activities and we should therefore avoid generalising from incidents of bad policing. There is secondly a danger that a focus on tackling unethical policing as a means of producing ethical policing suggests that if policing is not unethical, then it is by implication ethical. However, it is surely possible for policing to fall short of being seen as ethical without it being considered to be unethical. To think otherwise would, in my view, either set the bar too low for what is meant by ethical policing, or conversely, ethical policing becomes too unrealistic an aim, such that too many policing activities are portrayed as unethical in an unhelpful, demoralising way (Kleinig, 2002). Thirdly, the focus on unethical policing becomes particularly problematic for promoting ethical policing when it takes a punitive approach, which it invariably does. A punitive approach towards unethical policing is understandable, and at times fully justified, but it can make ethical policing harder to achieve (Waddington, 2013). This is especially the case if and when the shortcomings of one police officer are addressed through measures that impact on all police officers. Ethical policing can only survive and flourish within a learning organisation (Senge, 2010).

It is worth noting that the idea of policing being ethical is a relatively new idea. As Alderson (1998) argues, policing has been defined historically by its *amorality*. Good policing has been associated with ethical neutrality. It is only within the last five years, for example, that a policing code of ethics has been introduced within the UK (College of Policing, 2014). So is good policing *necessarily* ethical? Conversely, what is wrong with ethically neutral police?

I will discuss the limits of ethical neutrality in Chapter 2 but for the moment I will simply state that good policing requires doing more than following force policies and observing the law. This statement is at the heart of my understanding of ethical policing and it assumes that the police officer is what MacIntyre (2004) calls a moral agent. It is this understanding of moral agency that makes the idea of policing I am presenting here *necessarily* ethical. My argument is that police officers should embody a clear sense of moral obligation, duty and responsibility. I will qualify this claim somewhat in later chapters by emphasising the word *should* in this statement, to show that I am using the term 'ethical policing' throughout to express an *aspirational* ideal of policing. I will also emphasise criticisms of the term 'moral' as it is used from a Kantian perspective within ethical debates. However, the important point to note at this stage is that although there are notable exceptions (Kleinig, 1996; Alderson, 1998; Miller, 2004a; Delattre, 2011; Waddington, 2013), in general I do not believe that such a *moral* purpose is clearly identifiable within existing ideas of policing.

Aims of the book

There are three main aims of this book. First, it seeks to highlight the importance of ethical reasoning in shaping police practice and the role normative debate can play in developing police knowledge. It seeks to do so both in terms of contributing to the evidential base within policing through the presentation of moral arguments, and also with regard to enabling officers to make better sense of police research, and indeed to develop it further through reflective practice and action research. In the book I argue that policing is a highly contested practice (Wright, 2002; Reiner, 2015), which is continually reviewed, challenged, contested and subject to changes in law, policy and social convention. It would therefore appear inevitable that our understanding of policing requires an appropriate level of philosophical scrutiny to ensure conceptual clarity and accuracy.

Secondly, the book outlines different philosophical approaches to understanding ethical policing. It provides an opportunity to engage critically with the literature on police ethics, with a focus on the philosophical and theoretical reasoning underpinning research. I will make reference to the dominant schools of ethical and moral reasoning as they apply within the contexts of policing, most importantly the utilitarian, deontological and virtue approaches to ethical debate. I will also examine theoretical perspectives that add sociological context to normative debates by highlighting ways in which ethical concerns are shaped, and indeed distorted, by power relations, both within society and also within police organisations. With this in mind, I will endeavour to avoid presenting ethical policing as an all-or-nothing, unachievable, perfectionist ideal. Instead, my aim is to foster an understanding of ethical policing that is aspirational but nonetheless grounded in the day-to-day realities of police practice, within complex historical, social, political, economic and environmental contexts. There are powerful obstacles at play frustrating good ethical intentions that cannot be underestimated. While we should not allow such obstacles to subdue our ambitions completely, we need to be mindful of the dangers arising from an overly zealous pursuit of ethical perfectionism in policing.

Thirdly, the book aims to be philosophical in its approach. By this I mean that the book presents normative arguments and focuses on the way policing could and/or should be, as opposed to how it is and/or how it is perceived to be (Miller, 2004a). It seeks to establish an approach to ethical policing, as opposed to simply reviewing different accounts of police ethics. I hope that what it lacks in insights that can only come from direct policing experience is more than compensated for by an appropriate depth of ethical reasoning that complements the policing perspectives generated by thoughtful, reflective police officers.

There are three dimensions to the normative understanding of ethical policing I favour in the book. It is (1) an understanding that emphasises ethical reasoning over both principles and outcomes. Values (of the kind associated with deontological ethical reasoning) and results (understood in terms of consequential or utilitarian reasoning) are presented and explained in the book as important factors within ethical policing but the emphasis is placed upon the ability of an officer to make sense of competing demands within different contexts, as opposed to following ethical rules of one kind or another. The understanding presented also (2) acknowledges that ethical policing requires ambitious expectations to ensure the ethical bar is not set too low. Police ethics has to be more than the negation of unethical policing. Police corruption is clearly unethical but it is wrong to assume that ethical policing occurs when corruption is absent. However, at the same time we need to ensure that the ethical bar is not set too high. The potentially perfectionist sensibilities of a principled approach to police ethics can create too great a chasm between the abstracted policing ideal and the concrete reality of operational policing. Ethical policing needs to be aspirational but at the same time cognisant of human fallibility. Finally, within the book I argue that (3) ethical policing requires not only reflective police practitioners, but also policing organisations that allow for the development and nurturing of ethical, reflective police work. Policing, in short, needs to become a reflective practice in the fullest sense, and this needs to be embodied within police services and embraced by their respective workforces. The book, in this sense, is as much about understanding how we create the appropriate and necessary conditions within police organisations to allow ethical policing to flourish. These three dimensions taken together make virtue ethics of particular interest with regard to ethical policing.

The importance of reasoning within ethical policing

An aim of this introduction is to establish the role moral reasoning can play in developing our understanding of policing. The policing literature contains a rich and plentiful body of sociological canons (Banton, 1964; Skolnick, 1966; Bittner, 1970; Westley, 1970; Manning, 1977; Muir, 1977; Holdaway, 1983; Waddington, 1999; Reiner, 2010). More recently, the literature on policing has added to the sociological research (Chan, 2003; Loader and Mulcahy, 2003; Loftus, 2009; Cockcroft, 2013). There has also been a growing emphasis on a social scientific gathering of empirical evidence to address policing matters, notably through the procedural justice literature (Tyler, 2003; Bottoms and Tankebe, 2012; Tankebe, 2013; Bradford, 2014; Jackson and Bradford, 2019), but also more generally through evidence-based policing (Sherman, 1998; Sherman, 2011; Weisburd and Neyroud, 2013; Neyroud and Weisburd, 2014; Mitchell and Huey, 2018).

Analysis and reasoning play an important role in sociological and social scientific empirical research, but such research primarily derives its strength from the empirical data; the facts, so to speak, speak for themselves. The quantitative and qualitative researcher share a commitment to the sanctity of their respective empirical findings. The integrity of the data is of primary importance, and it remains stubbornly resistant to creative interpretation. Reasoning used to justify an empirical claim is readily contestable by reference to facts. It is scrutinised against a data set and no matter how persuasive an argument is, it is always limited and constrained by the unmoveable weight of the facts at hand.

Normative considerations have become more prominent in the policing literature. Policing scholars, for example, have argued for much greater recognition of different forms of policing other than the public police (Stenning, 1989; Johnston, 1992, 1999; Jones and Newburn, 1998, 2002; Bayley and Shearing, 2001; Shearing and Johnston, 2003; Wakefield, 2003; Kempa, Stenning and Wood, 2004; Wood and Dupont, 2006; Rogers, 2016). The nature of police work has also changed qualitatively over time in different ways (Edwards, 2005; Goldsmith, 2010; Brogden and Ellison, 2013; Brown, 2014). Perhaps most notably, there has been a tempering perception of what would once have been seen as excessively intrusive (Marx, 1988), such that today greater merit is seen in police use of covert methods, and this is perhaps now even celebrated if and when it is seen to be done under the guise of a duty of care to protect the most vulnerable people in society. Waddington et al (2017) note that police officers they conducted research on were particularly critical of colleagues for failing to demonstrate an adequate duty of care. And what would have been dismissed as an inappropriate level of covert spying is today lauded as a necessary use of intelligence-led policing in the fight against terrorism (Wilkinson, 2011). The changing nature of policing and the changing attitudes to the police within and across societies present challenges in establishing evidence-based police practice (Wood and Bryant, 2015; Fleming, 2018; Fleming and Rhodes, 2018); however, the logic of the evidence-based approach is always to gather more data. The more data we have, the less susceptible it is to fluctuations in policing norms.

A key argument in this book is that our understanding of ethical policing requires a rebalancing of intellectual energies more towards moral philosophy. Moral philosophy deals with the more enduring features of human behaviours and human societies. Here, reasoning plays a much more central role in establishing intelligible arguments that can offer insights and explanations for issues such as ethical policing. As Beardsmore (1969, p.x) notes, within moral philosophy, 'reasons play a quite different part from elsewhere'. Importantly, reasoning comes to the fore within moral philosophy and is therefore less constrained and limited by empirical data than it is within empirically driven research methodologies.

Beardsmore (1969, p.x) recognises that this difference can lead to the conclusion that reasoning within morality is reduced to 'persuasion', 'likes and dislikes' or 'expressions of approval and disapproval', but if this conclusion is correct, then morality ceases to be rational. It would make morality a highly subjective preoccupation and would make ethical policing either arbitrary (it is simply my likes rather than yours) or meaningless (we limit ethical policing to something unsubstantial to avoid conflict), or indeed both. So how do we develop an understanding of ethical policing that has meaning and purchase?

Avoiding accusations of trivialisation and/or selectivity in establishing objectivity within morality is impossible. As Hursthouse (1991) concedes, it afflicts all ethical reasoning; the issue is how this affliction is managed. Importantly, rejecting the overly subjective perception of moral reasoning does not necessarily require a commitment to an objective moral truth. As MacIntyre (1985) has argued, valid reasoning within morality occurs in different rational traditions; moral disputes are fought across competing rationalities. However, for Beardsmore (1969, p.29), 'at least one of the functions of a reason is to render a person's judgment intelligible'. This is an important point. It reminds us that in practice the reasons given to support moral judgements are not accepted or rejected because they follow or diverge from strict rules governing the use of moral reasoning. Reasons are rather accepted or rejected by degree on the basis of the extent to which they explain a judgement, or not. Arguments are either compelling, or they are not. They convince, or they do not.

Outline of the chapters

Chapter 1 establishes an initial sketch of what I understand ethical policing to be. There is a focus on the importance of appreciating the inherently moral characteristic of police work and the need to understand the police officer as a moral agent. Here I draw upon Simmons' (1979) distinctions between moral obligations, legal obligations and the positional duties of a public official. I stress the importance of moral space for the realisation of ethical policing.

Chapter 2 outlines the role that principles play within ethical policing. It shows how the idea of principled policing has been promoted and developed within the UK since the end of the 20th century. This is presented as a departure from the classical liberal ideas that shaped British policing from its inception and creation in 1829. I show how, in particular, British policing was premised upon the classical liberal ideal of ethical neutrality, such that values and morality were seen as inappropriate within the idea of policing associated with Peelian principles. I use Steve Uglow's (1988) book *Policing Liberal Society* to represent this perspective. I then show why ethical neutrality becomes so problematic within an increasingly democratic society, and how this leads to a growing sense of the importance of principles. I use John Alderson's (1998) *Principled Policing* to capture the shift in attitudes away from *amoral* policing, towards the kind of value-led policing promoted by Alderson (1998). The chapter considers the merits of Alderson's (1998) perspective but suggests that there are costs, in addition to benefits, associated with principled policing and that aspects of ethical neutrality, despite obvious shortcomings, retain significance for contemporary policing.

Chapter 3 focuses on the role human rights play in shaping policing in the UK today. I consider the extent to which human rights provide the moral basis for the kind of ethical policing that I am presenting within the book. While recognising the significance of human rights within contemporary policing, not least in terms of promoting ideas of proportionality, necessity and justification, I nonetheless raise concerns regarding the extent to which the adoption of human rights necessarily leads to ethical policing. This is partly to do with the nature of human rights, but perhaps more importantly, it concerns the way human rights are interpreted by police officers within legal frameworks. Within the chapter I develop Simmons' (1979) arguments about the nature of moral obligation and how it relates to the legal obligations and positional duties of police officers. I also extend here the importance of seeing police officers as moral agents (MacIntyre, 2004). I argue that a narrow, legal approach to human rights does not take us beyond the legal obligations and positional duties of a police officer, which do not in themselves entail ethical policing. I suggest that it is rather the moral power of human rights that can form the basis of ethical policing.

In Chapter 4, I develop the human rights-informed understanding of policing as principled by showing the underlying important influence of John Rawls in such thinking. In particular, I consider Rawls' (1971) seminal presentation of justice as fairness as the underpinning moral reasoning supporting contemporary ideas of police legitimacy within liberal democratic societies (Manning, 2010). I see police legitimacy as a critical dimension of ethical policing and note that the dominant influence on shaping our understanding of police legitimacy currently comes from a procedural justice perspective. I depart from the Rawlsian idea of justice as fairness, on the grounds that particularly within policing contexts, it pays too little attention to order as a primary political challenge. I also depart from the procedural justice approach to police legitimacy because of the extent to which it focuses on consensual dimensions of legitimacy, and conversely, the extent to which it pays too little attention to the moral dimension of police legitimacy.

The principled approach to policing, human rights reasoning and John Rawls' moral reasoning are all examples of non-consequential ethical reasoning. That is to say they approach ethical matters by establishing through reason what the right thing to do is, thereby creating obligations that are binding independently of what we think might occur when the obligations are carried out.

In Chapter 5, I turn my attention to consequential ethics, in particular utilitarian reasoning. Consequential ethical reasoning, as the name suggests, establishes an action to be the right thing to do if, and only if, it can be shown to produce a positive result. Utilitarianism is an example of consequential reasoning that classically prioritises the maximisation of welfare as the measure of ethical decisions. If an action can be seen to bring about *the greatest good for the greatest number*, to paraphrase Jeremy Bentham (1748–1832), then it is judged to be the right thing to do. I acknowledge the limitations of consequential ethical reasoning, and utilitarianism in particular, not least because of the extent to which such reasoning permits the suffering of a minority as a means of enhancing the welfare of the majority, and likewise fails to prevent seeing an individual as a means to another's ends. Nonetheless, drawing upon Wolff (2006), I argue that despite its philosophical shortcomings, utilitarianism has much to offer in practice, especially within public life. Drawing upon Kleinig (2002) I argue that consequences are important within policing. There is a danger that non-consequential ethical reasoning becomes too abstract and disconnected from the world in which police officers operate if consequences are ignored. I argue that we need to avoid perfectionist views of how the world should be because this ignores the ethical demands that confront those in positions of public authority (Brandt, 1979).

Chapter 6 focuses on the notion of reflective practice as a means of understanding ethical policing and embedding it within police practice. Aristotle's virtue ethics and his approach to ethical reasoning is used to emphasise the importance of context in understanding ethical policing. In particular I draw favourably on his idea of practical wisdom as it relates to police discretion and reflective practice. Similarly, I utilise Dancy's (2004) arguments that promote ethical reasoning over ethical principles. Dancy's (2004) approach to ethical questions is a form of particularism as opposed to the universalism found within human rights reasoning. I consider how this informs our understanding of ethical policing and argue that it is the capacity of officers to make ethical decisions rather than their compliance with principles that is critical from the perspective of ethical policing. This requires officers to be supported within their organisations and more broadly across society. This links to the full sense in which Schön's (1983) idea of reflective practice is presented.

The book concludes by drawing together the various positions explored within the previous chapters. It reiterates the value of philosophical research within policing and outlines the contribution made to police knowledge through the different ethical approaches explored within the book. The conclusion emphasises the importance of ethical reasoning in the approach adopted within the book towards understanding ethical policing and reiterates the importance of reflective practice in realising this end.

Suggested further reading

Delattre, E.J. (2011) *Character and Cops: Ethics and Policing*. 6th edition. Lanham, MD: Rowman & Littlefield. Chapters 1–3

Kleinig, J. (1996) *The Ethics of Policing*. Cambridge: Cambridge University Press. Chapters 1–3

Waddington, P.A.J., Williams, K., Wright, M. and Newburn, T. (2017) *How People Judge Policing*. Oxford: Oxford University Press. Chapter 1

1

Establishing the parameters of ethical policing

Introduction

The aim of this chapter is to establish what I mean by the term *ethical policing*. I will emphasise the importance of moral agency and the ability of police officers to reason, and in doing so hope to provide a flavour of the philosophical approach adopted in the book. Although the writing requires engagement with abstract ideas and technical concepts, it is nonetheless always being directed towards appreciating how ethical policing can be understood within and through police practices. Above all else, I hope to avoid any confusion that leads to an assumption that ethical policing is somehow idealistic fantasy unconnected to real police work. Likewise, I do not want to give the impression that there is in any sense a tension or contradiction between ethical policing and effective or good policing. The idea of ethical policing I am presenting is at the same time a view of what is good policing: good policing is necessarily ethical, and ethical policing is necessarily good.

Policing is not normally discussed in such moral terms, despite the inherently contested nature of police work (Wright, 2002; Reiner, 2015). Indeed, until fairly recently policing was assumed to be ethically neutral (Uglow, 1988; Alderson, 1998). Likewise, police officers tend to see their work more comfortably in legal as opposed to moral terms. I appreciate that this means challenging the way policing is normally approached but my central argument is that if we are to take the idea of ethical policing seriously, then we need to recognise the importance of seeing police officers as moral agents (MacIntyre, 2004), with a considerable degree of moral responsibility attached to their role as public officials.

It is important to stress two points about my approach to ethical policing. First, I pay little attention to unethical behaviour, such as police corruption, to avoid any misconception that ethical policing is achieved by the negation of unethical policing. Secondly, my focus on moral reasoning assumes that ethical codes are of limited use in establishing ethical policing. They can even be counterproductive to the extent that they disincentivise ethical reasoning. The College of Policing's (2014) *Code of Ethics* will therefore not feature prominently in the book. Hopefully, both of these omissions, which might seem strange at the outset, will make more sense to the reader by the end of the book.

An emphasis on moral obligation in understanding ethical policing

The idea of ethical policing I present in the book assumes that moral obligation is at the heart of good policing. I draw here upon a distinction Simmons (1979, pp.7–23) makes between *legal obligations* and *positional duties* on the one hand, and *moral obligation* on the other hand. Simmons (1979) is concerned primarily with understanding political obligation in general, rather than ethical policing specifically, but I believe his arguments apply readily within a policing context. The lesson we need to take from Simmons (1979) is that we should not assume that legal obligations or positional duties in themselves provide a moral basis for policing. In other words, meeting legal obligations and positional duties does not *necessarily* result in ethical policing.

The lessons of Nazi Germany can be used to show how state actors carry out unethical duties within the boundaries of the legal obligations and/or positional duties imposed upon them. Indeed, in Nazi Germany police officers were not only permitted legally to do morally abhorrent things to Jews, homosexuals, communists, people with disabilities and a whole host of others deemed subhuman by the Nazi regime, they were legally obliged to do these morally abhorrent things. Moreover, the positional duties of the police officers operating in Nazi Germany also obliged them to do likewise as a condition of their employment. They had what Simmons (1979, p.5) defines as, a 'political obligation ... to "support and comply with" ... the political institutions' of Germany at that time, and this is reflected through compliance with the law and the expected duties of a police officer within Nazi Germany.

Nazi Germany is by any standard an extreme example and we need to be cautious regarding its relevance when discussing more routine aspects of police work. On the one hand, it is helpful to consider extreme examples of immoral actions because it is much easier to see what is wrong when the wrong is exaggerated than it is to see more nuanced wrongdoing in everyday matters. But this can become unhelpful if we only see immoral action when it is presented in an extreme form. Likewise, historical examples of immoral actions provide an emotional distance and detachment that allows us to see things with greater perspective and hindsight. However, this can give the impression that we have learnt lessons from this dark period of history and that human rights and employment laws preclude such immoralities being permitted today. The institutionalisation of human rights in particular is seen as an explicit and proactive barrier to laws and social practices that contravene such basic levels of respect for human dignity. However, all this demonstrates is that we are diligent in avoiding a repeat of the Nazi atrocities in the form they took in the first half of the 20th century. We pat ourselves on the back for having rectified the moral errors of our predecessors, but to what extent does this make us sensitive to potential abuses in the here and now, especially if and when they present themselves in different forms?

History is littered with examples of bad laws (not least as they have been used explicitly to discriminate against women, homosexuality and different religious/ethnic groups), and although these laws are easily identified as bad laws with hindsight, at the time and place they were enacted they were perceived quite differently. There are times when legislators act in good faith with the intention of being highly moral and it is only later that the immorality of their endeavours becomes apparent. We only have to note Michael Sandel's (2010, pp.201–3) discussion on Aristotle's defence of slavery for an example of how even someone highly regarded as one the greatest moral philosophers of all time held such objectionable views to the modern eye. It is always much easier for us to identify immorality in the actions of others in different places at different times than it is to recognise our own moral shortcomings in the here and now. It is precisely for this reason that legal obligations do not in and of themselves necessarily result in morally justifiable actions.

Liebling (2004) has addressed the issue of what I am referring to as moral obligation in relation to what she describes as the *moral performance* of prisons. Importantly, Liebling (2004, p.473) describes moral performance as something that goes 'beyond legitimacy'. She also suggests that this approach to understanding moral performance applies 'to any organization' and is not necessarily specific to prisons (2004, p.455). At the heart of her argument is the view that legitimacy tends to be rooted within questions of power relations, whereas the concept of moral performance lends itself more to interpersonal and civic values. She says '... prisons are about more than power relations. They are, or can be, despite the stark imbalance of power, almost civic communities. Prisons can be moral communities and can be experienced as such, under certain conditions' (2004, pp.473–4).

The approach adopted in this book is premised upon the assumption that policing can be framed similarly in terms of moral performance. That is to say that ethical policing needs to be defined in terms of the extent to which it is experienced as being motivated by interpersonal and civic values that foster and promote a moral community of the kind described by Liebling (2004). I suggest that while this would require police officers to be cognisant of their own legal obligations and positional duties, and indeed their legitimacy as actors of the state, it would also require them to consider the consequences of their actions as police officers much more at the level of the interactions they have with those they encounter as part of their duties. I see Liebling's (2004) notion of moral performance as a reminder that ethical policing is realised through police interactions with other human beings. It is not found within policies or legislation, or even within a code of police ethics.

This sense of moral performance is not, in my view, found sufficiently within the policing literature. Perhaps it could be argued that a recent exception to this claim is the wealth of research conducted under the umbrella of procedural justice (Tyler, 1990, 2003; Bradford, 2014). I will say more on procedural justice in Chapter 4 but for now I will limit myself to saying that despite the undoubted influence procedural justice has had upon promoting the idea of police legitimacy in the UK today, and the similar degree of impact it has had on promoting fairness and human rights values within police practice, it is nonetheless important to stress that procedural justice is premised upon what Simmons (2001) calls an *attitudinal* approach to legitimacy. Procedural justice is a means of measuring the extent to which the police are *perceived* to be legitimate but it does not speak to the morality of a police action in and of itself. This is not a criticism of procedural justice as an approach to establishing police legitimacy, but rather a recognition of the extent to which it focuses on measuring one aspect of legitimacy (Bottoms and Tankebe, 2012). I will argue in Chapter 4 that the approach adopted within the procedural justice literature is framed within, and does not go beyond, the legal obligations and positional duties that frame police practice at any given time, in any given place.

The lack of attention to moral considerations is perhaps even starker when police ethics is addressed within the context of professional standards (MacVean et al, 2013). The focus on professional standards inevitably emphasises positional duties over the moral purpose of policing. As Hughes (2013, p.12) notes in his balanced and insightful contribution to the MacVean et al (2013) collection, 'some caution is needed in treating professional standards straightforwardly as instruments for promoting ethical behaviour'. Hughes (2013) notes that 'non-moral factors' (p.13) inform and shape professional standards, and that professional standards 'cannot be a substitute for ethical engagement on the part of practitioners' (p.14). Despite these qualifications, and a generally cautionary approach to the linking of professional standards to ethical policing, Hughes (2013) nonetheless sees the merit of professional standards as a guide to practice and as a means of motivating ethical behaviour in policing.

This to me gets things the wrong way around, for the very cautionary reasons Hughes (2013) himself alludes to throughout his chapter. We should not underestimate how difficult it is to change values within large public institutions such as the police. My concern is that a focus on professional standards as a way of achieving ethical policing will never get beyond a discussion about professional standards. This is because it is much easier to establish and maintain professional standards than it is to develop ethical behaviour. Professional standards, as Waddington (2013) notes, deal with unethical behaviour but do little to promote ethical behaviour. He says: 'Despite the plethora of rules and procedures that govern policing, this still does not impose upon police officers standards of conduct that are high enough. The reason is that such rules can only stipulate minimum standards, which if an officer falls below will merit his or her punishment' (2013, p.10). Indeed it could be argued that professional standards normalise and legitimise behaviours that fall short of what we might consider to be ethical. Negating unethical behaviour does not in itself produce ethical behaviour. Again, this is why a focus on police corruption can be unhelpful when discussing ethical policing.

Waddington (2013) highlights the imbalance currently found within our approach to ethical policing. He notes that there is far too much emphasis on uncovering unethical behaviour and punishing with severity officers found guilty of wrongdoing, and conversely, too little emphasis on rewarding and promoting the heroic endeavours of officers. He says:

> We need to reverse this emphasis and encourage officers to recognise the nobility of their calling; the opportunity they are offered to influence lives for the better; and the extent to which they can be relied upon when 'the going gets tough'; so that they aspire to live up to the values they espouse. (2013, p.12)

Waddington (2013) articulates here a strong sense of moral purpose for policing, which in turn delivers a far more appropriate, meaningful and ultimately effective guide to police officers than is provided through a focus on professional standards. If policing is to be conceptualised as ethical, officers need to be inspired, supported and motivated to act with moral purpose and to make ethical judgements. Moreover, the focus on professional standards is not only insufficient with regard to what I understand to be ethical policing, but more importantly, I suggest, it fosters instead compliance with minimal standards, risk aversion and a cautionary approach that falls short of the noble calling emphasised by Waddington (2013). A focus on moral obligation, however, not only promotes ethical policing but also requires a more meaningful and thorough engagement with professional standards.

Ethical policing is competent policing

To develop this point further, it is important to stress that I see ethical policing as *necessarily* competent. I certainly wish to avoid any confusion of seeing ethical policing as somehow at odds with being good at policing. One of the most positive aspects of my own experiences of working with police officers has been the extent to which so many of them have aspired to achieving the standards to which Waddington et al (2017) refer. Officers have been candid about the extent to which they are not always prepared to face demands, which chimes with Holgersson and Gottschalk's (2008) research. While officers have at times been overly defensive and reluctant to engage in reasoned debate – I recall in particular the difficulties of discussing the Winsor Report (2012) with officers – in the main they have been open to the idea that things could be better, and genuinely committed to make improvements.

However, even the most conscientious officers I have worked with rarely express their aspirations explicitly in ethical terms. They are more likely to discuss policing not in moral terms, but rather in terms of competence. Competence needs to be recognised as an important starting point in discussions about ethical policing because it engages immediately with an officer's sense of what good policing looks like. And while it is important to maintain that the ability of an officer to carry out his or her duties competently does not in itself constitute ethical policing, I argue nonetheless that competence is a necessary condition for ethical policing to be realised. An emphasis within this book is the view that policing cannot be ethical if it is incompetent.

Ethical policing requires reflective practice

A further theme in the book is that the notion of the reflective practitioner (Schön, 1983) supports the realisation of ethical policing in practice. I am confident that there is sufficient talent and goodwill among the police services in the UK to nurture the kind of reflective practice that I see as essential for the development of ethical policing. However, reflective practice is not something that the police can achieve in isolation. Reflective practitioners alone will not lead to ethical policing. An important but often overlooked dimension of ethical policing concerns organisational justice within policing (Sklansky, 2008). Ethical policing cannot be attained, and certainly not sustained, if officers are not valued in their working lives. As Wood and Williams (2016) have argued, policing needs to become a reflective practice in order to allow and encourage reflective practitioners to flourish. Indeed, we need to go further than this and consider how policing is understood within society. Too often, policing is idealised in ways that ignore the realities of policing and when this happens, attempts at police reform fail. For ethical policing to be realised there is a need for society at large to appreciate the contextual dimensions of police work. Policing happens in the margins, where and when society is failing to reproduce order through other means. Ethical policing is not established in the abstract, but rather in the real-life contexts within which it is practised. It is not enough to say that ethical policing is about doing the right thing; ethical policing is more precisely achieved through doing right within the specific parameters of each and every policing instance. Ethical policing is in this respect a socially reflective practice.

I see ethical policing as a journey and this is hopefully conveyed by the inclusion of 'towards' in the title of the book. This is a journey that involves individual officers and police organisations, but also various institutions across society and indeed also community groups and citizens more generally. The concept of ethical policing I wish to develop is in this respect a shared journey. It is certainly not something that can be achieved by simply admonishing the poor performance of particular officers, nor can it be imposed upon the police from above. Ethical policing requires informed, thoughtful and reflective officers operating within supportive organisations that are understood by, and have the backing of, the social and communal environments within which they operate.

A normative approach to understanding ethical policing

The focus on moral obligation dictates a normative approach to understanding policing. It is important to understand what this means, in particular in terms of what it can and cannot tell us about policing. There are different ways of understanding the world. At present, within policing, there is a focus on establishing what works and on developing an evidence base to establish best practice. The development of evidence-based policing is to be welcomed, especially given the extent to which it has fostered a discussion about police knowledge and its importance within establishing police authority. However, there are things that such an empirical focus cannot tell us about policing and no matter how much evidence we gather to inform police practice, there will always be aspects of policing that remain contested and unresolvable in any definitive manner.

Take, for example, the issue of police legitimacy. Procedural justice research can tell us whether a particular approach to policing is perceived to be the right thing to do, but just because something is popular does not mean that it is the right thing to do. In policing, the kind of consensual legitimacy that can be measured through the procedural justice literature is important, but it is only one dimension of police legitimacy. There remains a moral question about whether the police are doing the right thing, and this moral dimension of police legitimacy is much more difficult, if not impossible, to resolve in the way that other aspects of policing can be resolved through evidence gathering.

It is my contention that philosophical questions about the purpose of policing are necessary and vital components of establishing what makes policing ethical. At the heart of my argument is the assumption that ethical policing is founded upon the moral agency of police officers. This assumes that police officers will always need to make judgements and these judgements are inevitably moral in character. They require officers to make decisions about what is important. A reliable evidence base supports and shapes such judgements but it does not remove completely the need for moral decision making on the part of the officer. The focus of this book is to explore why moral philosophy is important within developing an understanding of policing, and a starting point has to be recognising the contested nature of policing (Wright, 2002).

The contested nature of policing within liberal democratic contexts

On the one hand, it is important that we do not lose sight of the fact that the existence of a standing body of police requires justification. The police are, in historical terms, still a relatively new institution, one that was resisted by Parliament in the UK over a period of some

50 years at the end of the 18th and beginning of the 19th century (Reiner, 2010). It is difficult for most people to imagine society without the police, and indeed the trajectory since the introduction of the Metropolitan Police in 1829 has been to make the police increasingly embedded within the fabric of our society. There have been questions about the extent to which the police dominate our thinking on policing (Shearing and Johnston, 2003; Brogden and Ellison, 2013), but the justification for the police to exist is largely taken for granted. However, I think that there is merit in occasionally asking the question, *do we need the police?* I say this not because I anticipate anyone putting forward a serious argument as to why we do not need the police, but rather because it forces us to question why we think the existence of the police is justified. It starts a conversation about the kind of police institutions that we want.

This brings us back to the question of legitimacy. As indicated earlier, there are different dimensions to police legitimacy, and within liberal democratic contexts there are important, ongoing processes of negotiating and renegotiating what constitutes legitimate policing in any given time and place. At times such negotiations are formal but there are also informal ways through which policing is legitimised (Walker, 2000).

The law is one means of establishing police legitimacy both in terms of specific legislation that establishes the legal parameters of police powers, but also through legal principles and conventions that are less prescriptive, and which require socio-legal reasoning, such as the rule of law, civil and political rights, social rights, human rights and environmental rights. The law can establish things that the police can and cannot do much more easily than it can establish what the police should or should not do in any given circumstance. Policing is such that there are often multiple legitimate legal options open to police officers. As Marshall (1978), Lustgarten (1986), Waddington (1999), Walker (2000) and Reiner (2010) have all noted, it does not make sense to see policing as merely law enforcement.

Policing also operates in political contexts and political will is important in shaping police legitimacy. If enough people think something is legitimate, then it becomes legitimate in one sense at least. As noted earlier, this aspect of police legitimacy is the focus within the procedural legitimacy literature and it accords with the ideal of policing by consent. We should note though that consent can take different forms. It can be something that is sought regularly, infrequently or even on just one occasion. It can be sought from a wide section of society or limited to an elite group, and it can be established through simple majoritarian mechanisms or captured in more sophisticated participatory and deliberative ways.

Perhaps most importantly for understanding how consent differs today from earlier periods of policing is the difference between (1) an *acquiescence* form of consent, in which consent is expressed tacitly through a lack of opposition, and (2) a *consensual* form of consent, in which the goal is to maximise the number of people expressing positive support. The acquiescence approach is clearly limited in terms of knowing whether people think the police are legitimate or not, and this approach certainly runs counter to the strong democratic sensibilities of contemporary society (Wood, 2016a). However, there are also dangers in seeking to establish consensus in society in that it can foster a high level of intolerance towards non-conformist views (Rescher, 1993). Waddington's (1999) observations regarding the oxymoronic tension within the term 'community policing' is appropriate here. As Waddington (1999) notes, the term 'community' assumes cohesion, whereas 'policing' is premised upon there being conflict.

Moral reasoning plays an important role in the interplay between the legal and political influences on policing. My contention is that moral reasoning is the keystone in understanding ethical policing. Ethical policing is necessarily influenced, shaped and constrained by legal and political institutions, but compliance with the law and political norms alone is insufficient to establish ethical policing. Moral reasoning is also required at times to make sense of the sometimes competing claims of legal arguments against political sentiments. Good policing requires a balancing of the obligations it has to the law, the government and the consent of those being policed (Neyroud and Beckley, 2001). It needs to balance pragmatic and principled approaches, and the interests of society, communities and individuals (Hopkins Burke and Morrill, 2004). Such balancing acts require philosophical thinking and cannot be easily or readily arrived at through adherence to rules, procedures and policies. The weight of argument will no doubt be swayed by these different considerations, which themselves will have been produced in light of available evidence and research. Nonetheless, the interpretation of all these factors, and understanding them in each and every context, requires moral reasoning.

Philosophical but not unnecessarily abstract

The philosophical focus of the book means that I seek to provide conceptual clarity regarding what it means to say that policing is ethical. This requires an engagement with key concepts and ideas within moral philosophy, but the book is not about moral philosophy per se, it is first and foremost about policing. Above all it is important to stress that I am not seeking to provide the reader with an abstract concept of police ethics. I share with Mary Warnock a concern that moral philosophy is trivialised if and when it becomes overly abstract. Her account of ethics from 1900 to 1960 (Warnock, 1966) highlights the technical characteristics of the dominant voices in moral philosophy at that time, in particular through the influence of A.J. Ayer's (1936) logical positivist approach to ethics. Ayer (1936) is primarily concerned with establishing the view that all meaningful statements can be categorised either as analytic or empirical. Warnock (1966, p.56) summarises Ayer's understanding thus: analytic statements are understood as 'necessarily true but not concerned with empirical matters of fact', and an empirical statement is one that 'can never be more than probable' and 'it must be capable of verification by sense-experience'.

The framing of meaningful statements in this way is problematic for ethical propositions as they do not fit neatly into either category. This leads Ayer to view ethical propositions as emotive statements (the emotive theory of ethics) and he sees the role of ethical philosophy as being limited exclusively to the study of propositions that define ethical terms. Warnock (1966, p.144) counters this approach to moral philosophy in the following way:

> How we describe the world cannot be the primary concern of moral philosophers ... Deliberating, wishing, hating, loving, choosing; these are the things which characterise us as people, and therefore as moral agents, and these are the things to which emotive theory ... paid insufficient attention.

My intention is to conceive of ethical policing as a practice in a way that I hope accords with the sensibilities expressed by Warnock (1966). I want the reader to be imagining police officers in action and *in situ* making judgements and decisions. I do not want the reader to be thinking about police ethics as something removed from the theatres of police work. For this reason my preference is to use the term *ethical policing*, as in the title, to conjure up an image of ethics in practice, rather than the term *police ethics*, which I feel lends itself more to thinking about ethics as a thing, such as a code, standard, theoretical perspective or a series of ethical propositions. Perhaps most importantly, I want to stress that codes, standards and theories of ethics can never determine what an officer should do within a given situation. As Kleinig (1996) has argued, ultimately police officers are required to make judgements, and ethical policing is located and found within the reasoning and decision making of officers, not in published codes, decision-making models, standards or theoretical treatises. My point here is not to dismiss the merit of such documents completely but I am concerned that within policing, perhaps more so than other areas of public life, there is a propensity to reduce everything to models, mnemonics and other such devices to provide simplified explanation and guidance.

In the UK, the National Decision Model (NDM) is a good example of what I have in mind here. Moreover, its inclusion in the College of Policing's (2014) *Code of Ethics* demonstrates the extent to which it is assumed that ethical direction can be given in this way, or more importantly, that ethical policing will be realised if officers follow a set of commands or directions. But as Nowell-Smith (1954, p.15) reminds us, the sobering reality is that ethics does not provide us with the kind of *truths* found in geometry or physics that assist surveyors or engineers to resolve their respective practical problems: 'although the subject has been studied for over two thousand years, it does not seem to have produced any established system of truths comparable to those of mathematics and the natural sciences'.

Part of the problem for moral philosophy is that human societies change and with these changes social norms are continuously modified and at times radically transformed. This is not to say that there are not aspects of humanity that remain fairly constant but these tend to be the least controversial aspects of what it means to be human and therefore the aspects least likely to give rise to moral disputes. A police officer is most likely to seek help and guidance when dealing with situations in which there are conflicting obligations between well-established ethical principles and/or where established ethical issues are presented in new or different contexts. There are also fresh ethical dilemmas arising from new technology that are not always captured easily by established guides. As Nowell-Smith (1954, p.19) argues,

> [a] detailed moral code, a sort of handbook to which we
> might turn for the answer to every moral problem, cannot
> help us, because the difficulties will always arise about the
> application of the rules to new cases and because the cases
> in which the need for practical thinking is particularly
> acute are just those which are new and those in which we

suspect that there is some good reason for breaking the accepted code.

I appreciate that officers might find the NDM useful and I recognise that it has been designed to promote reasoning. However, my concern is that any practical aid to ethical decision making is necessarily abstracted from the details and specifics of each police encounter. This can make it of limited use in the situations in which it is most needed. Moreover, there is a danger that it fosters unthinking compliance rather than intelligent, ethical reasoning. Attempts to simplify matters for police officers by providing them with prescribed direction limit the development of the kind of ethical reasoning that I see as being of such central importance in the development of ethical policing. The focus on ethical reasoning over an appeal to a set of principles, guidelines or instructions requires officers to be much more cognisant of exactly what it is they are dealing with, and much more practically minded in how they utilise their authority, power and skills to resolve a situation.

It is important for me to stress here that I recognise the difficulty of achieving this level of ethical reasoning in any organisation. It is perhaps more challenging in policing given the extent to which it has not historically promoted such thinking, and indeed many officers have voiced to me concerns that any discretion they once had has been all but completely eroded in recent years. I have included the word 'towards' in the title of this book in recognition of this challenge and to emphasise a sense of journey. This requires patience. There are no quick fixes and we need to avoid perfectionist expectations. The idea of ethical policing I present in the book has to be seen as aspirational and it needs to remain as such throughout the journey, a journey that never ends.

This aspirational understanding of ethical reasoning, and the idea of a never-ending journey towards realising it, also necessitate the police becoming a much more explicitly committed learning organisation (Senge, 2010). Officers will need to make brave decisions and be open and transparent about them. They will inevitably make mistakes. Here, police organisations need to be supportive, and to be supported themselves at societal levels, to allow learning to occur and for the flourishing of informed, ethical reasoning to be embedded within police practice.

Embedding ethical reasoning in routine police work

A final consideration by way of introduction is the need to acknowledge that there is a tendency when discussing police ethics to focus on what are perceived to be the most serious, but ultimately least frequent, aspects of police work. Undoubtedly, the most intense instances of crime and disorder, and the corresponding means of policing such incidents, provide a heightened sense of tension and drama to ethical questions. Dealing with the terrorist threat or a serial killer increases interest and polarises opinions because so much is at stake. But generalising from such extraordinary instances is problematic for informing our understanding of ethical policing. There is a danger of assuming that ethical policing is reserved for the most dramatic of situations, when in practice, we know that police officers are routinely required to make decisions and act upon them in much more mundane, everyday occurrences (Delattre, 2011).

Police officers need to remember that the most routine aspects of their work are often experienced as exceptional moments by those encountering the police. Making an arrest is an everyday occurrence within policing but for the populace at large it is an extraordinary moment of significance. Police officers need to be cognisant of this fact and aware of how their routine actions will be perceived and presented within different social contexts.

Conclusion

Within the chapter I have hopefully given the reader a flavour of what is to come and a sense of the approach adopted in the book. I appreciate that at times the philosophical tone of the writing may seem somewhat abstract and fairly distant from the operational practice of police work. This is perhaps an inevitability given the topic. However, my intention is very much to chime with a professional police audience, and in particular police officers who are still operationally active.

In setting the parameters of the book I want to reassure officers that although the writing is laden with moral philosophy, with an emphasis on the moral components of police work, this should not be seen as an attempt to establish unrealistic, abstract, ethical doctrines to be imposed on front-line police officers without any consideration of the difficulties and challenges they routinely encounter as part of their professional duties. Police failings, shortcomings and wrongdoing will all attract more than their fair share of attention. My intention is rather to focus on the public service provided by police officers and to appeal to the sense of pride and conviction that police officers articulate and demonstrate through their work. I save my critical attention much more for police leaders, policy makers, academics and the wider citizenry, by focusing on the necessity for institutional and societal support in realising ethical policing. I also want to stress that by ethical policing I mean at the same time good policing.

In the next chapter I focus on a significant contextual shift in policing that has seen liberal arguments that conceptualise police as ethically neutral (Uglow, 1988) being increasingly replaced by the idea that policing should be principled (Alderson, 1998).

Suggested further reading

MacIntyre, A. (2004) 'Social Structures and Their Threat to Moral Agency', in P. Villiers and R. Adlam (eds) *Policing a Safe, Just and Tolerant Society: An International Model for Policing.* Winchester: Waterside Press, pp.36–54

Reiner, R. (2010) *The Politics of the Police.* 4th edition. Oxford: Oxford University Press. Introduction and chapters 1–2

Waddington, P.A.J. (1999) *Policing Citizens.* London: UCL Press. Chapters 1, 2, 6 and 7

2

From ethical neutrality to principled policing

Introduction

The primary aim of this chapter is to consider the role that principles play within ethical policing. I will introduce two contrasting ethical approaches to policing:

- one that establishes principles at the heart of policing;
- one that favours ethical neutrality as the most appropriate policing strategy.

I will refer to the first approach as principled policing and the second as liberal policing in recognition of two important texts that help frame this chapter. The first text is John Alderson's *Principled Policing* published in 1998, which, as the title suggests, champions an approach to policing that is informed and shaped explicitly by moral priorities. The second text, which represents a liberal ideal of policing that favours ethical neutrality, is Steve Uglow's book *Policing Liberal Society* published in 1988.

It is important to recognise that I am using the term 'liberal' here in a very particular way, one which might not accord with how the term is commonly used. As Gray (2000) notes, there are at least two broad ways in which liberalism is conceived. These can be articulated with reference to Berlin's (1958) seminal paper that distinguishes between positive and negative concepts of liberty. When I refer to liberal, I am talking about Berlin's (1958) negative concept of liberty and a version of liberalism that favours limited interventions in society. It is the form of liberalism that champions ethical neutrality. This is the kind of liberal thinking that underpins Uglow's (1988) *Policing Liberal Society*. Without wishing to confuse the matter, it should be noted that Alderson's (1998) *Principled Policing* conforms to the other understanding of liberalism, which articulates a positive conception of liberty, and rather than seeking to limit interventions in society, it favours a form of value-led interventions that foster liberal principles concerning freedom and rights. My intention of using Alderson (1998) and Uglow (1988) as reference points is to avoid confusion.

Are principles necessary to achieve ethical policing?

The relationship between morally framed principles and ethical policing is my main concern in this chapter. More specifically, I want to explore how necessary such principles are for policing to be considered ethical. This might appear a strange question to ask. Contemporary policing bodies are overwhelmingly committed to the promotion of particular principles as an essential aspect of what they do. While the sceptic might reasonably question whether police practice lives up to policy aspirations in this regard, it is harder to deny the efforts made by police to adopt a principled approach to policing as advocated by Alderson (1998).

However, this has not always been the case and until fairly recently values were perceived as problematic within the context of a liberally framed policing ideal that emphasised the importance of the police officer's impartiality and disinterestedness (Reiner, 2010). Uglow's (1988) representation of liberal policing is supported by Johnston's (2000) notion of an optimal society, in which policing is neither excessive nor extensive. Similarly, liberal police can be seen as the antithesis of Gary Marx's maximum security society, in which privacy is severely limited (Marx, 1988). Indeed, Uglow's (1988) account of liberal policing clearly favours ethical neutrality as being a more appropriate policing strategy, as opposed to one premised upon particular values.

Uglow (1988) promotes an approach to policing that deliberately avoids committing to moral principles. Liberal policing conforms to the law but is not explicitly or excessively predicated on *moral* grounds, and it is certainly not committed to promoting any particular values, nor is it premised upon any conception of what it means to be human. However, by the time Uglow's book was published in 1988, the tide was shifting away from this classic liberal position, and by the end of the 20th century the emphasis had gravitated more towards the idea that policing should be grounded on a strong moral footing.

This shift in thinking is expressed most clearly by John Alderson, a former Chief Constable of Devon and Cornwall. For Alderson (1998), policing had historically lacked principles. He argues that policing lacked a clear and coherent mission and that this was to its detriment. Alderson (1998) suggests that policing had been defined not in terms of principles but rather by its *amorality*, and he illustrates his argument with reference to the continuity of police staff in the transition from

Tsarist Russia to the Bolshevik-led Soviet Union in 1917 and similarly, in the transition from the liberal democracy of Weimar Germany to Hitler's Nazi Germany in the 1930s. In both cases he argues that police officers performing duties for such diametrically opposed political regimes is evidence of a lack of moral perspective among officers.

I will say more on both the principled and liberal approaches throughout the chapter but for the moment I will simply state that principles address shortcomings within the liberal policing ideal, and in particular its emphasis on ethical neutrality, but in doing so present policing with different challenges. Notwithstanding the positive contribution Alderson (1998) has made, there remain limitations in understanding ethical policing simply as principled policing. I will show that principles are *necessary*, but in a more limited sense than suggested by advocates of principled policing, and perhaps more importantly, I argue that principles are certainly not *sufficient* to establish ethical policing. Indeed, I suggest that an unthinking adherence to principles can lead to unethical policing. I also draw out the positive aspects of Uglow's (1988) *Policing Liberal Society*, with its emphasis on ethical neutrality, which I will also return to in later chapters.

The classical liberal perspective and the role of ethical neutrality within liberal individualism

The classical liberal perspective I am considering here is one that favours and promotes ethical neutrality (Boyd, 2004). Key to understanding ethical neutrality is the extent to which it places the individual as a primary concern within society. Liberal individualism lies at the heart of the liberal policing perspective promoted by Uglow (1988) and understanding this helps to explain why ethical neutrality, and its associated concepts of disinterestedness, impartiality and tolerance, shaped British policing for so many years.

There are four aspects of liberal individualism that need to be drawn out here, before we can understand the appeal of ethical neutrality. First, liberal individualism implies that individuals can and will differ significantly in how they perceive the world. This is not about people's physical and/or intellectual attributes, but rather what they perceive to be important in terms of what it means to be human. If everyone thinks the same, individuality becomes a trivial matter. Its importance arises from the extent to which we recognise that people perceive the world differently, and the differences are substantive.

Secondly, the logic of liberal individualism is that each perception of what it means to be human is defensible, within certain parameters.

Again, individuality has less importance if we establish that only one perception of what it means to be human is valid, while all others are not. If there is only one legitimised perception of what it means to be human, then the role of ethics is reduced to ensuring compliance and consistency in accordance with the accepted values, over and above recognition of individual differences. It would favour social conformity over individual expression. So while it is not unusual for a liberal society to deny validity to particular expressions of what it means to be human, it is recognised that such denials cannot be extensive or excessive if the society is to retain its liberal character. Liberal individualism favours pluralism, which requires a high degree of toleration towards many different perspectives (MacIntyre, 1999; McKinnon, 2006; Scanlon, 2003), some of which will undoubtedly be regarded as offensive to many in that society (Raz, 1988; Mendus, 1999; Williams, 1999). Toleration is therefore central to the classic liberal position; indeed Rawls (2000, p.7) sees it as 'one of the historical origins of liberalism'. It has been defended on different grounds (Mendus, 1988) and is a key component of Mill's (1859/1973) arguments in *On Liberty*. More recently, its virtue has been championed by Furedi (2011, p.25) who sees it as 'a precious resource that is in need of constant intellectual renewal'. For Ryan (1988, p.41), perhaps the most straightforward defence of toleration was presented by Hobbes, who saw intolerance on the part of the state as 'the foolishness of causing needless anxiety and resentment'. Toleration is an important component of ethical neutrality.

Thirdly, the classical liberal perspective assumes that the individual is an autonomous being who can think for him- or herself. This limits the extent to which those in authority can dismiss the thoughts of individuals simply because they are deemed to be foolish or ill-informed. Again, Mill's (1859/1973) influence on the architecture of this liberal perspective is noteworthy. A liberal government will engage its citizens in debate and challenge different perspectives, but will fall short of compelling or even cajoling others into agreeing with an officially sanctioned view of the world. The idea of individuality is stripped of its content if restricted to persons who are deemed worthy of such status by self-appointed guardians of reason. Advocates of a classical liberal perspective are aware that many people in society fall short of the autonomous ideal assumed within liberal individualism, but nonetheless support a form of governance that *assumes* all individuals are autonomous.

Importantly here we need to recognise that the individual is a concept. It represents an ideal person that should be used as the common measure in deciding the appropriateness of government interventions. From a classical liberal perspective, there is more harm done when governments intervene unnecessarily in the lives of strong, autonomous people, than when they fail to protect those who are more vulnerable and in need of support. From a contemporary policing perspective, this is a significant weakness of liberalism.

Fourthly, and perhaps most disconcerting from a policing perspective, liberal individualism presupposes conflict as a natural consequence of recognising the equal validity of competing expressions of individualism. This is recognised by the 17th-century English philosopher Thomas Hobbes (1588–1679). Although Hobbes is more commonly disassociated from the liberal canon because of his anti-democratic sentiments, Gray (2000) argues that it is Hobbes who revolutionises the way we think about individuals, and in this respect he lays the foundations for liberal individualism. For Hobbes (1651), humans are by their very nature individualistic, and within the state of nature this individualism inevitably results in conflict, in *a war of all against all*. For Hobbes (1651), disorder, crime, conflict and chaos are not pathological but the norm in the state of nature; order and peace are therefore only arrived at through the imposition of society against our nature. As Martinich (2005, p.105) puts it, for Hobbes, where 'no laws existed, no behaviour would be immoral'.

Hobbes (1651) is not arguing against peace and order here, nor is he challenging the imposition of society. Indeed, he argues that the best form of governance is in the form of a benevolent dictator, someone who is willing to impose order across society, albeit for the good of society. Hobbes favours a benevolent dictator because of the extent to which he sees conflict as an inevitability of individual differences regarding what it means to be human. He sees these differences to be so profound that any form of government that involves more than one leader will inevitably result in these differences being given representation by the different leaders. This in turn, for Hobbes, means fractures at the heart of governance, which will inevitably tend towards civil war. For Hobbes, democracy is the worst of all forms of governing because of the extent to which it empowers different, conflicting views on what it means to be human. Importantly, as Gray (2000) argues, for Hobbes there can never be consensus in society, therefore, the best we can ever hope for is *peaceful coexistence* between the different factions in society.

Taken together, these four aspects of liberal individualism lead to the adoption of ethical neutrality at the heart of liberal governance. Liberal individualism is premised upon the idea that moral pluralism is a natural human condition and that therefore there are many ways of realising and expressing our humanity. The individual is conceived as an autonomous being who cannot be compelled to act or think against his or her nature, and from this, there is a tension between the various perceptions of what it means to be human that leads inevitably towards conflict if not checked. The role of government and police is to ensure that conflict is avoided (Waddington, 1999; Delattre, 2004; Miller, 2004a; Reiner, 2010). Peaceful coexistence is argued to be the primary substantive aim of those in authority from this perspective.

It is worth remembering the historical context within which liberal individualism was born, in particular as it develops in 17th-century England (Hill, 1999). Liberal individualism can be seen as both contributing to the anarchy in England at that time, and being a strategy to overcome the chaos and violence. On the one hand, liberal individualism challenges deeply ingrained privileges that had existed for centuries through religious and monarchical traditions (Held, 1984). In removing these traditional and long-established institutions of authority, liberal individualism creates a power vacuum and a radical questioning of all forms of authority. In 17th-century Britain, religious and political tensions intensified and competing values came to the fore, resulting in unprecedented levels of violence during the English Civil Wars. Liberal individualism, as Boyd (2004) notes, emerges from this chaos as a radical departure from the rigid social hierarchy characteristic of pre-liberal societies. Social order, and a person's place within it, are suddenly no longer predetermined and fixed as had been the case within traditional societies, and legitimate authority is no longer preordained by God but rather established through human reason. Ethical neutrality becomes a necessary tool within liberal individualism for dealing with the inevitable conflict that arises within a society liberated from the tyranny of privilege and a rigid social hierarchy.

Ethical neutrality plays a limited role in the principled liberal perspective that aligns with Alderson's (1998) *Principled Policing*. It is limited to being a temporary mechanism to permit an initial flourishing of moral thinking. But as Gray (2000) notes, this perspective assumes that differences will be resolved through reasoned discourse. As particular expressions of what it means to be human are dismissed as irrational, ethical neutrality becomes less important. It is assumed that each time we dismiss a particular set of values, we move closer to establishing a consensus regarding what it means to be human. In the aftermath of the Second World War, for example, racial ideologies were rejected as irrational and immoral, and restricted accordingly over time through laws and other measures. This is reflected within policing in the UK, which moves from being premised upon a race relations model – what we might see as attaining peaceful coexistence across ethnic divides – to the conceiving of police as an explicitly anti-racist organisation post Macpherson (Rowe, 2002). From this principled perspective, we dismiss ideas of what it means to be human and over time also begin to promulgate particular human attributes as universal values, for example through the language and institutions of human rights. Human rights are clearly not underpinned by ethical neutrality, but are rather explicit expressions of particular values that are claimed to be universally representative of what it means to be human.

Within Uglow's (1988) *Policing Liberal Society*, ethical neutrality is seen not as a temporary means of correcting errors in our reasoning, but rather as a permanent requirement to ensure peace. Gray (2000) argues that this strand of liberal thinking emphasises the inherently pluralistic nature of humanity. Here differences are not seen as a clash between right and wrong conceptions of what it means to be human, but simply as a tension between substantially different perceptions. This perspective favours pluralism and is expressed through the Latin term *modus vivendi*. It favours peaceful coexistence between incompatible and mutually hostile factions in society (Gray, 2000). As Rescher (1993) says, consensus is an unachievable folly and efforts to achieve consensus are more harmful than they are helpful. Moreover, consensus is argued by Rescher (1993) to be unnecessary. He argues that people do not need to agree with one another, they simply need to find acceptable ways of living together.

MacIntyre (1985), in a similar vein, states that there are different intellectual traditions that shape people's views on questions of what it means to be human, which cannot be resolved rationally because they draw upon different, equally valid, rationalities. MacIntyre (1985) illustrates his argument by showing how entrenched disputes are on issues such as abortion. He argues that each side of the dispute is able to present empirical evidence within rational and logical structures to support their competing perspectives. As MacIntyre (1985) demonstrates, such conflict is explained not by logical or factual errors, but rather by the substantially different and deeply held convictions of what it means to be human on each side of the dispute.

This poses a problem for advocates of principled policing. How do we establish what the principles should be? As Gray (2000) notes, principles are prone to being either (i) *too indeterminate*, so broad or general that they become meaningless and trivial, or (ii) *too arbitrary*, overly selective in what is accepted as a core principle and what is ignored. Gray's (2000) observations are directed at the role principles play generally in defining a good society, but they are arguably even more pertinent when looking specifically at policing. As Reiner (2010) and Waddington (1999) have both argued so eloquently, the existence of policing presupposes conflict and discord. In this respect they both argue that community policing is oxymoronic, a contradiction in terms. This poses a very real problem for our understanding of ethical policing, which is likewise susceptible to being seen as oxymoronic. The level of consensus required across society for us to establish clearly defined and specified policing principles that are at the same time meaningful, systematic and logical is such that policing would hardly be needed. The less we need police, the easier it is for policing to be ethical, and for it to be seen as such. However, policing is needed where and when it is most contentious. It is this that makes ethical policing difficult to define, and more importantly, to put into practice.

From a policing point of view, it is arguably much easier to maintain order if a particular idea of what it means to be human is given privilege over competing conceptions. Religious authority and political dictators overcome the kind of conflicts identified by MacIntyre (1985) by imposing one view on all. However, the primary challenge confronting the liberal society emerging in 17th-century Britain was how to reconcile mutually hostile perspectives on what it means to be human without appearing to favour one faction over another. The emergence of liberal society necessitates an authority that can resolve conflicts and ensure peace without having recourse to religious authority or arbitrary use of force. For such an authority to be regarded as legitimate by all parties it needs to be seen as impartial, disinterested and neutral. This is the basis of ethical neutrality.

There are two specific aspects of ethical neutrality that I want to emphasise here. First, ethical neutrality favours tolerance and a spirit of *live and let live*. It stops us from being overly judgemental and forces us to consider different perspectives. Ethical neutrality fosters understanding and a more empathetic appreciation of the needs of others. Such understanding and empathy can only be achieved by detaching ourselves from the immediacy of the warring parties, and by distancing ourselves from the outcomes of any conflict resolution.

Ethical neutrality also reminds us that even when dealing with the most extreme behaviours, the morality of an action is always likely to be more ambiguous than its legality: one person's terrorist is another's freedom fighter. Likewise, all legal judgments, no matter how difficult and complex, are always in one respect more straightforward than moral judgements, no matter how easy and simple they appear: a person can be legally convicted of child abuse, and while the fact that the perpetrator had also been a victim of child abuse does not absolve them of their legal guilt, or diminish the devastating impact of their actions on others, the dual status of the convicted, as both offender and victim, creates moral ambiguities and clouds moral judgements.

The impartiality of those in authority is deemed necessary to ensure that all parties involved in a conflict recognise the legitimacy of any resolution. Authority needs to be seen as neutral or it will be challenged for being part of the problem rather than a means of resolving disputes. This was a key issue in the review of policing arrangements in Northern Ireland as part of the peace negotiations in the late 1990s (Patten, 1999). The Royal Ulster Constabulary (RUC), the police at the time of the peace process, were deemed to have been too involved with the conflict. Replacing the RUC with a new police service was therefore seen as essential to the success of the peace process.

The second aspect of ethical neutrality that I want to draw upon here is the favouring of minimal and limited intervention in society. This is a defining feature of Uglow's (1988) *Policing Liberal Society* and it recognises that the involvement of authority in a conflict can have the unintended consequence of escalating problems. The escalation occurs because the involvement of an authority raises the stakes for the conflicting parties. What might have started as a neighbourly dispute becomes potentially much more if and when the police become involved. The question of who is right and who is wrong can have much more serious implications when the police are involved, and this makes it less likely for warring parties to make peace, or indeed to simply stop fighting. Ethical neutrality encourages those in authority to step back and not get involved unless it is absolutely necessary to do so. It restricts government intervention to matters that can be clearly seen as public law, as opposed to those that are characterised as private morality concerns. This perspective, captured within John Stuart Mill's (1859/1973) 'harm to others' principle, suggests that interventions should be prioritised around instances where there is clear evidence of harm, and the only justification for intervening in the affairs of a person is to prevent them from harming others. Importantly, those in authority should not, according to Mill, intervene because people are acting immorally or foolishly. Indeed, Mill emphasises that individuals are best placed to decide what is in their own best interest, as opposed to those establishing enlightened social norms. Mill (1859/1973) articulates the virtue of ethical neutrality, which has at its heart a clear distinction between public matters of law and private matters of morality.

The limitations of ethical neutrality

Ethical neutrality, as I have argued earlier, is a valued policing strategy within a liberal society that prioritises the pragmatic pursuit of peaceful coexistence in the face of moral pluralism. However, Alderson (1998) manifests the changing sensibilities that mean that by the end of the 20th century such classical liberal ideals have lost their appeal. Indeed, Oakeshott (1991) had documented much earlier in 1949 the extent to which privacy had come to be seen as a trivial matter. The decline of classical liberalism has been mirrored by the unstoppable rise globally in the dominance of democratic sensibilities (Wood, 2016a). Within the contexts of increasingly democratic societies, the liberal favouring of ethical neutrality has diminished and is increasingly rejected as a valid basis for policing. This is evidenced not least by the proliferation of different articulations of proactive policing (Wilson and Kelling, 1982; Goldstein, 1990; Hopkins Burke, 2004; Ratcliffe, 2016).

One criticism of ethical neutrality is that it is a misnomer. It is argued that far from being neutral on ethical matters, liberalism promotes and favours values that advocate liberal individualism (Bellamy, 2000). Ethical neutrality, by championing the freedom of the individual and favouring limited police intervention in society, gives preference to those with social, economic and political power to act unabated against the interests of the vulnerable, the poor and disenfranchised groups in society with minimal moral condemnation.

Ethical neutrality in this respect does little to challenge embedded inequalities in society and indeed, by appealing to the separation of law and morality, those in authority have been able to ignore serious injustices on the grounds that they take place in the private worlds where individual morality precludes the kind of legal interventions that are reserved for matters of public concern. Ethical neutrality thus permits violence against women and children within the confines of private, familial relationships, almost without public sanction. Moreover it is suggested that the police are not, and nor should they be, impartial when confronting conflict. This is because values shape society and create societal expectations that require the police to make value judgements about who is in the right and who is in the wrong within a given conflict.

This was illustrated in October 2012 when Commander Peter Spindler of the Metropolitan Police Service in London announced that he would be leading the police investigation into the accusations of child sex abuse against Jimmy Savile. Commander Spindler made his announcement on television wearing an NSPCC (National Society for the Prevention of Cruelty to Children) badge on his lapel. The lack of a response to this demonstrates that societal expectations of police ethical neutrality are at the very least passive. I suspect that if asked explicitly about the appropriateness of having a lead investigator into child sex abuse identifying so candidly with a charity set up to protect children, people would generally see no conflict of interest and they may even see it as a good thing. I suggest that increasingly there is an expectation that the police take sides against bad people and support good people, thus justifying what Commander Spindler did. Having spoken to him on this matter, he confirmed that it was a deliberate and conscious act on his part. I am not concerned here whether Commander Spindler was right or wrong to do what he did. I simply refer to his actions and the lack of any negative response to them as evidence of the retreat away from liberal ideals and the arguments favouring ethical neutrality.

There are other characteristics of liberal policing that are increasingly rejected today. Uglow (1988) argues, quite rightly in my view, that liberal policing is by definition limited and restrained, and as such, it should not be anticipatory, preventative or proactive. Nor should it be the means of resolving social problems. For Uglow (1988), liberal policing is also necessarily reactive because to be otherwise would constitute excessive or overly intrusive police activity: liberal police respond to symptoms; it is for others to address the causes of social ills.

The shift away from such liberal ideals is evidenced within police policy and operations. During the 1990s, police services across the UK presented themselves more and more as being proactive. Proactive policing became the norm and it was used as a positive term in opposition to the pejorative characterisation of traditional police approaches as fire brigade policing. The reactive character of liberal policing was presented as an ineffective and inefficient use of resources (Audit Commission, 1993), with officers either sitting in a police station or police car, or aimlessly and randomly patrolling an area, waiting for something to happen. By the mid-1990s, less than a decade after Uglow's (1988) publication, the liberal ideal of policing was in serious retreat. The liberal virtue of restraint, and the corresponding strategy of avoiding unnecessary interventions, were no longer associated with the idea of good policing. Instead, good policing was established by the extent to which it could predict, prevent, disrupt and solve crime problems, whether it was through zero-tolerance policing (Punch, 2007), intelligence-led policing (Ratcliffe, 2016) or problem-oriented policing (Goldstein, 1990). The proactive policing models differed significantly and in substantive ways, but they all shared the common assumption that good policing is purposeful and directed, with explicit values underpinning its interventions in society. Even the introduction of the Human Rights Act 1998 (HRA), sometimes portrayed as limiting police interventions, has played an important role in moving policing away from the classical liberal perspective. It has placed obligations on those in authority to protect the vulnerable, which in turn has fostered preventative legislation, requiring the police to intervene in more aspects of our lives, and to do so proactively before problems manifest themselves fully. The HRA thus imbues policing with moral purpose and requires them to be guided more by a sense of mission and purpose that is deliberately absent within the ethically neutral ideal of liberal policing.

This approach to policing, informed and shaped by HRA, is anticipated and promoted within Alderson's (1998) *Principled Policing*, which characterises the shift away from a classical liberal perspective. It is much more aligned to the changing sensibilities that favour value-led, preventative and proactive interventions. Whereas Uglow (1988) represents liberal policing, Alderson (1998) is the standard bearer for an approach to policing that embraces moral obligations. His articulation of principled policing is explicit in criticising the kind of ethical neutrality that has characterised policing historically. For Alderson (1998), policing is necessarily purposeful, and therefore needs to be driven by moral values and this approach is captured by Miller (2004a, p.167) when he says the purpose of policing is 'the protection of moral rights'.

My objective here is not to explain why this change has taken place, nor is it primarily to support or critique the diminishing importance of a classical liberal perspective within policing. Indeed, my views on this matter are somewhat in the balance. On the one hand, I agree with those who criticise the liberal ideal of ethical neutrality as being anything but neutral (Bellamy, 2000). More substantively, I agree that ethical neutrality favours the powerful over the disenfranchised. It also appeals to particular human traits, such as the capacity to reason and rationalise, over other human qualities such as compassion, intuition and emotional intelligence. On the other hand, I also recognise the pragmatic value that comes from a classical liberal perspective. Social good can be achieved from restrained and limited intrusions, just as social harm can come from well-intended interventions. In particular, the progressive thinking of many classical liberal thinkers is something often overlooked by contemporary critics (Wolff, 2006). For the moment, though, I want to emphasise how the declining influence of a classical liberal perspective has brought values to the forefront of policing in a way that was unimaginable for the majority of the police's history in the UK. Today it is clear that values are integral to shaping policing and in particular in establishing what is ethical policing.

A distinction within moral philosophy between amorality and immorality

It is worth noting here two different ways in which we can consider policing to be principled, by looking at what we consider to be the opposite of each approach. So far, I have treated principled policing as moral policing, or more precisely as morally informed policing or value-led policing. But we need to be mindful of an important distinction in how we use the term 'moral'. This distinction is highlighted within moral philosophy by the articulation of two discrete *opposites* to the term moral. Montefiore (1958), for example, notes moral can be represented,

(i) as an affirmation of what is good, or,
(ii) in relation to matters that are treated with special importance, as matters of principle.

The 'affirmation of what is good' is grounded in the Latin origins of 'moral' found in the word 'mores', which relates to the behavioural norms and customs of a community (Montefiore, 1958, p.148). Within this meaning, the term *moral* distinguishes between those acts that conform to the norms and customs of a community and those that do not. The opposite to this understanding of moral is the word *immoral*. Immoral acts are those that are identified as bad because they go against the standards, expectations and rules governing the community. A person, in this respect, acts immorally when they act in a way which they know and understand, or at least should know and understand, to be wrong. So we might say that policing is unprincipled if the reasoning upon which it is founded is deemed to be immoral. Corrupt policing, by definition, is always immoral in this sense because it is underpinned by bad intentions. As an aside, it is for this reason that Kleinig (2002) objects to the term 'noble cause corruption' (see Chapter 5). Similarly, we would say today unequivocally that policing in Nazi Germany or apartheid South Africa was immoral because it was premised upon what we now see as morally abhorrent ideas of racial supremacy.

In relation to Montefiore's (1958) second understanding of morality, we consider policing to be unprincipled if there is an absence of principles at the heart of the police's strategic thinking. This label of unprincipled would apply, for example, to the kind of liberal policing outlined by Uglow (1988). It is deemed to be unprincipled, indeed it is self-proclaimed as unashamedly so, to the extent that it explicitly champions ethical neutrality rather than any particular moral principles. But when we say that liberal policing is unprincipled in this second sense, we are not saying that it is immoral. Liberal policing is still based upon understanding the difference between right and wrong, but does not reserve a special place for particular values to be treated with greater importance. This second opposite to morality is called *amorality*.

Liberal policing approaches right and wrong in legal terms, and moreover focuses attention on what is deemed immoral, rather than on what it means to be moral. A liberally framed legislation does not start with an idea of how a good person acts, and then criminalise all behaviours that fall below this civic standard. Instead it identifies specific acts and behaviours that are deemed immoral and prohibits them. If an act is not prohibited, the assumption is that it is permissible. Does its permissibility mean that it is a morally good thing to do? No, it is viewed neutrally unless or until it is deemed to be so bad that it requires prohibitive legislation.

Importantly, it is much easier, although still contentious and open to challenge, to establish what an immoral behaviour looks like than it is to recognise and agree upon what we understand a moral act to be. This is reflected in debates about police ethics, which will often focus on identifying and responding to the unethical (Westmarland and Rowe, 2018), and in particular tackling corrupt policing (Punch, 2009). This is understandable, given the detrimental impact that corruption has upon police legitimacy (Jackson et al, 2014), and it is also much easier to agree on what bad policing looks like than it is to establish what constitutes exemplary policing.

There is a danger here that by implication we define ethical as the absence of unethical. This is a problem within the permissibility of a liberal approach that focuses exclusively on tackling the unethical, without making any firm or explicit articulation regarding what is ethical. The absence of corruption does not in itself produce ethical policing. Tackling corruption is a given within an ethical policing context but when Alderson (1998) speaks of principled policing I suggest his target is not the *immorality* of some police practice, but rather the *amorality* of policing as a whole.

In establishing the idea of principled policing, Alderson (1998) is therefore not saying that policing historically has been *immoral*, even though at times it may well have been, but rather that it has in general tended to be *amoral*. Alderson's (1998) concern is not that policing has been founded upon bad principles, but rather that it has lacked a strong moral base upon which officers could prioritise morally what they should be doing. Consequently, he argues the police have found it too easy to simply go with the flow and adapt to whatever changes are thrown their way. The police have been, he argues, overly compliant and defined narrowly by what is established in law and through social norms, at any given place and time.

Moral obligations, Immanuel Kant and a deontological ethic

The dominant thinking in terms of what constitutes a principled approach to ethical policing comes from ethical theories that are founded upon notions of duty. In particular, the influence of the German philosopher Immanuel Kant (1724–1804) looms large here. As MacIntyre (1966) notes, Kant's (1788) approach to ethical reasoning transforms the way we think about duty by defining it in terms of the moral obligations we have as individuals to act in particular ways, as opposed to a narrower understanding of duty as something we are tasked to do within specifically defined occupational roles. This is called a *deontological* ethical approach because of its emphasis on duty and obligation (deontology is derived from the Greek word for duty, *deon)*. The contemporary dominance of the Kantian notion of duty within public life owes much to the seminal influence of American philosopher John Rawls (1921–2002). In particular, through his notion of *justice as fairness* (Rawls, 1971), Rawls is pivotal within moral, political and legal philosophy, widely recognised for his contribution to understanding ethics in public life by disciples and critics alike. The influence of Rawls can be seen in Alderson (1998) but also in Manning's (2010) articulation of democratic policing and it is implicit within the increasingly influential procedural justice approach to understanding police legitimacy.

A key feature of Kant's reasoning is that the obligatory nature of his notion of duty means that the actions of a police officer are to a large extent predetermined and shaped by values that are established and imbued by officers prior to arriving at an incident. A Kantian understanding of duty thus necessitates policing to be proactive rather than reactive in a truly substantive way, such that it completely contradicts the liberal idea of policing presented by Uglow (1988). In stark opposition to the ethical neutrality of liberal policing, principles express *explicitly* moral values that shape our actions in at least three substantive ways.

First, principles are presented as being independent of contingent facts. That is to say they have a non-consequential quality, which in turn means they are justified, more or less, without reference to outcomes. I say *more or less* because there are degrees to which advocates of a principled approach insist upon the primacy of obligation over results. I will say more on this in Chapter 5 when I consider the difference between seeing principles as aspirational as opposed to obligatory. However, for the moment I am considering principles as they are presented in an obligatory manner, in which the right (or not) of performing an act, as opposed to the good (or not) achieved from performing it, is emphasised. Principles preclude us from doing certain actions if they are not deemed to be the right thing to do, even if it can be established that doing such actions would bring about a positive outcome. So, for example, principles preclude us from racial profiling because it discriminates against individuals on ethnic grounds, irrespective of whether such discriminatory actions are likely to lead to the apprehension of individuals guilty of the most serious of offences.

This aspect of a principle mirrors the binding and incontrovertible quality of a peremptory norm in law (Simmonds, 2002). Human rights, for example, have this peremptory quality in that they prevent us, at the level of our conscience, from considering particular solutions to problems, even though they would be considered rational options outside of a human rights framework (Brandt, 1979). As Gray (1995) notes, in this respect rights can stop us from doing good things, at the same time as allowing us to do bad things. Principles are set above achieving good, for example, when they prevent us from telling a lie, even when we know that it could save another person's life. Imagine being confronted by an enraged and jealous husband asking where his wife is. You know she is hiding under the bed in fear of her life. Do you tell the truth knowing that he will violently attack her, or lie and say that you saw her leave the house by the back door as he arrived through the front door? At the same time though, principles do not stop us from doing things that we know are not good. For example, a principle of allowing people to make choices regarding what they consume does not stop them from smoking or drinking excessive amounts of alcohol, both of which we will readily accept do considerable harm. Principles are thus detached from the consequences of our actions. Freedom of choice, for example, is deemed a good thing in and of itself, even if we choose to do bad things with our freedom.

Secondly, the kind of principles that Alderson (1998) has in mind are public in nature. As such they challenge the legal positivist view that separates law and morals (Hart, 1957), or what Green (2008) presents as the separability of law and morals. Legal positivism sees morality belonging to the private world as opposed to the public orientation of law. This position was set out and challenged within the Hart–Devlin dispute against the backdrop of Sir John Wolfenden's Report of the Departmental Committee on Homosexual Offences and Prostitution published in 1957. The Report, which was underpinned by Hart's (1957) legal positivism, was challenged by Lord Devlin, a British judge who countered the recommendations of the Wolfenden Report to decriminalise private acts of homosexuality and prostitution, arguing that public authorities had a duty to protect the moral fabric of society. For Devlin (1965), homosexuality and prostitution undermined the family, which he saw in very traditional and conservative terms. Moreover, for Devlin (1965), families were the building blocks within our society, and community cohesion was dependent upon their existence. He therefore saw it as a public duty to intervene in the private lives of those individuals whose private moralities had what he perceived to be a detrimental impact on the public good. Lord Devlin lost the argument at that time, and his specific views on homosexuality and family have come to be seen as increasingly archaic and antiquated. However, his arguments about the blurring of the distinction between law and morality, and his questioning of the separability of the two along a public/private divide, have become more widely accepted.

Principled policing in this respect is not about the individual morality of particular officers, but rather the collective will of the police organisation as a whole. It captures a public expression of police values and priorities. Moreover, principled policing operates not in isolation but with the consent and in the name of the public. Police principles need to be shared by the majority in society or at least be representative of the dominant sensibilities of the day if they are to have meaning. Principled policing thus has the qualities of a recognised public morality, something that sits between the private morality of individuals and the public law of any given jurisdiction.

Principles oblige us to take affirmative action to proactively prevent particular values from being contravened. This is partly born out of the role principles play within a public setting, for example in relation to establishing what ethical policing is. It is not enough that we personally refrain from being unprincipled, or even that we chastise others for acting in an unprincipled manner. The understanding of principles I am presenting here also places obligations upon us to anticipate and prevent actions that contravene the principles we have established. Using the example discussed earlier, we are required to proactively prevent racially discriminatory police practice from occurring.

Principles are thus positive statements about the way the world should be; they are normative statements that promote a particular idea of what it means to be a good person, and perhaps even more profoundly, what it means to be human. Principles play a role within society in promoting specific values in an impersonal manner (Haldane, 2017). Unlike an individual's private morality, principled policing has a more impersonal characteristic that imposes itself upon all as a matter of public interest rather than simply a private concern; however, unlike public laws, the imposition of principled policing takes the form of normative expectations as opposed to legal instruction.

Thirdly, this normative dimension of principled policing means that for ethical policing to have meaning, an officer needs to be able to justify his or her actions with reference to these principles that are both impersonal and shared. Drawing on Beardsmore (1969, p.xiv), this sets parameters to what constitutes ethical reasoning: 'Reasons in morality cannot be just whatever the agent chooses to mention.' Indeed, where morality remains at a private level it has minimal bearing on ethical policing. It is perhaps more correct to say that ethical policing requires the subjugation of an officer's *private* morality.

If ethical policing is to be articulated through principles, the underlying values that give it shape need to be clear and transparent. This requires addressing the dual challenge of avoiding both trivialisation and selectivity if the principles are to provide meaningful and indiscriminate guidance to officers in situations that require ethical decisions to be made.

John Rawls, for example, captures and represents the ethical thinking that underpins liberal democratic societies that emerged largely as a revolt against the arbitrary imposition of power in pre-modern communities. Rawls' understanding of justice as an integral part of liberal democracies, as *the* means by which a valid form of authority is instituted, is important to appreciate here. Justice, in this sense, replaces hereditary lineage and other forms of privilege, as the instrument for establishing legitimate sources of power (Held, 1984).

It is possible within illiberal, undemocratic societies to elevate justice as a primary concern. For example, in both Plato's (1955) philosopher king in *The Republic* and Hobbes' (1651) benevolent dictator in *Leviathan* we are presented with just rulers; however, in both cases the respective authorities of these leaders are absolute and in this respect are not *dependent* upon being just. There is very limited capacity for removing either if they fail to live up to expectations. As such, justice is aspirational and incidental to each leader's authority. However, liberal and democratic authority *needs* a concept of justice in order to have meaning. The relationship between policing and justice is in this respect taken for granted within liberal democratic contexts. Justice underpins and establishes the legitimacy of police authority in an *essential* way: our understanding of liberal democratic policing is dependent upon a notion of justice and is rendered meaningless if it is not at the same time conceptualised as being just.

We are starting to see a move away from the principles that shape Rawls' thinking. For example, his focus on wealth distribution as a political priority captures the mood in the context of the relative peace and harmony of the post-World War Two consensus. Although still a dominant force, different critical voices that depart from Rawls and the Kantian notion of duty in important ways are gaining influence (Sandel, 1982; MacIntyre, 1985; Sen, 2009). Rawls is seen as too committed to liberal individualism but there is also growing concern about security within liberal democratic contexts, which are reshaping policing ideals (Wood, 2016a). A growing sense of insecurity and chaos is elevating order above wealth distribution as the primary political objective (Tralau, 2011), with the redistribution of 'bads' rather than 'goods' being seen as the most pressing need (Giddens, 1991; Beck, 1992). Saying principles are important is one thing, establishing what they should be is something else.

Conclusion

I will conclude this chapter by arguing that principles are important in shaping our understanding of ethical policing, but are ultimately insufficient in providing a coherent and workable definition. The idea of policing in the UK has been, for the most part, shaped by a classical liberal perspective that fosters a deliberate strategy of ethical neutrality (Boyd, 2004). This strategy of ethical neutrality excludes morality as much as possible from police practice, and policing is characterised, historically, more by its impartiality and disinterestedness than it is by being principled. Policing has avoided moral values and this explains why the kind of principled policing favoured by Alderson (1998) was until very recently regarded as highly problematic.

The situation has changed steadily over recent decades. As I have argued elsewhere (Wood, 2016a), support for the classical liberal perspective has diminished so much that today the idea of policing being value led has become an expectation receiving little critical objection. Uglow's (1988) favourable articulation of the idea of liberal policing is in stark contrast to Alderson's (1998) promotion of principled policing.

Principled policing and the adoption of an explicit promotion of particular moral values becomes necessary in the face of obvious shortcomings arising from the liberal policing approach. Society has become much more attuned to the suffering of the vulnerable and the inequalities across society that manifest themselves as crime and disorder policing problems. There is a growing expectation that the police should be proactive in identifying and responding to the suffering of the most vulnerable and disenfranchised in society, and that more should be done to redress imbalances in the power relations between the *haves* and *have nots* across our communities. We are no longer willing to tolerate the strategy of ethical neutrality, and non-intervention is rejected. We want and expect the police to do more, to do more protecting and serving, and in this regard ethical policing today is represented much more as being involved than it is by the liberal ideals of neutrality, disinterestedness or impartiality.

I have given some indication already in this chapter of the difficulties and shortcomings of a principled policing approach. These concerns will be explored further in the remaining chapters. For the moment though, I will end this chapter by stating that the explicit articulation of values within policing is essential in framing an understanding of ethical policing. However, this is only one aspect, or one dimension of ethical policing. While welcoming the adoption of such values within policing, we should not lose sight of other qualities that shape ethical policing. These include aspects of the liberal policing approach. We need to remain mindful of the virtues of tolerance, disinterestedness, ethical neutrality and an ethos of limited intervention, without accepting any of these tactics uncritically and without ignoring the role values can play in helping us understand better the extent to which any one of these mechanisms is appropriate or not.

Suggested further reading

Alderson, J. (1998) *Principled Policing: Protecting the Public with Integrity*. Winchester: Waterside Press

Berlin I. (1958) 'Two Concepts of Liberty', in I. Berlin (1990) *Four Essays on Liberty*. Oxford: Oxford University Press, pp.118–72

Gray, J. (2000) *Two Faces of Liberalism*. Cambridge: Polity

Uglow, S. (1988) *Policing Liberal Society*. Oxford: Oxford University Press

3

The role of human rights in providing the basis for good policing

Introduction

In Chapter 2 I argued that principles play an important role in framing our understanding of ethical policing. At the same time, I suggested there are limitations in understanding ethical policing exclusively and simply as principled policing. In this chapter I look to develop both aspects of this argument by focusing on human rights as an example of principled policing.

In the first part of the chapter I provide a brief overview of the emergence of rights-based thinking, outlining different forms rights have taken. I also contextualise the emergence of human rights in the second half of the 20th century, in both intellectual and institutional terms. I draw a distinction between the moral and legal representations of human rights, between human rights-based ethical reasoning, and formal human rights institutions such as the Universal Declaration of Human Rights (UDHR), the European Convention on Human Rights (ECHR) and the Human Rights Act 1998 (HRA).

The distinction between the moral and legal representations of human rights is important in understanding ethical policing because within policing, I argue, a legalistic approach to human rights dominates. This can consequently limit the extent to which human rights impact upon policing *ethically*. I argue that it is the moral power of human rights that primarily establishes ethical policing. Moreover, I suggest that institutionalising human rights principles has the potential to unintentionally foster a culture of compliance, and thereby undermine the capacity for officers to think ethically. It is more appropriate, I suggest, to engage with human rights as moral aspirations, principles that we strive to achieve in practice, as opposed to understanding them as legal obligations and/or positional duties, expressed through compliance within a professional code of ethics.

As Scanlon (2003, p.113) notes, human rights are portrayed as 'a particularly important class of moral considerations' that have largely remained immune from the political controversy of other political and economic matters. However, this is changing, and I draw upon different arguments that challenge the moral basis of human rights (Gray, 2000; Tralau, 2011) and I explore various critical voices that have questioned the appropriateness of human rights for the 21st century (Ignatieff, 2001; Dershowitz, 2006). In particular, the universal claims of human rights reasoning, in many respects its most powerful component, appear to be increasingly hollow and unsustainable (Gearty, 2006). I refer to Coady's (2008) concept of moralism, which captures a disconnection between moral claims and what they actually deliver. I conclude the chapter by arguing that human rights have an important role to play in shaping ethical policing, but only if we ensure that the moral dimension of human rights reasoning is not lost, and conversely, that we avoid treating human rights from a narrow legalistic or formulaic perspective. It is worth bearing in mind Sen's (2009, p.363) observation that human rights are not, as Bentham argued, to be understood as law's children, but rather H.L.A. Hart (1957) was closer in seeing human rights as the '*parents of law*'.

The emergence of rights: a brief overview

The idea of human rights emerges from an understanding of natural law, which has antecedents in Ancient Greece. It has also been a dominant feature within Western Philosophy since at least the time of St Thomas Aquinas (1225–74). The basis of natural law in relation to moral philosophy is the idea that rights are an inherent quality of being human. Natural law is in this respect contrasted with positive law, the idea that laws are created by humans in specific places at particular times. From a natural law perspective, there are inherent, universal human values that need to be discovered and recognised within the laws of any given jurisdiction. A good law is seen as one that accords with natural law; a bad law, conversely, is at odds with natural law. An appeal to natural rights and natural justice goes hand in hand with this idea of natural law, and from this perspective a law will be seen as unjust if it is deemed to contravene human nature.

An early expression of natural rights led to the signing of the Magna Carta by King John in 1215 at Runnymede. This Great Charter was imposed upon King John by his subjects, the feudal barons, who asserted their political rights such that it limited the King's power over them. They argued that the King's arbitrary rule contravened their inherent rights and demanded that the King ruled justly in accordance with natural law. The Magna Carta is still celebrated today as a significant moment in the development of rights and democracy, despite its limited scope; it did not require the King to act justly to all, but rather to an elite group of barons. The Charter of the Forest 1217, which established rights beyond an elite group, was also limited in scope, albeit in a different way. This second Charter allowed commoners to live off the forest but with very strict limitations in terms of what was permitted in practice. The step towards modern-day human rights was extended through the Peasants' Revolt led by Wat Tyler and John Ball in 1381, but it is not until the 17th century that the elevation of rights as a concern for all takes centre stage. It is only at this point that the individual becomes a dominant concern, allowing for the eventual flourishing of contemporary human rights.

Immanuel Kant (1724–1804) needs further mention here. While there is debate regarding the extent to which Kant's moral philosophy can be seen as the basis for the modern legal, political and moral human rights infrastructure (Follesdal, 2014), it is hard not to see strong Kantian influences upon the nature of human rights discourse. Kant's emphasis on human dignity, on ensuring that an individual is not treated as a means to an end, and Kant's focus on moral obligation, and the duties that arise from our moral reasoning (his deontological approach to ethical reasoning), are all clear to see within human rights reasoning. Kant is a giant of the *Enlightenment*, an intellectual revolution that shaped modern ideas of science, art, literature and governance, but also the political revolutions of the 18th and 19th centuries that gave life to the modern idea of rights.

There are other intellectual influences from the 17th and 18th centuries worthy of note. The modern idea of rights also owes much to the English philosopher Thomas Hobbes (1588–1679), who is more commonly disassociated from liberal and democratic traditions. Hobbes is most famous for the conclusions he drew towards the favouring of dictatorship over democracy but, as Gray (2000) argues, Hobbes is influential in rooting the idea of natural right firmly at the level of the individual. This becomes increasingly important in the development of human rights reasoning in later centuries. However, it is a contemporary of Hobbes, John Locke (1632–1704), who had a more immediate and substantial impact on the development of political rights that are today expressed as human rights. Locke (1690) provided a political blueprint for how governments could be organised and shaped from the underpinning idea that natural rights were derived from natural law. The political revolutions of the 18th century in France and America drew upon Locke's ideas in particular, which have in turn shaped liberal democratic societies as the natural home for human rights throughout the 19th and 20th centuries.

The French Revolution in 1789 in particular became a focus for wider discussions about rights at the end of the 18th century (Sen, 2009). In response to Edmund Burke's (1790) *Reflections on the Revolution in France*, in which he attacked the revolutionaries and defended aristocracy and constitutional monarchy, Mary Wollstonecraft (1790) published *A Vindication of the Rights of Men*, in which she drew upon Enlightenment arguments that championed reason and rationality over privilege and tradition. She later published *A Vindication of the Rights of Woman* (Wollstonecraft, 1792), to present an early expression of feminist philosophy, challenging not only the substance of Burke's defence of tradition, but also what she saw as the misogynistic manner in which he presents his arguments. Wollstonecraft (1792) represents an early example of how rights become the dominant language through which many political causes have been pursued since.

Thomas Paine's (1791) *Rights of Man* likewise challenged Burke's defence of, in particular, the French aristocratic regime. Paine (1791) sees human rights as natural and from this challenges the status quo by questioning the rights of government to exist. Governments, for Paine (1791), are granted the authority to govern by the people. Rights reside in each person by nature, whereas governments only exist because people have created them. The legitimacy of a government, its right to rule, can therefore only be granted by the people who create it.

The political influence of the French and American Revolutions initiated a global move towards democracy. Building likewise on the democratic sensibilities of the Magna Carta, subsequent revolutions around the world in the 19th and 20th centuries ensured that rights provided the philosophical and political language to challenge traditional forms of authority. The drive for greater equality throughout this period has ensured that rights remain the primary language used by campaigners across a range of issues.

However, it is not until the second half of the 20th century in the aftermath of the horrors of two world wars, and the scale of the sheer brutality and inhumanity of the supposedly civilised nations of the world, that human rights were enshrined through various international treaties, most prominently the United Nations' UDHR. The systematic and industrial manner in which the German State under Nazi control murdered millions of Jews and other groups deemed undesirable represented a most extreme expression of inhumanity. However, beyond the extremities of Nazi Germany's brutality, most Western nations had committed significant state crimes against different sections of society in the first half of the 20th century.

The reaction and response from those in authority following the Second World War was to give human rights an institutional form, most notably on a global scale through the UDHR, but regional variants also arose. Blau and Esparza (2016) refer to this as a revolution in global human rights. The 1948 American Declaration of the Rights and Duties of Man, which was largely superseded by the American Convention on Human Rights in 1978, was sanctioned by the Organization of American States, and the 1950 ECHR was ratified in 1953 and overseen by the Council of Europe under the jurisdiction of the European Court of Human Rights. The United Kingdom was an early signatory of the UDHR and the ECHR, and the incorporation of human rights formally within British law was achieved later through the HRA 1998.

An important component of human rights reasoning is that it shifts ethical thinking away from a consequential perspective, where the focus is on what actions achieve in practice, towards a Kantian-informed deontological approach, one in which doing the right thing is expressed as a moral obligation, something that we are committed to do irrespective of what we think will be achieved. Moreover, the UDHR, ECHR, HRA and a whole host of other globally situated examples of institutionalised expressions of human rights represent not only a quantitative growth in the influence of human rights reasoning, but a qualitative shift also. As Neyroud and Beckley (2001, p.216) note, during this period human rights became 'the *lingua franca* of liberal democracy' and Ignatieff (2001, p.53) makes reference to human rights as the 'world-wide secular religion', suggesting that the language of human rights is to 'global moral thought' what English language is to 'the global economy': 'Human rights has become the major article of faith of a secular culture that fears it believes in nothing else.'

Similarly, Gearty (2006, p.9) argues that human rights have become the dominant expression of morality within most nations and at an international level: 'Where once we had ideas like "socialism", "social justice" and "fairness", nowadays increasingly "human rights" is being called upon to do all the moral work.'

We should not underestimate the scale and scope of this institutionalisation of human rights internationally. It has transformed the role of rights from being a tool of the oppressed in a battle against those in authority, to become the dominant expression of authority itself, and the language through which it is administered.

There are many positives to be taken from these developments. Not least, the institutionalisation of human rights in this way places obligations upon those in authority to proactively prevent the oppression and victimisation of the most vulnerable in society. Likewise, it gives greater protection to minority groups and limits the expediency of those in authority and the extent to which they can ignore their duty of care to all within their jurisdictional reach. However, there is a danger that institutionalising human rights in this way means that we lose sight of the moral component of human rights reasoning as human rights takes on a formalised, legalistic and constitutional form. It is easy for us to approach institutionalised human rights in a rather compliant, legalistic, tick-box, bureaucratic manner.

Moreover, by establishing human rights as formalised obligations within an institutional setting we can overestimate the extent to which human rights issues are met, and in this regard we can become complacent. In the next part of this chapter, I turn my attention to how the institutionalisation of human rights poses challenges for the understanding of ethical policing I am presenting in the book.

Challenges of embedding human rights in policing

There are a number of questions that need to be addressed regarding the role human rights play in establishing ethical policing. Some of these relate specifically to the nature of policing, but others arise from changes in the world and perceptions of human rights. I consider first the challenges that relate specifically to policing before exploring more general difficulties of establishing human rights as the basis for legitimate authority.

There are two issues I wish to consider in relation to the specific challenges of embedding human rights within police practice. First, I want to highlight the tension between human rights reasoning and the idea of policing by consent. The police are in this respect subject to potentially contradictory pressures: on the one hand, human rights establish expectations that the police will do the right thing; at the same time, policing by consent establishes majoritarian expectations that the police conform to public will, that is, do what is popular. Secondly, and perhaps most substantively, I will argue that a challenge of embedding human rights in policing in a transformative way that fosters ethical policing comes from the tendency of police to be more comfortable thinking of their role in *legal*, as opposed to *moral*, terms. Human rights are enshrined in law and are expressed in legislation but I argue they have a strong moral component and it is this moral component that is most significant in promoting ethical policing. A question remains, though, as to whether the moral dimension of human rights is recognised sufficiently within police practice.

Within the UK there is an established commitment to ensuring that police services are responsive to local communities. This has existed since the inception of modern Peelian policing and is manifested through the notion of policing by consent (Reiner, 2010). The introduction of Police and Crime Commissioners (PCCs) has reasserted, re-emphasised and reframed the notion of policing by consent (Joyce, 2011; Newburn, 2012; Sampson, 2012; Lister, 2013; Rogers, 2013; Turner, 2014; Wood, 2016a), by giving greater priority to the idea of democratic accountability within policing. Critics may argue that the democratic credentials of PCCs are limited in a number of ways. For one, the electoral turnout for the PCC elections falls well below what would normally be considered a legitimate democratic mandate, and the form of democracy promoted by the introduction of PCCs is seen as narrow and lacking in real community engagement. The constituent base for the PCCs is also challenged as being far too dispersed, such that local communities are not adequately represented by their respective PCCs. Nonetheless, the role of PCCs emphasises an aspect of policing that is potentially at odds with human rights and is at the very least in tension with the universal claims of human rights.

The tension between the universalism of human rights thinking and the particular interests of any given jurisdiction can be manifested as a conflict between an individual's rights and the rights of a community. The idea of community rights arises from criticisms of the kind of liberal individualism discussed in Chapter 2. Mulhall and Swift (1996, p.71), for example, refer to Alasdair MacIntyre's criticism of 'liberalism's failure to perceive the importance of the community in the moral life of the individual'. Such critical voices have been labelled as communitarianism and the growing influence of such perspectives is acknowledged by Hopkins Burke and Morrill (2004, p.236) in considering how the use of Antisocial Behaviour Orders (ASBOs) as a form of 'civil law for crime control' emphasised community concerns over individual rights.

It is important here to understand the nature of human rights and in particular the need to recognise that they are founded upon points of principle as opposed to popular will. On the one hand, they are widely supported in general, and when discussed in the abstract, those promoting human rights are seen as the good guys; conversely, anyone criticising human rights would be characterised in negative terms. On the other hand, people's attitudes to human rights change within specific contexts, and at times, the support for human rights diminishes. However, diminishing support for human rights, or an increased willingness to contravene human rights, does not weaken the importance of human rights; if anything it reflects a greater need for them.

Human rights are largely invisible for most people, most of the time, particularly in societies that have well-established liberal democratic conventions and institutions. It is primarily at extraordinary times, for example following a terrorist attack, that human rights become more meaningful in ways that test liberal democratic conventions and institutions. The point at which human rights become meaningful to the majority in society is invariably within a context in which human rights are less appealing.

In policing terms, this paradox is manifested as a tension between principled policing and policing by consent. On the one hand, policing is committed to upholding particular values, but at the same time it has a consensual, majoritarian dimension that requires officers to be sensitive to popular, community expectations and desires. This point needs emphasising. Human rights are important for everyone but in everyday matters they are always of greater significance to only a minority of people. It is always likely to be a minority of people who are most clearly affected adversely by any illiberal measures that contravene human rights.

Moreover, liberal democratic governments tend not to undermine human rights unless they feel they really have to. Even then, they will always seek to limit the extent to which human rights are breached. Nonetheless, as Edwards (2005, p.10) reminds us, governments remain 'the biggest single restriction on liberty'. However, in practice when liberal democratic governments breach human rights, it is within a context in which a majority of people are more likely to see the merit in such a breach. To repeat, human rights are needed most when they are least popular; conversely, support for human rights is strongest when they are least needed. However, human rights are powerful not because they are popular, but because they stand outside popular sentiments, and, when necessary, against them.

The notion of policing by consent, on the other hand, manifests democratic values. It emphasises the idea that the police serve the community and are responsive to their needs. In this respect, human rights sit outside democratic processes. Human rights exist irrespective of whether people in a given jurisdiction at a particular time think they should exist. They prevent legislators from introducing laws that are deemed to contravene human rights, regardless of the extent to which there is popular support for such legislation. From a human rights perspective, the legitimacy of a police action cannot be established exclusively by public support for such action, but despite the fact that policing by consent alone cannot achieve police legitimacy, it nonetheless retains significant influence, even to the extent that it qualifies the embedding of human rights within police practice.

Do human rights provide a moral basis for policing?

While I acknowledge that consent is an important aspect of policing, I am suggesting here that consensual policing is not necessarily ethical. The extent to which consensual policing can be determined as ethical is dependent upon the nature of the popular, democratic influences shaping policing. We might assume that the popular will of the people has a strong moral foundation but this cannot be guaranteed. For policing to be ethical, it needs to do more than simply respond to the general will of those it serves. Delattre (2004) likewise says that in its mission statement the police should not mimic the values of the community it serves but rather use this to inspire the community to the highest ideals expressed within constitutions and through human rights. There needs to be a moral framework underpinning ethical policing that is conceptually distinct from the policing-by-consent requirements.

Police officers have often suggested to me that human rights provide precisely the kind of moral framework that I have argued underpins ethical policing. This view is also represented within the policing literature. Villiers and Adlam (2004), for example, suggest that human rights provide officers with the moral language to pursue genuinely moral discussions. Others have also highlighted the positive impact human rights have upon how we think about policing (Neyroud, 2006; Manning, 2010; Reiner, 2010). Neyroud (2003) refers to the extent to which police training has shifted its emphasis towards core values arising from human rights, and Neyroud and Beckley (2001) stress the impact that this has upon police officers' decision-making processes. Even if we accept more sober assessments that suggest the HRA 1998 has had a much more limited impact on policing *in practice* (Bullock and Johnson, 2012), we should not underestimate the significance of introducing concepts such as proportionality and necessity into the police officer's lexicon.

Likewise, we should not underestimate the significance of the HRA's impact in establishing a clear constitutional basis upon which the protection of rights and liberties is based within the UK. Stone (2014), for example, notes that prior to the HRA 1998 the primary constitutional documents in England and Wales were the Magna Carta 1215 and the Bill of Rights 1688. But these, he argues, 'dealt with such matters as the limits of power of the monarch and Parliament, they did not tell us what are the freedoms of the individual citizen' (Stone, 2014, p.10). He emphasises the point by showing that the only reference to freedom of speech in the Bill of Rights 1688 is restricted to what is said within Parliament.

The ECHR, which, as Bradley et al (2014) note, has been of such importance in Britain, was ratified by the UK in 1951 and came into force in 1953. The ECHR itself is derived from the 1948 UDHR, which explicitly sought to address the barbarities of the first half of the 20th century. Bradley et al (2014, p.359) emphasise that the UN Declaration established that 'the acts of public authorities may be challenged even though they are in accordance with national law'. This logic has been carried through into the ECHR and the HRA 1998.

So, on the one hand, it appears self-evident that human rights provide policing with a strong moral grounding, particularly following the HRA 1998. Human rights explicitly seek to embed moral obligations within police practice and express a Kantian, deontological approach to ethics. This 'morally binding' dimension of human rights stresses 'ethical actions that must be done' (Haggard, 1993, p.11), thereby removing consideration of consequences as a primary motivating factor for performing, or not performing, a policing action. The Kantian flavour of human rights is also noted by Kleinig (1999) in his references to the importance of human dignity within establishing an ethical approach to policing and within Alderson's (1998) call for a more principled approach to policing.

There remain challenges though, as Bullock and Johnson (2012) have observed. For one, the hierarchical structure of police and the extent to which there is a culture of following orders and enforcing laws raises problems for principled policing and the embedding of human rights. There is undoubtedly a tension, for example, in establishing moral obligation in contexts where officers routinely follow orders. As Wirrer (2006, p.74) notes, 'respect for others can hardly be an order'. There is a concern here that the police ethics narrative has led to an overly formalised and centrally controlled model of rule, following, rather than inspiring, a sense of moral duty within police officers. Neyroud (2003, p.592), for example, observes that 'the right things police officers should be doing have become increasingly nationally defined and nationally prescribed'. It is easy to see from this how police officers might experience discussion of police ethics as an imposition, rather than being something they own, especially as it tends to attract most attention when raised in response to a crisis (Neyroud, 2006).

This returns us to the point I raised in the introduction regarding the importance of moral obligation as something beyond legal obligation and positional duty. Whether the HRA 1998 establishes in practice the required level of moral underpinning to establish ethical policing in England and Wales remains unclear. The complication is that human rights are enshrined in law through the HRA 1998, and therefore clearly place upon police officers and police organisations legal obligations and positional duties. It is not as self-evident whether the moral reasoning embedded within the HRA 1998 is reflected and manifested within police practice as much as I suggest it needs to be.

Throughout my years of working with the police I have been struck by how much more comfortable officers are when discussing legal obligations as opposed to moral obligations. The law is seen as somehow more objective than moral philosophy, a more solid base upon which to justify police actions. However, human rights legislation is framed explicitly in a way that challenges a narrow and exclusively legal interpretation of written law. It requires and necessitates a level of moral reasoning at the point of law enforcement.

Within policing contexts we need to be mindful of a tendency to understand human rights in a legalistic way because where this happens, it does not provide the necessary degree of moral obligation required to establish the kind of moral agency promoted by MacIntyre (2004). At best, such an approach might imbue an officer's legal obligations with moral flavouring, but at worst it will be completely devoid of any moral purpose. Human rights legislation is perceived from this perspective as an unambiguous decree that elicits an unequivocal legal obligation upon an officer to act with certainty.

It is not only policing scholars who would question such a rigid interpretation of the law (Lustgarten, 1986; Waddington, 1999; Reiner, 2010; Stenning, 2011). Academic lawyers also emphasise that in practice, the law is 'not always as it appears on the statute book or in the case law', and that even when the greatest of clarity is found within law, 'it often gives wide discretionary powers to those whose duty is to apply it' (Padfield, 2010, p.103). Stone (2014, p.1) likewise notes that '[t]he borderline between law and politics' regarding human rights 'is so narrow that the influence of one on the other cannot be ignored'.

What is true generally within law is especially true within human rights legislation. Human rights legislation has been forged institutionally through various constitutional arrangements globally, as an explicit remedy to the kinds of instances of gross inhumanity captured by MacIntyre's (2004) narrative of officials operating in Nazi Germany, in which legal obligations form part of the defence by those engaged in inhumane activities. The important point to emphasise here is that the law is subject to a higher authority, which is framed in moral terms, and irrespective of how morally flaky the foundations of a natural law conception of human rights are (Gearty, 2006; Sen, 2009), we need to recognise that without such a moral foundation human rights become more arbitrary (Gray, 2000; Ignatieff, 2001). They lose the importance they are granted within contemporary legal, criminal justice and political orders the world over.

Beyond the particular challenges of embedding human rights within policing, I will now consider more general concerns about the role human rights institutions play in addressing contemporary global inhumanities. It is suggested that human rights, which emerged in response to the horrors of two world wars in the first half of the 20th century, are less appropriate at the start of the 21st century (Dershowitz, 2006), which is characterised more by weak, fragmenting states (Gray, 2000).

There are two issues to consider here. First, we need to note that the universalism of human rights reasoning is challenged. It is increasingly argued that human rights are far from being universal and are rather expressions of Western, Enlightenment thinking. In other words, human rights are located in specific times and places. Human rights are framed as international in scope but the world is still dominated by national interests, something that has been strengthened following the 9/11 terrorist attacks on the USA in 2001. This is illustrated most starkly in policing terms. The police remain stubbornly national despite facing increasingly transnational and global challenges.

Secondly, it has been suggested that the atrocities being committed in the world today are different from those committed in the 20th century. Importantly, it appears to be the absence, rather than presence, of strong government that leads to atrocities today. There is a concern that human rights express a form of what Coady (2008) calls moralism, that human rights establish the way things should be, without necessarily helping to realise this envisioned world. Shue's (1978) seminal paper on torture is pertinent here. It illustrates that despite being able to establish an almost universal condemnation of torture throughout the world, torture has nonetheless been on the increase over the past half century. The same could be said of slavery, which is unanimously condemned by all governments and universally prohibited through global human rights institutions but still appears to be on the rise.

The universalism and international character of human rights versus national self-interest

Human rights are framed as international values. They are international to the extent that they explicitly restrict the intentions of national jurisdictions. This tension has existed since at least the time of the peace settlements that culminated in the Treaty of Westphalia in 1648, which established national sovereignty as a fundamental aspect of the world order. As Zifcak (2005, p.34) argues, the focus on international matters changes the way we think about individuals, who 'have gradually come to be regarded by the international community as holding internationally material rights and interests', thus undermining the traditional authority of sovereign states. Sampford (2005, p.23) makes a similar point from the converse perspective when he says that the sovereignty of nation states 'historically and, still, ideologically, is an argument against the international rule of law'. Den Boer (2010) refers to the enduring struggle over sovereignty between supranational and intergovernmental perspectives and Held (2006) notes the increasing number of legal challenges that express international views against nationally framed laws. Human rights play a significant role in promoting international perspectives over national sovereignty.

There is a long-standing counter-view that see rights as having legal meaning *only* within national jurisdictions. From this perspective, rights become meaningless when conceptualised abstractly beyond national judicial controls. This view is captured famously by Jeremy Bentham's (1843, p.501) much-quoted summation of natural rights, which he sees as 'simple nonsense', and moreover, he portrays 'natural and imprescriptible rights' as 'rhetorical nonsense,—nonsense upon stilts'. Bentham's approach to rights, first published in 1796, was part of the attack on the presentation of political rights, underpinned by the notion of natural rights, by supporters of the 1789 French Revolution. Bentham is not against rights per se, but rather the idea that rights can be more than positive legal expressions. As Dworkin (1986, p.152) notes, there is a pragmatic view towards rights that argues we should 'sometimes act *as if* people had legal rights' (emphasis in original) even if we do not think that human rights exist, because it is to the long-term benefit of society to do so. Bentham's understanding of rights is consistent with the view that sees legal rights as necessary to establish a nation state's authority, whereas the kind of natural and imprescriptible rights that shape contemporary approaches to human rights are deemed to undermine national sovereignty.

Today, the majority of nation states voluntarily subscribe to international human rights conventions, and for the most part nation states are committed to recognising and upholding the universal claims of human rights. However, it is not agreed by all that the moral claims underpinning human rights are as universal as they are claimed to be, which in turn raises questions about the extent to which such moral statements about what it means to be human should have such authority in the world. This is becoming increasingly problematic because, as Gearty (2006) notes, the philosophical foundations upon which human rights are established are looking increasingly fragile.

Gearty (2006) suggests that historically the moral authority of human rights was founded upon either religious beliefs or rationally based universal truths concerning what it means to be human. This is also illustrated by Davis (2016, p.4) when he introduces the general idea of human rights by emphasising human dignity, which he argues gives 'practical effect to an intuition or a feeling which, it is believed, all reasonable human beings share' (Davis, 2016, p.4). Intuitions, feelings and beliefs hardly provide the kind of objectivity that police officers often perceive to be found within law. However, what is perhaps even more unsettling for those seeking objective foundations is that Gearty (2006) argues both religious and rational authorities have much less purchase in the world today than they once had, which means despite the recent and contemporary success of human rights in legal and political terms, its philosophical base is much less secure. Gearty (2006, p.11) cautions that 'the subject of human rights needs a better answer to the question of the basis of its authority than it seems currently able to provide'.

We should note that there has existed resistance to the institutionalisation of human rights internationally from the outset. For example, Ignatieff (2001) refers to the challenge that arose against human rights from Islamic perspectives. The Saudi Arabia delegation at the inception of the UDHR in 1947, for example, raised objections and refused to sign up to it because of Articles 16 and 18 relating to marriage and religion respectively. Whatever we may think about the motivations of the Saudi regime on these matters, their position challenges claims of universalism underpinning the UDHR. Moreover, opposition was heightened following the Islamic Revolution in Iran at the end of the 1970s. Ignatieff (2001, p.60) says the very substance of a universal claim of individual human rights was deemed deeply offensive by Iran's religious leaders: 'In Islamic eyes, universalizing rights discourse implies a sovereign and discreet individual, which is blasphemous from the perspective of the Holy Koran.'

More recently, we have seen a growing interest in questions of national sovereignty and a resurgence in expressions of national self-interest. There are growing disputes over the extent to which international legal treaties, such as the ECHR, should override the democratic procedures of establishing national legislation (Ewing, 2010). Such arguments have been articulated most strongly by those advocating the UK's departure from the European Union, which has been premised upon an appeal to national sovereignty against the influence of the transnational institutions of the EU.

Perhaps more significantly, beyond the criticisms of particular states, most nation states have probably found themselves at one point or another wanting to opt out of global commitments, even if only for a limited period of time and/or in relation to a particular national emergency or incident. National self-interest has a powerful influence that reasserts itself against commitments to international treaties and conventions. This has been a particular feature in the world since the 9/11 terror attacks on the USA in 2001 (Ip, 2013).

In the UK, for example, the introduction of control orders through the Prevention of Terrorism Act 2005 was highly controversial, from their inception to their being repealed in December 2011. Control orders were challenged on the grounds that they were incompatible with human rights legislation, and human rights groups such as *Liberty* and JUSTICE challenged, for example, the use of 18-hour curfews against suspected terrorists (Horne and Berman, 2011). Likewise, the UK's Parliamentary Joint Committee on Human Rights (JCHR), which comprises cross-party members from both the House of Lords and the House of Commons, challenged the standard of proof proposed within the Prevention of Terrorism Act 2005 for the issuing of controls. With regards to derogating control orders, those deemed to be incompatible with Article 5 of the ECHR, the JCHR argued that the standard of proof should be in line with criminal cases, where *beyond reasonable doubt* is the norm, as opposed to the suggested *balance of probabilities* found within civil law cases (Horne and Berman, 2011). The JCHR also expressed concern that non-derogating control orders required more than *reasonable suspicion* to have legitimacy under human rights legislation.

It should be noted that despite the controversy regarding control orders, they were used sparingly and there was judicial oversight and an annual review of their use. Lord Carlile of Berriew QC was given the responsibility of this oversight role and in his sixth and final report he noted that 48 people had been subjected to control orders between 2005 and 2011 (Carlile, 2011). These were all non-derogating control orders. There had been no derogating control orders issued.

However, the point of interest for me here is the extent to which the justifications for these measures being introduced in the first place comes from national political concerns with order and security as priorities over and above transnational human rights legislation. This is evidenced within statements by the different Labour Home Secretaries responding to legal rulings limiting the use of control orders. Horne and Berman (2011) cite, for example, Alan Johnston, 'Protecting the public is my priority' (p.17) and Jacqui Smith, 'My top priority is national security and protection of the British people' (p.13), illustrating that national security at times will be of greater concern to politicians than human rights legislation. At the very least, we can say that politicians are prepared to push the boundaries of human rights legislation as far as possible and interpret its meaning in ways that are not only challenged by human rights advocates, but also ultimately dismissed as incompatible with human rights legislation through the courts.

To be clear here, I am not talking about people who are opposed to human rights. My point is rather that people in authority who support human rights are prepared to take measures that are incompatible with human rights at times of national crisis and in response to national emergencies. This political context has a powerful influence upon policing, both in relation to the pressures upon policing from the government of the day, but also with regard to policing by consent and the expectation that police are responsive to popular sentiments.

Measures that contravene human rights tend to be limited in both scope and time, and it is often these limitations that are the focus of disputes between governments and human rights advocates. As Lord Carlile (2011) notes, proportionality is key in determining whether counter-terror measures, for example, are compatible with human rights legislation or not. Governments will always present such initiatives as transitory responses to emergencies but they will be challenged by human rights activists as being representative of a trend towards a more permanent move away from a human rights-based order. The police will be directed by governments to act in ways that would normally be seen as unethical and will be criticised by human rights groups for acting thus. This presents an ethical dilemma for the police, both in terms of organisations and individual officers, which is not easily and readily resolved through reference to human rights legislation. Lord Carlile's (2011) reference to proportionality, however, hints at the need to retain human rights reasoning when dealing with this ethical dilemma.

The importance of human rights reasoning comes to the fore given the extent to which human rights legislation appears to lose its primacy within heightened terror contexts. Ip (2013) refers to the increase in the use of *sunset clauses* within counter-terror legislation in the USA, Canada and the UK post 9/11. He notes that sunset clauses have a long legal history dating back to the 1500s. They are intended to avoid unnecessary legislative constraints in society as a consequence of knee-jerk legislative responses to emergencies. The idea of sunset clauses is to set time frames within which legislation applies, forcing legislators to reconsider the justifications of specific laws within a given period of time to make sure that they retain their validity. However, there is a concern that reviews can become routine paper exercises and Dershowitz (2002, p.11) suggests that such extraordinary counter-terror measures are only likely to become ever more normal: 'The "emergency" steps that we take today to combat terrorism … are likely to become part of the permanent fabric of our legal and political culture.'

Counter-terror measures illustrate a difficulty for advocates of human rights. Such measures are generally introduced following an atrocity, at a time when people feel vulnerable and angry, and are consequently more likely to accept intrusive state interventions and police actions. Counter-terrorism inevitably has a negative impact on a person's freedoms and will on occasions result in the mistreatment of individuals who have no connection to terrorist groups or their activities. The police are likely to be central within such injustices and thereby seen to be overriding human rights precisely at the point they are most needed. This is a significant challenge for ethical policing.

In understanding the role human rights play within policing we cannot ignore that there is a tension between the international characteristic of human rights and the local focus of policing. While human rights are established in transnational, global terms, policing, meanwhile, remains stubbornly embedded within national contexts. Even when policing operates beyond the national stage, it does so predominantly through intergovernmental, temporary and constrained operations, in which the national sovereignty of the police is retained. A good example of this comes from policing within the EU. Despite the increasingly supranational characteristics of the EU in general, especially following the Treaty of Lisbon 2009 (Disley et al, 2012), policing across EU jurisdictions remains limited and almost exclusively intergovernmental in form. This is expressed most clearly within a House of Lords (2008, p.9) report in the UK:

> Contrary to popular misconception, Europol is not a European Police Force; the European Union does not have a police force, and is unlikely to have one in the foreseeable

future. Law enforcement remains the responsibility of the Member States. What the EU does have in Europol is an organisation whose task is to help the police forces of the Member States to help each other.

This statement was made prior to the Treaty of Lisbon 2009, which enhanced 'the EU's ability to act in the field of policing cooperation and home affairs' (Disley et al, 2012, p.4) but has nonetheless remained a valid take on policing within the EU. To the extent that Europol has grown in influence following the Treaty of Lisbon 2009, it has primarily been with regard to facilitating intergovernmental Joint Investigative Teams (JITs). Furthermore, the dominance of national sovereignty in policing was expressed most clearly by the then UK Home Secretary, Theresa May, when she announced on 15 October 2012 that the UK would withdraw from over 130 EU policing and criminal justice measures. The emphasis on national sovereignty is reinforced by the extent to which counter-terrorism has become an increasingly routine aspect and expectation within UK policing, and the consolidation of the PCC role in providing policing with a local emphasis exacerbates matters further. Despite the dominance of human rights thinking within British policing, it is clearly curtailed by this focus on national sovereignty.

Human rights do not necessarily achieve what they are supposed to achieve

Another feature of the counter-terror focus within contemporary policing is that it is framed by a growing sense of insecurity in society. While there are many measures that suggest life in the UK is relatively safe and secure, and that people's life expectancy and quality of life are both improving, there is nonetheless a growing perception that things are getting out of control. This might be manifested through discussions about immigration or in relation to knife crime and, in particular, the number of young people being stabbed. The August 2011 riots were treated as symptomatic of a wider crisis in social order, and as Tralau (2011) has noted, there has been a growing interest among academics in Thomas Hobbes and other thinkers who have stressed the importance of order maintenance as a primary political objective. It is in this context that Tralau (2011) considers the insights of Carl Schmitt, a German jurist largely discredited and ignored because of his association with and participation in the Nazi regime in the 1930 and into the 1940s.

The point here is that the institutionalisation of human rights and the intellectual framing of liberal democracies through ideas of fairness and equality occur against the backdrop of a relatively peaceful world order. The presumption and existence of order allows for political authority, including policing, to be seen as primarily distributing wealth and welfare in a fair and equitable manner. This consensual world is shaped by human rights reasoning and allows for the establishment and growth of human rights institutions. The absence of order today, whether real or perceived, is giving rise to different priorities for those in positions of authority. From this perspective, the primary objective for those in authority today is safety and security; human rights are consequently relegated to second-order concerns. As we saw from the statements of previous Home Secretaries mentioned earlier, it is argued that human rights lose their meaning and power if people are unable to enjoy them safely and securely.

Another way of thinking about this matter is to consider what or whom human rights protect us from. The momentum that led to the international institutionalisation and expansion of human rights following the Second World War quite rightly saw the problem in terms of strong nation states abusing sections of their respective societies. These abuses were on political, religious and/or ideological grounds, or simply an expedient way of dealing with a particular national challenge. But to what extent can we say that the worst abuses of humanity today are committed within or by strong, stable nation states? It is arguably the absence of state authority that has led to the worst acts of barbarism in the latter stages of the 20th century and the early part of the current millennium. This is not to downplay the enduring discrimination experienced by different sections of most, if not all, societies. Nor is it to suggest that the most powerful and stable Western governments are perfect havens in which human rights thrive. However, Gray (2000) quite rightly asks whether strong states are the primary problem today in the way that they clearly were in the first half of the 20th century. He suggests, to the contrary, that it is the absence of legitimate government that is a greater problem today.

Hughes (1998) approaches this matter by considering how we view criminal justice bodies from the perspective of human rights. While it is important that the criminal justice system is held to account in line with human rights measures, the greatest abuses of individuals and minority groups is increasingly found within societies where the criminal justice system is weak or absent. Hughes (1998, p.109) cites Etzioni's (1993) concerns on these matters: 'the greatest threat to public safety is not excessive police powers but rather the danger of the public turning to "extremists"'. The concern here is that if the police are unable to tackle crime and disorder problems adequately, then vigilante groups will emerge to do the job. Whatever shortcomings a criminal justice system may have in upholding human rights, vigilante groups are invariably much more likely to be considerably worse.

The issue at stake here is ultimately a question of how authority is practised as opposed to how it is conceptualised. A concern for Gray (2000, p.116) is the extent to which the elevation of human rights institutions means we 'inflate the role of rights and hollow out the practice of politics'. I interpret the practice of politics here to include policing, and as Gray (2000, p.132) reminds us, 'rights are conventions, upheld – in the last resort – by force'. From a realist perspective, the focus is always on understanding how things operate in practice and for Coady (2008) there is a concern that the influence of human rights institutions internationally has reduced our capacity to make difficult but necessary decisions. Brandt (1979) likewise suggests that adopting a deontological approach to ethical reasoning, one that establishes what we are obliged to do at the level of our conscience, precludes us from even asking questions that would, by any other measure, appear to be reasonable, rational concerns.

Coady (2008) sees the emergence of the human rights movement as a primary factor in what he refers to as a decline of political realism within international politics. He introduces the notion of moralism here to highlight the tendency within political institutions to exaggerate the extent to which human rights modify behaviour positively in intended ways. He laments the loss of pragmatic endeavours to resolve problems in the world and he criticises the extent to which there appears to be a greater willingness to engage in moral debates about international affairs. Coady (2008) uses the term *moralism* as a pejorative expression for what he sees as inappropriate moral attitudes and/or actions. He sees the growing influence of religious fundamentalism on the world stage as illustrative of this move away from pragmatic resolutions towards explicitly and aggressively value-led, entrenched positions.

It is important to stress that Coady (2008) is not challenging all moral reasoning here. Rather, he is challenging principled positions that offer little or no scope for genuine political and moral debate. From a policing perspective, I think that Coady (2008) presents a challenge, which relates to how we embed human rights within policing in a way that is meaningful and supportive of the kind of reflective practice I have suggested is required for ethical policing to be developed.

There are six types of moralism identified by Coady (2008, pp.15–49), which I will briefly outline to provide a better sense of what he means.

(1) Scope – the concern here is that we increasingly moralise about things that are trivial. People use the phrase *it's my right* inappropriately by presenting individual preferences through the language of rights.

(2) Unbalanced focus – this occurs when we favour one moral concern excessively over other equally important moral concerns. This is a fundamental challenge within any principled approach; it is one thing to establish that principles are important, but quite another to establish which principle champions all others. Principles are different from rules in this respect. There can be no tensions or contradictions in a system of rules but there can be competing principles that require ethical reasoning.

(3) Imposition – there is an understanding that a moral principle differs from a law. Moral principles establish arguments as to how one *should* live, whereas laws prohibit certain behaviours. The moral principle is deemed to extend its authority too far if and when moral advice becomes a form of moral bullying. The imposition occurs when the moral principle is asserted so forcefully that it becomes prohibitive.

(4) Abstraction – both law and morality manifest human endeavours to make the world a better place. In order to do this they must engage with the problems and challenges that confront us. It is at times possible for policy makers and legislators to become so embroiled in their own world experiences, and too disconnected from the experiences of the majority, that their endeavours become excessively rational. Where this occurs, moral principles lose sight of the emotional and more broadly human dimensions found within specific contexts. This is a danger when establishing universal moral principles. I suggest that policing by consent is in this respect a useful barrier against ethical policing becoming too abstract and disconnected from the operational realities of police work.

(5) Absolutism – the more certain we are that we have established through reason how we should live, the more confident we become in imposing our moral world view upon others and the more willing we are to establish that there can be no exceptions. The classical liberal strategy of ethical neutrality is established to avoid the inevitability of such moral absolutism in a society that

prescribes only one officially sanctioned conception of what it means to be human.

(6) Deluded power – when we approach problems in the world from an exclusively or excessively human rights perspective, we run the danger of deluding ourselves into thinking that establishing through reason what the right thing to do is will automatically resolve the problems we are encountering. As noted earlier, human rights do not in and of themselves stop the return of slavery or an increase in torture.

Conclusion

The aim of this chapter is not to dismiss the significance of human rights. It is rather to show how essential moral reasoning is in ensuring that human rights support ethical policing. Human rights legislation has embedded within it an explicit moral component and it is this that makes human rights legislation so powerful. However, we cannot assume that this embedded moral component will necessarily come to the fore. Conversely, when this reasoning does come to the fore, we need to be mindful of the connection between what we seek to achieve and the contexts within which we seek to achieve it. There are two pitfalls that we need to avoid when thinking about the role human rights play in establishing ethical policing.

The first pitfall is the danger that the moral component within human rights legislation is ignored or given too little attention. This danger is particularly strong in policing contexts in which there is greater comfort in the assumed legislative objectivity than in the perceived subjective uncertainty of moral reasoning. However, if the moral dimension of human rights is diminished, then human rights cease to provide the basis for the kind of moral agency promoted by MacIntyre (2004), and they do not provide moral obligations above and beyond the narrower legal obligations and positional duties provided by the law. Stone's (2014, p.6) suggestion that it is more precise to think of human rights not as a thing, a precise entity that is easily defined and articulated, but rather 'as a description of a *relationship*' (emphasis in original), is helpful here. It is particularly helpful in redressing the impulse to adopt an overly narrow, legalistic approach to understanding human rights. Relationships are clearly more dynamic, complex and volatile than a fixed entity, and understanding human rights in this way implies that moral obligation is only met through the moral deliberations and judgements required in enforcing, or not enforcing, human rights legislation in practice. The legislation in itself proffers only legal obligations; engaging with the legislation in practice provides the opportunity for moral agency to be demonstrated but this will only be realised if the challenge to deliberate morally, inherent within human rights legislation, is met.

The second pitfall is the counter-danger of elevating the importance of the moral component of human rights legislation to the point that our principled approach to policing becomes excessively moral, leading to what Coady (2008) defines as moralism. To tackle the impulse towards moralism, I suggest that we need to think about the moral component of human rights in aspirational terms, rather than as obligations or duties in a Kantian sense. Sen's (2009, p.63) stress on the important distinction 'between being "rational" and being "reasonable"' is apt here. There is a danger that the rationality that produces human rights reasoning and the kind of morally binding obligations associated with this way of thinking become unreasonable in practice.

I appreciate that thinking about human rights as aspirational rather than as obligatory weakens and undermines them to some extent, and this is something that needs to be monitored closely. I will simply stress that understanding the moral component of human rights as aspirational should not be interpreted to mean that it can be taken lightly. I emphasise that it needs to be seen as a strong, substantive aspirational goal; it needs to be something that we are striving towards with conviction. We should avoid at all costs seeing aspirational as simply being a nice idea that is ultimately unrealisable in practice.

So, human rights have the potential to provide the moral underpinning required for ethical policing, but there is a requirement for a continuous balancing and rebalancing to ensure that our approach to human rights avoids both a narrow form of legalism and likewise an overreaching moralism.

Ethical policing requires a commitment to human rights when they are most unpopular, and when they are most difficult to achieve, without losing sight of the responsibilities the police have regarding the safety and security of the communities in which they serve. This places police organisations at odds with governments just as it places police officers in conflict with their respective employers. Proportionality and ongoing critical reflections are required both at the police institutional and individual officer levels to ensure that there are appropriate and balanced responses to the demands placed upon policing. This applies as much to the demands that originate from criminal activities, critical incidents and moments of disorder as it does to the pressures from governments, communities, activists and international protocols.

Ethical policing is never achieved through simple compliance and adherence to rules. It always requires thoughtful, considered and balanced reflection on the competing demands faced within policing as they are manifested within particular contexts and situations.

I will continue these themes in the next chapter by looking at the concept of police legitimacy as an important component of ethical policing. I will draw upon the influential work of political philosopher John Rawls and the extensive procedural justice literature.

Suggested further reading

Bullock, K. and Johnson, P. (2012) 'The Impact of the Human Rights Act 1998 on Policing in England and Wales', *British Journal of Criminology*, 52(3): 630–50

Ewing, K.D. (2010) *Bonfire of the Liberties: New Labour, Human Rights, and the Rule of Law*. Oxford: Oxford University Press

Gearty, C. (2006) *Can Human Rights Survive?*, Cambridge: Cambridge University Press

Ignatieff, M. (2001) *Human Rights as Politics and Idolatry*. Princeton, NJ: Princeton University Press

4

Justice as fairness, procedural justice and police legitimacy

4

Introduction

So far I have argued that ethical policing needs to be shaped by principles but without this becoming slavish compliance to preconceived values. Likewise, I have considered the extent to which human rights shape ethical policing. While recognising that human rights have the potential to guide the ethical reasoning of police officers, I have also highlighted the challenges of embedding human rights within police practice. These challenges are partly related to the specifics of police work (Bittner, 1970) and in particular the strong consensual dimension of police legitimacy (Reiner, 2010, pp.48–50). However, they also concern questions of whether human rights have the same purchase philosophically speaking in the 21st century as they did previously (Gray, 2000; Ignatieff, 2001; Gearty, 2006). A particular challenge arises from validating the universal claims of human rights. We are today more sensitive to the rich diversity of humanity globally, manifested through different ideas of what it means to be human, expressed in a multitude of ways. Human rights are increasingly seen as just one expression of what it means to be human, one that is imbued with a Western, Enlightenment focus on the individual and the centrality of a scientific rationality (Sen, 2009). Likewise, the international logic of human rights becomes ever more problematic when confronted by expressions of national self-interest in what are perceived to be increasingly insecure times. Indeed, the relative peace and security enjoyed during the second half of the 20th century, which allowed human rights to flourish, is seen from a Hobbesian perspective as an aberration, a break from the norm of chaos, war and disorder (Tralau, 2011).

The focus of this chapter shifts the debate towards the question of legitimacy as it relates to the idea of ethical policing that I am presenting in this book. I focus primarily on the political philosophy of the American John Rawls (1921–2002), whose ideas have been a dominant force in moral philosophy with far-reaching influence beyond academia in shaping contemporary public institutions in liberal democratic societies. In particular, Rawls' (1971) seminal text, *A Theory of Justice*, produced a detailed philosophical blueprint for establishing legitimate liberal democratic authority. It has spurned an ongoing debate that has continued for some 50 years about the legitimacy of our political institutions, and despite a number of powerful counter-narratives (Nozick, 1974; Brandt, 1979; Sandel, 1982; Walzer, 1983; MacIntyre, 1985; Taylor, 1989), it retains significant influence today. Rawls (1971, 1993) provides above all else the underpinning values that define our liberal democratic processes and procedures, captured most prominently through his idea of *justice as fairness*.

Philosophical and empirical accounts of legitimacy

It should be noted that legitimacy is a complex concept that is approached from different perspectives (Bottoms and Tankebe, 2012; Waddington et al, 2017; Morrell and Bradford, 2019). Of most importance for the purposes of this chapter, these different perspectives tend to fall into either (1) a moral philosophical approach or (2) an empirical, social scientific approach (Hinsch, 2010). Rawls falls firmly within the moral philosophical approach and, given the overarching narrative of this book, it is this approach that is of most interest to me. However, this is not to underplay the significance of the empirical, social scientific approach. It would be remiss of me not to mention the significance of the procedural justice literature that has developed from the work of American psychologist Tom Tyler, in particular regarding the extent to which it has elevated the issue of police legitimacy to a position of significant prominence today (Tankebe, 2013; Waddington et al, 2017). If I did not mention this substantial and growing body of work, the reader would justifiably question its omission. However, given the extent to which the procedural justice literature has come to dominate discussions of police legitimacy, I feel there is space and a need for some rebalancing of the debate to include more philosophical insights into understanding police legitimacy (Bottoms and Tankebe, 2012).

The philosophical and empirical approaches to understanding legitimacy will often use the same terminology, but with different meanings and interpretations attached to them (Morrell and Bradford, 2019). The notion of procedural justice is a good example of this. What is identified as procedural justice in the empirical research on police legitimacy (Tyler, 1990, 2003, 2009; Sunshine and Tyler, 2003; Bradford, 2014; Tyler and Jackson, 2014; Jackson, 2018; Jackson and

Bradford, 2019) differs significantly from the use of the term within moral philosophy (Rawls, 1971; Simmons, 1979, 2001; Sen, 2009). From Tyler's original work, procedural justice measures the extent to which the public perceive the police as being *just* in the way they perform their duties, whereas for Rawls, procedural justice is arrived at through moral reflection and reasoning. The same difference applies to the concept of fairness, which is likewise central to both the empirical procedural justice research and the moral philosophy of John Rawls. For advocates of empirical procedural justice research, fairness is captured from the perspectives of the policed, whereas for Rawls it is established again through moral reasoning.

With these potential confusions in mind, the approach I take in this chapter is to understand the distinction between the philosophical and empirical approaches to understanding legitimacy as they relate to (1) moral and (2) consensual dimensions of police legitimacy. I argue that for the police to be considered legitimate they need to satisfy both the normative expectations that are established through moral philosophy, for example in relation to human rights, but also by being perceived to be fair and just in relation to the expectations established through the notion of policing by consent.

Procedural justice, consensual legitimacy and policing by consent

An important message that has been conveyed to the police in recent years is that public perceptions of police conduct, expressed as procedural justice, are a powerful indicator of police legitimacy. Moreover, public perception is primarily concerned with how the police conduct themselves, as opposed to what they achieve. It thereby shifts the debate about policing away from outputs, for example the number of arrests made, towards the fairness of police processes, expressed in terms of how the police are perceived to treat those they encounter. Indeed, more than this, Skinns (2011, p.198) notes that procedural justice adds 'humanizing aspects' to police proceedings in a way that takes it beyond compliance with due process.

Procedural justice stresses the importance of public support and takes the willingness of people to comply with the law as a primary defining feature of police legitimacy. Debates about police legitimacy today are almost exclusively discussed in these terms. I have no doubt that the procedural justice literature has a positive impact on the professionalisation of policing and in providing measures for addressing examples of bad policing. However, at the same time, it is important for me to stress that I do not see this aspect of police legitimacy alone as being sufficient to establish ethical policing.

Procedural justice research is an example of what Simmons (2001) defines as attitudinal approaches to legitimacy because it measures the attitudes of recipients of actions, rather than the actors themselves, or indeed the actions that they perform. As such, I suggest, the approach taken within the procedural justice literature relates more closely to the consensual dimension of police legitimacy captured by the notion of policing by consent. The consensual dimension of police work is an integral part of police legitimacy and always has been. It features prominently in the principles associated with Sir Robert Peel through the establishment of the Metropolitan Police in 1829 (Waddington, 1999; Reiner, 2010) but it has come to the fore more forcefully in recent years (Wood, 2016a). This is evidenced in the UK by the introduction of PCCs (Newburn, 2012; Sampson, 2012; Rogers, 2013). Policing by consent has been boosted by the shift away from liberal ideas towards the increasingly democratic sensibilities identified by Wood (2016a) and I see the procedural justice approach to understanding police legitimacy as consistent with this heightened democratic awareness. Indeed, procedural justice has an explicitly democratic approach to defining legitimacy with no *necessary* commitment to liberal values, in particular values that champion the importance of the individual, for example privacy, toleration, liberty.

A focus on perception is critical within the empirical, social scientific approach to understanding legitimacy. As Jackson and Bradford (2019, p.3) note, it is used to 'describe whether – *as a matter of fact* – those that are subject to authority confer legitimacy on that authority'. I have added the emphasis here to illustrate a distinction between (1) empirical facts and (2) the conjecture of philosophical argument. This distinction can be exaggerated but is nonetheless worthy of note. Jackson and Bradford (2019) are emphasising the merits of an empirical approach that derives theoretical statements from a factual basis. However, it is important that we do not assume that this distinction means that empirical facts are somehow inherently more reliable than philosophical conjectures. It is worth reminding ourselves that perceptions 'may be false, distorted and even contradictory' (Waddington et al, 2017, p.28). They rely 'on what people *believe*' and we know that 'people voice with certainty claims that are palpably *untrue*' (Waddington et al, 2017, p.4 (emphasis in original). It is the task of the social scientist to account for such inherent errors in establishing reliable and valid claims, but nonetheless, facts are not necessarily as clear cut as they appear to be, just as there is much validity and longevity in the philosophical arguments of Aristotle and Plato. Rather than positing one approach against the other, it is important to recognise that insights can come from both empirical and philosophical studies. At the same time though, we need to be mindful of what each approach can, and cannot, tell us.

Procedural justice presents a rather one-dimensional view of police legitimacy as Bottoms and Tankebe (2012) have argued. Waddington et al (2017, p.149) bemoan this diminished view of legitimacy 'as merely a felt obligation to obey the police during future encounters'. Jackson and Bradford (2019) acknowledge that the procedural justice approach is but one approach to understanding police legitimacy. More than that, they emphasise that procedural justice is not the same thing as police legitimacy. They stress that procedural justice should not even be seen as a component of legitimacy, but rather as an 'important predictor of legitimacy' (Jackson and Bradford, 2019, p.2). Furthermore, and notwithstanding the remarks of its detractors, the impact of the procedural justice research on our understanding of policing generally, and more specifically as it relates to police legitimacy, is quite remarkable and needs to be acknowledged as such.

Tom Tyler developed his procedural justice theory in the USA, but its use as the basis for empirical research into questions of police legitimacy has expanded internationally (Jackson, 2018). Within the UK, Professors Jonathan Jackson and Ben Bradford have contributed significantly to this research and developed the understanding of procedural justice from its initial starting point (Jackson and Bradford, 2019). Jackson and Bradford (2019) are at pains to emphasise the empirical nature of their research and their understanding more broadly of procedural justice as it relates to police legitimacy. Indeed, in his inaugural lecture, Professor Ben Bradford defined himself as *radically empirical*, to emphasise the degree to which he goes to ensure that his research is driven by empirical findings as opposed to preconceived ideas. Jackson and Bradford (2019) acknowledge that there are other ways of conceptualising legitimacy, in particular the use of moral philosophy to establish normative components of legitimacy, but their focus is clearly and explicitly on 'discovering *bottom-up* the normative content of legitimacy' (Jackson and Bradford 2019, p.24, (emphasis in original). They emphasise the need to be clear on what the procedural justice research can tell us, and how concepts such as procedural justice, along with other concepts such as distributive justice, effectiveness and legality, can be used as predictive measures of legitimacy through empirical research. Indeed Jackson and Bradford (2019) are critically sensitive to the incorporation of empirically untested normative arguments into the analysis of empirical enquiries. As such, they are critical of Tankebe (2013) and even more so Sun et al (2018) for introducing top-down, a priori ideas of what constitutes the normative basis of legitimacy into their research, thereby blurring the distinction between empirical and moral enquiry in a problematic way.

Waddington et al (2017) consider the emergence of the procedural justice literature in the context of research that focuses on what happens when the police come into contact with the public. They argue that a 'theoretical framework' was required to bring 'conceptual order to the kaleidoscope of experience' garnered through this 'contact' research, and they see procedural justice as filling this void (Waddington et al, 2017, p.23). They raise concerns about the excessive focus on perceptions, but nonetheless argue that through the procedural justice thinking, perceptions become more dynamic and dialogic. So while procedural justice research is focused on perceptions, it nonetheless breaks from previous behavioural approaches which present the police 'as *stimuli* to which members of the public *react*', by introducing a 'more humanistic perspective', from which 'people are deemed to *construct* trustworthiness and to *interpret* the actions of others through active processes' (2017, p.27, emphases in original).

I suggest that the strength of the procedural justice literature is in establishing consensual legitimacy rather than moral legitimacy. By this I mean it does not tell us whether the police have acted legitimately in accordance with preconceived ideas of what constitutes legitimate performance, ideas that have been established through careful, considered moral reflections. To be fair, and to be clear, nor am I suggesting that this is something the procedural justice literature claims to do. However, what the procedural justice literature can do is to establish the extent to which the public perceive the police to have 'the right to rule' and 'the authority to govern' (Jackson and Bradford, 2019, p.4).

I see the empirically framed procedural justice research as an important dimension of ethical policing. It captures the consensual dimension of police legitimacy and is a stark reminder that ethical policing is not something that can be simply conceptualised in the abstract. Ethical policing is realised through the operations of policing. The interactions between the police and public, indeed what Jackson et al (2013, p.7) describe as a 'bond', are an integral part of what it means to say that policing is ethical. However, consensual legitimacy alone cannot produce ethical policing. Moral legitimacy, of the kind that cannot be established through empirical, procedural justice research, is likewise of integral importance in understanding and establishing ethical policing.

The liberal democratic understanding of legitimacy related to ethical policing

Legitimacy is a central concept within liberal democracies in qualitatively different ways from within other regimes. It is the liberal democratic sense of legitimacy that I see as a defining feature of ethical policing. Ethical policing becomes somewhat redundant and meaningless if it is operating in a society that lacks the kind of legitimate authority found within liberal democratic societies. My argument here is that ethical policing is not possible within authoritarian societies.

Ethical policing needs to be more than simply garnering popular support and public compliance with legal authority. It is for this reason that I do not think that policing can be ethical in any meaningful way within authoritarian regimes, or more precisely, the lack of an independent means of measuring the legitimacy of those in authority limits the moral space required for ethical policing to be fostered. I am using the term 'independent' here not to suggest that it is a neutral or unbiased means of measuring legitimacy, but rather simply that it is distinct from what is captured within attitudinal constructions of legitimacy. The measure does not need to be independent from values and bias for this purpose, but it needs to be independent from popular opinion, even if it draws the same conclusions.

This is ultimately the strength, importance and significance of human rights reasoning and to a lesser extent its representation in legislation. The values established through human rights reasoning exist irrespective of, and independent from, popular will and/or government dictates, as a reminder of the basic human values we hold dear. Without having such independent values, we can do no more than hope that the popular will of the people spontaneously reproduces principles akin to human rights as opposed to discriminatory, inhumane values. This is most likely to occur within contexts that require human rights protections the least and, conversely, are most unlikely to be produced in contexts where human rights are most needed. We know that at times the majority might support governmental measures to curb freedoms excessively. But it is invariably the case that we only know this through hindsight, which does little to protect those on the receiving end of the curbs at the time they are being administered. Human rights emerge to redress this deficiency by providing values that stand outside political expediency in a more reliable and permanent way than provided by the popular will of the people.

Consider the following as a thought experiment.

A democratically elected authoritarian government has passed legislation requiring all men aged 50 and over to be transported to specially designed internment camps. The government has been elected by a significant majority on the promise of introducing the camps for a period of ten years to redress a crisis in the regime's welfare provision and to alleviate environmental pressures. Those who survive the camps are promised a full and generous pension for the remainder of their lives but it is recognised explicitly that many will not endure the journey to the camps and only a small percentage are expected to survive the ten-year period. The camps are overcrowded and there are no medical provisions. The men are to be given physically demanding tasks to complete in the camp, working long hours seven days a week, with little more than a subsistence diet on which to survive.

Police officers operating within the regime are required to ensure that the legislation is enacted. They are tasked accordingly to track down, pursue and capture any individuals covered by the legislation who are attempting to avoid internment. The legal obligation placed on the police officers is unambiguous and the positional duties of the officers are likewise articulated with clarity in clear operational directives. The regime has specifically legislated such that it establishes a sunset clause revoking without exception the human rights of all men aged 50 and over for a ten-year period.

I appreciate that the *imagined* regime portrays an extreme measure to reduce the welfare bill and address environmental concerns. Likewise, I recognise that those who favour a more factual base to discussions about police legitimacy will feel somewhat aggrieved by the excessively unrealistic nature of the imagination here and indeed will no doubt feel vindicated in their own preference for concrete data over such fanciful creations. My point though is simply to amplify the inherent logic of the argument by showing that in such a situation it would be impossible for a police officer to act ethically in a meaningful way. The circumstances under which the officers are asked to carry out their duties are so unequivocally immoral, so lacking in any recognition of basic human rights, that the moral space within which officers are operating is too limited to allow for ethical decision making. I suggest that there is simply not the opportunity for a police officer to demonstrate what MacIntyre (2004) calls moral agency within such a context.

There are three points of clarification required here. First, I am assuming that if the logic is accepted in this extreme example, then we can move to ever more realistic examples that are nonetheless still such that the ethical space is so limited that it precludes sufficient levels of moral agency to realise ethical policing. Secondly, when I say that arresting all men aged 50 or over and interning them into labour camps, which are explicitly designed to reduce the population, is *unequivocally immoral*, I am assuming that it is possible to establish that a law is immoral independent of whether it is perceived as such or whether it has popular support. In the thought experiment I have stated that the government enacting the legislation was democratically elected and had campaigned explicitly on a commitment to do just this. While I appreciate that it might seem somewhat far-fetched to imagine a scenario in which people would willingly vote for such inhumane policies, my point is that from an empirical, procedural justice perspective, this would most likely produce normative alignment to, and compliance with, the police enforcement of the legislation. It would be seen as legitimate, unless a majority changed their minds after experiencing the societal consequences of the enforcement of the laws for which they had previously voted.

By saying that the enforcement of this law is nonetheless *unequivocally immoral* I am expressing a human rights perspective that favours particular ideas of what it means to be human that are independent of what the public and government think is necessary in order to reduce the welfare bill and avert environmental catastrophe. This expresses a moral perspective found at the heart of Kant's moral philosophy through his formulation of the 'categorical imperative', defined as both '(1) act only on maxims that you can at the same time will as universal laws, and (2) treat others never merely as means but always also as ends in themselves' (Uleman, 2010, p.2). This human rights sentiment can also be found within the deontological character of Rawls' (1971, p.26) notion of justice as fairness, which he defines as a theory that 'does not interpret the right as maximising the good'. These moral arguments act as constraints, limitations or correctives against what can be legitimately established as consensual norms. Of course, one might reject human rights morality and argue, for example from an ecological perspective, that culling the human population is the morally right thing to do. However, this would entail a radical departure from the understanding of ethical policing considered here.

Thirdly, when I say that there is no space for the moral agency of the police officer to be manifested in a meaningful way I am not saying that all decisions made by officers in such circumstances are equally valid. We can imagine some officers relishing in the inhumanity of their tasks, whereas others will perform their duties with a high degree of reluctance and regret. The former will conduct themselves with purpose, indeed they may even imbue this purpose with a degree of moral conviction, such that it leads to an exaggerated level of mistreating those interned in the camps. The latter are more likely to look for opportunities to treat the interns with as much dignity as possible, and to minimise their suffering as much as possible. However, these small pockets of humanity are ultimately crushed by the overall inhumanity of the situation. And while it is possible to argue that the latter is preferable to the former, I suggest it is too much of a stretch to articulate this preference in moral terms. Making the best of a situation, no matter how bad the situation is, might be preferable but it does not equate to moral agency, and it does not produce what I see as ethical policing.

MacIntyre (2004) uses the backdrop of the concentration camps in Nazi Germany to discuss his idea of moral agency. He provides a hypothetical example that illustrates for our purpose how moral agency requires a police officer to think beyond the immediacy of what he or she is told to do. He imagines a person, 'J' (from the German *Jemand* meaning *anybody* in English), who inhabits a social order with a strong and explicit political vision, with very clearly defined laws and positional duties for its public servants. J is given the responsibility 'for scheduling passenger and freight trains, monitoring their drivers' performance and coping with breakdowns' (MacIntyre, 2004, p.37). J is initially curious as to what the trains are carrying but is told categorically that it this is not his concern. He observes this instruction only to find later that he was tasked with the transportation of 'Jews on their way to extermination camps' (2004, p.37). To what extent is J implicit in the deaths of those being transported to the concentration camp? For MacIntyre, J's initial ignorance of the facts is no defence. He suggests that a moral agent is judged not simply on his or her intentions, but also on the 'incidental aspects' and 'reasonably predictable effects' arising from them (2004, p.37). He therefore rejects J's defence that he is not responsible for the extermination of the Jews because he did not know that this is what he was doing.

Beyond this though, what could J have done? In such a regime self-preservation is normal and understandable. Indeed, it is not only oneself that is being preserved but also family members and close friends. If J openly refused to carry out his duties, he would endanger not only himself but also those closest to him. Even if he were to perform his duties inefficiently, to be deliberately bad at his job in order to slow things down, he would put himself and others at significant risk. Nor is it possible for him to simply walk away from his duties without raising suspicions about his loyalty to the regime. In such circumstances, an individual is placed in an almost impossible position and any decisions he or she makes need to be appreciated as such. So while I agree with MacIntyre (2004) that J has moral responsibility for the transportation of Jews to the concentration camps, and the subsequent suffering of those transported, in such circumstances it is not possible to act morally while continuing to perform these duties. Self-sacrifice might be seen as a morally preferable option but this is complicated by the implications it might have for family members and/or friends who have not necessarily agreed to, or even been consulted on, this course of action.

There are two points that I wish to make in relation to the kinds of decisions an official is asked to make in such scenarios. First, to the extent that they can be seen as ethical decisions, it is important to note that all decisions are bad decisions ethically speaking. Such decision making is referred to as lesser evil ethics (Ignatieff, 2004). It can be portrayed as a form of consequential ethical reasoning that applies utilitarian logic but in a way that attempts to minimise harm, rather than maximise happiness.

Secondly, and more substantially in terms of my argument, J is limited further by being asked to make choices in isolation, without the institutional support or societal framework to make ethical decisions. Indeed J, like the officers in my own thought experiment set out earlier, is under pressure from his employer and the society in which he is operating to act immorally. Ethical policing cannot be realised through the will of individual officers acting in isolation. There might well be instances of ethical good practice and indeed exemplary moments of officers performing well beyond, and indeed at times against, the expectations of their employers, government and the general public. However, these are only recognised as such with hindsight or from afar. At the time they will be seen much more problematically and potentially as criminal or even treasonous.

It is for this reason that I argue that ethical policing only has meaning in a society that strives for moral legitimacy above and beyond consensual legitimacy. For ethical policing to be realised, the existence of morally just institutions operating within morally legitimate societal processes and procedures is as important as the moral character of the officers carrying out policing duties. Legitimate liberal democratic authority thus provides the most appropriate underpinning for ethical policing to be realised.

The dual characteristics of legitimacy as a defining feature of liberal democratic societies

When I use the term 'liberal democracy' I have in mind a society that demonstrates both a strong commitment to liberal values, *as well as* democratic sensibilities. Although often associated together, we need to recognise that liberal and democratic ideals express very different values that are in tension with one another (Wood, 2016a). Liberalism, for example, places great value on privacy, whereas democracy favours transparency and openness. Likewise, liberalism prioritises expertise, whereas democracy gives equal weight to all voices. A liberal democracy is one that tries to balance these competing ideals. Democracy favours consensual legitimacy, expressed, for example, through the notion of policing by consent, whereas liberalism champions the rights of the individual, the non-conformist and other minority voices that sit outside popular opinion, such that it favours moral legitimacy, in the form of, for example, principled policing or through human rights.

From a purely democratic perspective, human rights are only as important as the majority of people deem them to be. If the majority determine that a particular human right should not apply in a specific context, then from a purely democratic perspective, that particular human right loses its consensual legitimacy. Conversely, from a liberal perspective, establishing the moral legitimacy of an action is independent of its popularity. Moral legitimacy is established through ethical reasoning, and while it might be true to say that for such reasoning to be established as a legitimate authority there needs to be a consensus, any such consensus is nonetheless achieved only within an elite group of experts within society. As Johnston (1994) notes, liberalism is sometimes portrayed as elitist in this way. This applies whether we are establishing the facts concerning climate change (where there is limited controversy) or the costs and benefits of Brexit (where there is as much conflict between the experts as there is between the public at large). For the purposes of this chapter, we see this most evidently when human rights legislation is tested. While a basic understanding of human rights is shared by many, we know that applying human rights legislation in practice gives rise to conflicts and such matters are not resolved through a people's vote, but rather by legal experts, for example a judge or a panel of judges through an appropriate court of law. Indeed, as Delattre (2004) argues, this is a factor within policing because officers are required to make decisions quickly without the time to consider carefully whether their actions are lawful or in line with human rights. Likewise, as Alison (2008, pp.12–15) states, 'decision inertia' is not to be welcomed in policing contexts. Police officers interpret and apply the law in quick time, but it is only later, over a much longer time frame, that legal experts pass judgement on the initial interpretation and application made by the officer.

To illustrate further the independence of liberal and democratic ideals, consider the fact that what we generally consider to be authoritarian regimes can have either liberal or democratic intentions, but not both together. For example, with Plato's philosopher king in *The Republic* (Plato, 1955) and Hobbes' (1651) *Leviathan*, we are presented with absolute rulers who are characterised as benevolent, all-knowing, wise and compassionate dictators who act first and foremost for the well-being of all. They are driven by doing what is best for all and carry the burden of responsibility to achieve highly moral societal values; that is to say the values are highly moral whether we agree with them or not – they pertain to reasoned conceptions of what it means to be human. They are not in any sense democratic, in terms of how they come to positions of power, nor with regard to how they conduct themselves. This is what makes them authoritarian. Their respective authorities are not curtailed by democratic forces. The populace have virtually no legitimate power to resist such authority and can only hope that the dictator lives up to being as benevolent as they were conceptualised to be. While clearly not democratic, both the philosopher king and the Leviathan are presented as having liberal intentions. They are paternalistic in how they carry out these liberal intentions but they are legitimised through the high morality of what they seek to achieve. We can imagine in the face of increasingly significant ecological challenges, for example, establishing the moral legitimacy of a benevolent green Leviathan acting on behalf of the environment to bring about actions that are simply not achievable through democratic means (Ophuls, 1977 – see Wood, 2016b).

Conversely, Zakaria (2004) has suggested there is a growth around the world in what he refers to as *illiberal* democracy. This relates to specific measures, or governments more generally, that have popular support but are far from having liberal intentions. Indeed, the term 'populism' (Müller, 2016; Eatwell and Goodwin, 2018) is used to portray movements that are often discriminatory but supported by a substantial proportion of the electorate. The electoral success of such movements provides them with consensual legitimacy that justifies democratic representation, but the movements themselves may portray values that are seen to be immoral, or at least lacking the kind of moral legitimacy expected within liberal democracies. This is identified as 'competitive authoritarianism' by Dryzek and Dunleavy (2009, p.25), because there is an electoral competition of sorts that results in the imposition of an authoritarian order.

I suggest that ethical policing is limited within a benevolent dictatorship because there is no capacity to step outside of the dictator's stated intentions and question his or her authority. At best, we could have a form of principled policing but it would always be susceptible to the kind of moralism (Coady, 2008) discussed in Chapter 3. Likewise, ethical policing is limited within *illiberal* democracies because of the extent to which consensual legitimacy dominates and thereby removes the moral dimension of its legitimacy. Policing in such societies is stripped of its morality: it becomes amoral, and thereby readily permits and indeed at times enforces immoral acts.

Legitimacy is an integral concept within liberal democracies. This is because of the extent to which power is negotiated and mediated, with a focus on ensuring that there are checks and balances in place to avoid a concentration of too much authority in one place. For example, the prefix 'liberal' operates as a qualification limiting democracy by establishing principles that stand outside of electoral processes. At least this is a liberal democratic ideal that is used as a measure of a liberal democracy's legitimacy. It establishes certain values that are deemed to be too important to leave to the populace to decide upon. Similarly, a social democracy emphasises social values, rather than liberal individual ones, to set appropriate parameters for what can and cannot be decided through voting. There are hundreds of different sub-types of democracy that qualify democratic processes in this way (Wood, 2016a).

Liberal democratic legitimacy is manifested through its processes and procedures, which are portrayed as being particularly important, indeed as important if not more so, than what they achieve. This is reflected in the procedural justice literature, which emphasises the importance of how the police conduct themselves over what they achieve. Liberal democratic legitimacy assumes that citizens are free to make choices. People in liberal democracies have a say on important matters. They can be incentivised, motivated and perhaps at times even cajoled, but never more than this. This is the basic argument of John Stuart Mill in *On Liberty*, his seminal statement on liberal thinking (Mill, 1859/1973). People are given the space and freedom to decide what is in their own best interest, even when this is at times clearly against what those in authority think is best.

Liberal democracies differ in this respect from authoritarian regimes, which are much less dependent upon legitimacy because they are more willing to resort to the imposition of authority to compel people to do what the regime wants them to do. Where compulsion is a norm or a regular feature within a society, I suggest, the less meaningful legitimacy becomes. Of course, liberal democratic incentives and motivations are seen by some as a form of imposition, and liberal democracies are prone at times to cajole excessively and even compel. However, all forms of authority are constantly criticised within liberal democracies, by at least a minority but at times by substantial movements, in ways that are impossible within authoritarian societies (Waddington, 1999). It is through this constant questioning of authority that legitimacy becomes so central to liberal democracies.

This understanding of legitimacy is manifested and articulated through liberal democratic constitutions, which establish rules that apply as much to those in authority as they do to the general populace. As Walker (2000) notes, constitutions constrain and limit the authority of governments. This is especially true of liberal constitutions, which are consciously restrictive with regard to those in authority, but it is also the case, at least in relative terms, even where constitutions empower governments to assert their authority. The very nature of a constitution is to set limits and constraints on what governments can do. A constitution that permits those in authority to do whatever they desire ceases to be a constitution in any meaningful sense. It simply becomes redundant.

My understanding of ethical policing is highly dependent upon liberal democratic constitutional arrangements. However, as Manning (2010) notes, despite the general commitments made by police leaders and policy makers to the assumptions underpinning liberal democratic constitutions, and to the values eschewed by human rights thinking, we do not ask of the police to what extent this or that policing measure has led to a more equitable, fairer society. Manning's (2010) observations here are critical and they are supported further by Reiner's (2013) questioning of the police's role in society and how they are held accountable. The idea of ethical policing I am presenting in this book demands a much greater alignment between liberal democratic ideals and the aims of policing.

Rawls' liberal democratic thinking as it applies to ethical policing

The title of this book is *Towards Ethical Policing* and it is important to keep stressing that it is an aspirational approach to ethical policing. Moreover, its realisation is dependent not only on how police officers conduct themselves, nor even how policing is organised institutionally, but also how policing is understood, supported and held to account within society. As I have argued earlier, ethical policing can only be realised within just societies. Here I turn to Rawls' political conception of a just society. 'Only against the background of a just basic structure, including a just political constitution and a just arrangement of economic and social institutions, can one say that the requisite just procedures exist' (Rawls, 1971, p.76). By discussing the idea that a just society is a prerequisite of ethical policing, my intention is not to suggest that there is nothing that can be done towards achieving ethical policing until we have first established a perfectly just society. I do not wish to absolve police institutions or police officers from having any moral responsibility on the grounds that they are operating within an imperfect, unequal, unjust society. Indeed, although I see the actions of individual officers, the organisation of police institutions and the establishment of a politically just society as three conceptually distinct entities in the abstract, I nonetheless see the striving towards ethical policing as a process that engages all three dimensions simultaneously in practice. My concern here is that too often debates about police ethics will focus on the actions of police officers and/or the organisation of police institutions, but very little attention is paid to wider questions of how a politically just society relates to ethical policing. The next part of this chapter seeks to redress this deficiency.

I will use Rawls' (1971) idea of *justice as fairness* as a starting point for understanding the kind of social setting required for ethical policing to be realised. For Rawls (1971, p.3) the key 'virtue of social institutions' is justice, such that 'laws and institutions no matter how efficient and well-arranged must be reformed or abolished if they are unjust'. It is important to remember that the approach Rawls (1971) adopts is primarily to establish the ideal conditions under which just public institutions would be created. Rawls (1971) presents his ideas about justice within the social contract tradition associated with Locke, Rousseau and Kant. This involves thought experiments that require us to imagine 'what a perfectly just society would be like' (Rawls, 1971, p.8).

Rawls sees justice as the means by which a society is both ordered and regulated: 'a society is well-ordered when it is not only designed to advance the good of its members but when it is also effectively regulated by a public conception of justice' (Rawls, 1971, p.4). For Rawls, the focus of justice has to be at the level of what he calls the 'basic structure of society', which he defines as 'the way in which the major social institutions distribute fundamental rights and duties and determine the division of advantages from social cooperation' (1971, p.6). He argues this needs to be the focus of justice because the effects of the basic structure 'are so profound and present from the start' (1971, p.7). Rawls quite rightly stresses that where someone starts in society has such a profound impact on their life chances and this leads to 'especially deep inequalities' that 'cannot possibly be justified by an appeal to the notions of merit or desert' (1971, p.7).

From this, Rawls (1971) establishes two principles of justice that define justice as fairness. The first of these principles relates to the basic liberties within society and asserts that 'each person is to have an equal right' to these liberties (Rawls, 1971, p.53). These liberties should be as extensive as possible. His second principle of justice relates to 'social and economic inequalities' (1971, p.53). Such inequalities need to be assessed by the extent to which they exist to the benefit of all, especially those at the bottom of society, and by the extent to which they are 'attached to positions and offices open to all' (1971, p.53). Rawls thus seeks to establish principles of justice that (1) maximise basic liberties, ensuring all have equal access to them, and (2) minimise the impact that socio-economic inequalities have by attaching societal responsibilities to those enjoying privileges of office, and arranging them such that they benefit most the least privileged. For Rawls (1971), these two principles of justice articulate the most reasonable calculations that would be arrived at by rational individuals if asked to establish just procedures in the abstract, behind what Rawls (1971) describes as a *veil of ignorance*.

It is important to note the abstract character of Rawls' argument. He is not describing how principles of justice have been established throughout history, nor is he assuming that a perfectly just society is achievable. Rather he is asking that we think abstractly about 'an original position of equality ... a purely hypothetical situation' (Rawls, 1971, p.11), under which people come together to form a society that is just. Rawls (1971) recognises that there are inequalities between people and therefore the only way that the principles of justice can be deemed fair is if they 'are chosen behind a veil of ignorance' (Rawls, 1971, p.11). Thus the idea of a perfectly just society becomes a means of assessing the validity of proposed principles of justice. We are asked to consider whether such principles would be chosen by rational individuals in such an original position, operating behind a veil of ignorance.

The veil of ignorance is an important tool in Rawls' thinking. It assumes that for institutions to be just, the conditions under which they are created need to be fair. By this Rawls means that those entering into a social contract do so without knowing their own position within the ensuing social order. In other words, those constructing the principles of justice do so not knowing how they will be affected personally. The logic here is that I am less likely to support slavery if there is a chance that I will be selected as a slave. The veil of ignorance ensures that I thereby act as a 'rational and mutually disinterested' party (Rawls, 1971, p.12); not knowing how I will be affected personally encourages me to think rationally and impartially, rather than in a partisan, self-serving manner. I am still likely to seek to maximise my own gain, but since I cannot do this in a targeted way that explicitly addresses my own personal circumstances, I must do so in a way that I consider to be most likely to benefit people in general, myself included. This is what makes the principles of justice fair. Rawls (1971, p.11) does not use justice as fairness to mean that justice *is* fairness, that they 'are the same', but rather that 'it conveys the idea that the principles of justice are agreed to in an initial situation that is fair', in other words justice comes *from* fairness. The veil of ignorance is thus a conceptual construct conceived to 'nullify the effects of specific contingencies which put men at odds and tempt them to exploit social and natural circumstances to their own advantage' (1971, p.118).

Rawls (1971, p.125) emphasises the need to ensure that the procedures for establishing principles of justice are free from what he describes as 'destructive feelings', such as 'envy', to allow rational thought to come to the fore. For the principles of justice to be fair, it is essential that their creators are not swayed by personal preferences that are shaped by the specifics of their respective circumstances, but rather that they are motivated by a sense of good that would apply more generally. However, it is important to recognise that Rawls (1971) positions his thinking against utilitarianism, which posits the maximising of welfare in terms of the greatest good for the greatest number. Rawls (1971) argues that utilitarianism lacks an important reciprocal dimension between equal members and suggests that it is not rational for an individual to support a notion of justice that is to his or her own detriment, irrespective of what overall good it might achieve. He says 'the principle of utility is incompatible with the conception of social cooperation among equals for mutual advantage' (Rawls, 1971, p.13).

Rawls (1971) distinguishes between three types of procedural justice to illustrate his thinking further. As noted at the start of this chapter, Rawls' approach to procedural justice differs from Tyler's (1990) use of the term in relation to police legitimacy. What follows here relates specifically to Rawls' use of the term. This is not how the term is generally used in the procedural justice literature relating to police legitimacy.

Rawls (1971, p.75) sees 'pure procedural justice' as the primary goal within his notion of justice as fairness and he defines this as a process that is just in and of itself without reference to 'independent criterion for the right result, ... such that the outcome is likewise correct or fair, whatever it is, provided that the procedure has been properly followed'. This *pure* form of procedural justice is contrasted with 'perfect' and 'imperfect' procedural justice (1971, p.74).

Perfect procedural justice is illustrated by Rawls with the analogy of a person being presented with the task of cutting a cake in such a way as to ensure its fair and equitable distribution among a group. Rawls (1971) proposes the best way of achieving this task is for the person cutting the cake to be given the last slice. Assuming that everyone in the group, including the person cutting the cake, wants as much of the cake as possible, the rational thing to do is to divide the cake in equal proportions among the group. If there are different-sized portions then the person cutting the cake will receive the smallest slice. The cutter is thereby incentivised to slice the cake in equal proportions and to do otherwise would be irrational. This is an example of perfect procedural justice because 'there is an independent standard for deciding which outcome is just and a procedure guaranteed to lead to it' (Rawls, 1971, p.74).

Rawls makes it explicitly clear that considering such perfect settings has little if any practical use. He says 'perfect procedural justice is rare, if not impossible, in cases of much practical interest' (Rawls, 1971, p.74). We should not therefore get too preoccupied with the logistics of the cake-cutting analogy. Nor should we assume that the cake-cutting analogy captures what Rawls understands as justice as fairness. The point of the cake-cutting analogy is rather to illustrate through abstract reasoning that procedural justice can take a form in which (1) establishing what we understand to be just, and (2) the means of realising such aims, are independent of each other.

This logic is developed further by Rawls (1971) when he considers what *imperfect* procedural justice looks like. He states that imperfect procedural justice occurs if and when the procedures designed to achieve a just outcome cannot be so guaranteed. The aims of justice and how they are achieved remain independent of each other but with imperfect procedural justice there is no guarantee that the means of achieving justice will actually produce the stated goals, even if the proposed procedures are followed as intended. Rawls (1971) illustrates imperfect procedural justice with reference to criminal trials. He argues that the innocent can be found guilty just as the guilty might be set free even when criminal proceedings have been followed appropriately. The miscarriages of justice that ensue are feasibly a consequence of fortune or misfortune, and not necessarily the fault of anyone specifically, or indeed the proceedings in general, but rather they occur because of the inherent difficulty of establishing legal rules that can guarantee just outcomes in the way that was easily achieved in the cake-cutting exercise.

Pure procedural justice, as noted earlier, is what Rawls (1971) wants to establish through his notion of justice as fairness. It differs from the perfect and imperfect manifestations of procedural justice in that the design of pure procedural justice eradicates the distinction between the aims of justice and the processes for achieving these aims. Pure procedural justice establishes fair processes that are guided by Rawls' (1971) two principles of justice, such that by their very nature these processes are so conceived as to ensure fair outcomes, providing the processes have been followed appropriately.

Given what Rawls (1971) has said about the nature of criminal trials, and considering John Stuart Mill's (1863/1973) observations about the inherent difficulties of establishing a system of morality, I will assume here that imperfect procedural justice is never intentionally established as such, but is rather an example of pure procedural justice that has fallen short of its intended aims. I will therefore consider pure procedural justice as an aspirational concept that can be used to measure the legitimacy claims of those in authority, rather than as an achievable aim. However, I do not wish to infer that this is how Rawls sees it.

I see Rawls as expressing a moral understanding of justice as the primary means of establishing political legitimacy. He articulates what he sees as the reasonable and necessary moral obligations required for establishing political authority as legitimate. Rawls, in this sense, is aligned to the kind of human rights reasoning that dominates the second half of the 20th century. His thinking is also much more liberal than it is democratic. Indeed, much of the criticism of Rawls has come from communitarian perspectives that challenge Rawls' commitment to liberal individualism (Mullhall and Swift, 1996).

Conclusion

The police are an integral part of any liberal democratic society. They are one of its most prominent social institutions. They not only reflect, but also help to shape, the legitimacy of authority in liberal democratic societies. Ethical policing is dependent upon procedurally just social institutions and processes, understood both in terms of the kinds of consensual legitimacy captured through the empirical procedural justice research, but also in relation to the moral legitimacy established through moral reasoning, and the construction of procedures and institutions that reflect basic human rights. Consensual legitimacy reminds the police that they are public servants with responsibilities for protecting citizens, communities and society more generally. It helps to ensure that the police are responsive to public expectations and mindful of what the public want from the police. Moral legitimacy, on the other hand, constrains police actions by setting limits to what is acceptable and by establishing aspirations as to what constitutes the right thing to do through reason. It imposes obligations on the police to act in accordance with values and principles that foster ethical behaviour.

The insights from the procedural justice research are having a profoundly positive impact on policing, especially viewed from an ethical policing perspective. However, I feel that for ethical policing to be realised, there needs to be a greater understanding of the moral dimension of police legitimacy to complement and balance the understanding that has arisen regarding its consensual dimension. The moral dimension of police work is arguably a more challenging matter. I will consider this further in the next chapter by exploring the challenges of embedding moral agency within highly conflictual settings. But for the present I will end this chapter by emphasising that ethical policing is dependent upon the kind of legitimate constitutional arrangements, institutions, processes and procedures envisioned by Rawls (1971). Such a liberal democratic infrastructure helps shape not only the performance of its police officers, or simply its organisational policing structures, but also the ideas and institutions of justice across society more widely.

Suggested further reading

Bottoms, A. and Tankebe, J. (2012) 'Beyond Procedural Justice: A Dialogic Approach to Legitimacy in Criminal Justice', *Journal of Criminal Law & Criminology*, 102: 119–70

Bradford, B. (2014) 'Policing and Social Identity: Procedural Justice, Inclusion and Cooperation Between Police and Public', *Policing and Society*, 24(1): 22–43

Manning, P.K. (2010) *Democratic Policing in a Changing World*. Boulder, CO: Paradigm Publishers. Chapters 1–3

Rawls, J. (1971) *A Theory of Justice*. Cambridge, MA: Belknap. Chapters 1–3

Simmons, A.J. (2001) *Justification and Legitimacy: Essays on Rights and Obligations*. Cambridge: Cambridge University Press. Chapter 7

5

Ethical policing in practice: consequences matter

Introduction

> It is not the fault of any creed, but of the complicated nature of human affairs, that rules of conduct cannot be so framed as to require no exceptions ... There exists no moral system under which there do not arise unequivocal cases of conflicting obligation. (Mill, 1863/1973, p.427)

So far, I have focused on moral values and principles as they shape the way we think about ethical policing. Starting with a focus on such values in this way reflects the extent to which police ethics are increasingly dominated by deontological human rights considerations. But this is not without its problems. There are, as Mill (1863/1973) observes, inherent difficulties in establishing a meaningful moral blueprint for society, and in this chapter I shift the focus away from an abstract understanding of a police officer's moral obligations by introducing greater emphasis on the highly pragmatic nature of police work.

Policing operates in 'dirty' situations (Klockars, 1980; Delattre, 2011) and under conditions that are simply not conducive to ethical reasoning in any pure sense. From the perspective of a police officer, a Kantian-inspired deontology or a Rawlsian sense of *justice as fairness* might appear somewhat removed from the rough and tumble of operational policing. Likewise, human rights thinking might seem to be primarily concerned with the way things *should be* ideally, but perhaps less useful when dealing with things *as they are* in reality. This certainly captures the view that the police deal with the dysfunctional chaos on the periphery of normal society, where social norms and values have a significantly diminished presence and influence.

There are a number of issues raised by this perspective, that policing in general operates within the worst areas of society and deals with the worst individuals who behave in ways that fall short of societal expectations. First, it is important that we do not exaggerate the point.

Policing is not quite as remote as this account suggests. A significant proportion of police work deals with everyday matters involving individuals who are far from being outside social norms. The majority of people are prone to behave badly at some point in their lives, just as those we classify as bad people are rarely, if ever, bad all the time. We need to avoid an overly simplistic view of policing as the thin blue line protecting a well-ordered, just society from total chaos and disorder. Nonetheless, we do need to take seriously a concern that the contexts within which policing generally operates do not readily permit the kind of moral space required for ethical policing to flourish.

In the previous chapter I suggested that policing cannot be ethical in any meaningful sense within authoritarian regimes because such regimes lack the moral space created by liberal democratic constitutions. The question to consider here is whether it is possible *within* liberal democracies for policing to be ethical in a meaningful way. By this I mean that if policing is denied the moral space it requires, and if the circumstances under which police operate fall outside the norms of the liberal democratic constitutional arrangements, then the possibility of policing being ethical in a meaningful way is diminished. I raise the question in this way to emphasise the need to be more sensitive to operational policing demands when considering what we understand to be ethical policing. Ethical policing is always much easier to conceptualise and embed in policies than it is to realise through operational activities. We need to be mindful of this when discussing ethical policing so that we avoid becoming too idealistic in our thinking.

A challenge that this chapter addresses is how we maintain the importance attached to moral values and principles, especially in terms of human rights and the creation of just societal institutions and processes, while at the same time recognising the realities of police work. Miller (2004a) approaches this question in a slightly different way by drawing out the tension between (1) the purpose of policing, understood as the protection of moral rights, and (2) the kinds of things the police are required to do in order to realise this purpose, for example use of coercion and violence. Ethical policing requires a pragmatic level of thinking and an appreciation of how important consequences are in policing (Kleinig, 2002).

Utilitarian ethics as a form of consequentialism

Utilitarianism is a form of consequential ethics, ethical reasoning that prioritises the good over the right. Utilitarianism has antecedents in classical times but was developed in its modern guise in the 18th and 19th centuries, primarily by a number of English philosophers, for example Jeremy Bentham (1748–1832), William Godwin (1756–1836), John Stuart Mill (1806–73), Herbert Spencer (1820–1903) and Henry Sidgwick (1838–1900). Simmonds (2002) summarises utilitarianism as being defined by (1) its singular focus on one good, which is expressed as happiness or welfare, and (2) the singular pursuit of maximising this good. These two complementary aspects of a utilitarian ethic are captured most succinctly by Bentham's maxim of pursuing *the greatest good for the greatest number.* This specific aspect of classical utilitarianism has been modified by different consequentialists and there are many approaches to utilitarianism and consequential ethics which have been developed over time (see Smart and Williams, 1973; Weinstein, 2011). All utilitarian arguments are consequentialist, but not all consequential reasoning is necessarily utilitarian. However, I will use the terms 'utilitarianism' and 'consequentialism' more or less interchangeably as shorthand for a general approach to ethical reasoning that places greater emphasis on what actions achieve, as opposed to establishing the right motivations upon which to act.

It is important to keep in mind the distinct ways in which the terms 'right' and 'good' are used within moral philosophy (Simmonds, 2002). By way of simplification, deontological ethics focus on the concept of right, which is established a priori, independently of the good brought about by doing the right thing. Consequential ethics, on the other hand, place greater emphasis on the good achieved by performing or not performing a particular action. A consequential logic is expressed when we say that the ends justify the means. Indeed, any ethical discussions that are framed through a *means and ends* discourse articulate consequentialist reasoning (see Singer, 1979, chapter 9). This can be seen, for example, in relation to each of the following:

- *Ticking time bombs* (see Kleinig, 2005), a hypothetical scenario that involves a potentially catastrophic consequence. Someone has hidden a bomb and we are asked to consider what is permissible in ascertaining the whereabouts of the bomb in order to avert considerable loss of life.
- *Noble cause corruption* (see Delattre, 2011, pp.207–34) relates to police wrongdoings that are motivated by just intentions or, put another way, where police use corrupt and/or illegal methods to achieve just aims.
- *Dirty Harry* scenarios (see Klockars, 1980) relate to the series of films starring Clint Eastwood in which he plays a rogue cop who breaks the rules in order to bring the bad guys to justice.

All of these focus on the relationship between means and ends. Indeed they are different expressions of the same thing:

- they involve a police officer who is willing to bend the rules (or more) in order to bring about justice;
- there is a need for someone to do something to avert a disaster, a miscarriage of justice or bad things in general; and,
- there is an unambiguous sense of what justice is.

It is important to note that utilitarianism specifically, and consequentialism more generally, have come to be regarded as flawed because of the potential moral abuses that arise from such *means and ends* reasoning. In particular, the classical utilitarian pursuit of maximising aggregate welfare without considering how this affects all individuals is largely rejected today. It is deemed, quite rightly, especially unfair and unjust for the happiness of the majority (ends) to be achieved by measures that cause considerable pain and misery to the minority (means).

Throughout the second half of the 20th century there was a shift in ethical thinking away from a utilitarian perspective towards one in which rights and a focus on moral obligation became dominant. This was noted in Chapter 3 when discussing the rise of human rights thinking in the aftermath of the Second World War. Human rights thinking challenges the consequentialist logic that establishes a hierarchical, relationship between ends and means (Kleinig, 2019), in which what is achieved (ends) is presented as superior to how it is achieved (means). Through human rights, and likewise a Kantian approach to moral questions, such an expression is deemed inappropriate and morally indefensible. The Kantian approach considers means as an end in themselves and from a human rights perspective this is especially so when it comes to treating an individual as a means to another's end. For example, from a human rights perspective, the torture of one individual (means) can never be justified on the grounds that it will save many other lives (ends). The distinction between means and ends is thus rendered meaningless within deontological thinking.

Noble cause corruption

The weakness in utilitarian reasoning arising from potential human rights abuses is well noted. It is discussed within policing contexts through the idea of noble cause corruption (Miller, 2004b). As Crank et al (2007, p.104) note, the term 'noble cause' within police ethics is so 'grounded in a utilitarian ethic' that it is invariably associated with corruption. It is assumed that it is not possible for a police officer to be motivated by noble causes without this leading to the use of illicit means to gain noble ends. We do not tend to speak of noble cause justice. The framing of noble cause within a utilitarian framework leads to an association of prioritising just ends with corruption.

Kleinig (2002) criticises the term 'noble cause corruption' and questions its usefulness. For him corruption by definition can have no noble cause, just as noble causes cannot in and of themselves be corrupt. A noble cause might be corrupted but if and when this happens it ceases to be a noble cause at the point it becomes corrupted. Kleinig (2002) presents five illustrative case studies to question the use of corruption as an appropriate term for what he argues are more precisely cases of deviating from rules, which he argues arise from police having to operate in a climate that gives 'no weight to consequences' (Kleinig, 2002, p.299).

All of his illustrative examples, in different ways, relate to police officers taking shortcuts in dealing with low-level crimes and misdemeanours, predominantly to avoid over-complicating what are already overly complex means of dealing with petty criminal and disorderly activities. In essence the cases Kleinig (2002) uses illustrate the extent to which we have over-formalised the policing of minor offences and thereby undermined the discretionary underpinnings of policing in democratic societies. Reasonable doubt, which plays such an important role in serious offences, where the consequences of error are themselves so serious, can quickly become unreasonable in situations that would be better dealt with swiftly and informally. The over-formalisation of everything the police do has been highlighted as a problem in the UK (Flanagan, 2008), and it is a far cry from the idea of police established by French philosopher Montesquieu (1914 [1752]), who says: 'The business of the Police consists in affairs which arise every instant, and are commonly of a trifling nature: there is then but little need of formalities' (§24).[1]

Montesquieu is primarily concerned with making a distinction between the relatively rare, extreme events in society that require a robust legal response and the more everyday matters of disorder and petty crime that need to be policed in a more timely, less formal way. It is much more difficult today for police to deal with matters pragmatically through using consequential reasoning. Policing is increasingly characterised by its legalistic, bureaucratic and formal presence in everyday life.

However, we should not underestimate the extent to which police officers are motivated by getting a just result. As Kleinig (2002) argues, we do not want police officers to ignore low-level crimes, or bend rules to avoid what are seen as unnecessary complications. This can even lead to vigilantism or a normalisation of rule bending that leads towards more serious acts of corruption. The *noble cause* reasoning raises considerations regarding what motivates police officers to act corruptly and, correspondingly, how we encourage them to act otherwise.

Bayley (2002) illustrates how police will tend to resent the rule of law, not because officers are immoral but because they see the rule of law as a barrier to achieving morally just ends. The officers are thus presented as acting on moral grounds, albeit where their morality is mistaken. In simple terms we might say they are wrong, rather than bad or lacking in any sense of justice. Indeed, Bayley argues that we need to appeal to the police officer's sense of justice to show how the rule of law has pragmatic qualities that help police bring about more and better prosecutions. Bayley's (2002) logic here is to re-present the rule of law to officers so that they appreciate it in consequential terms, rather than in deontological terms. His approach gets officers to be more accepting of the limitations that the rule of law is perceived to impose on them, by encouraging them to see these limitations as short-term losses that allow for more substantial, long-term gains.

Notwithstanding its *philosophical* flaws, and without wishing to defend all aspects of utilitarianism, I suggest that we need to recognise certain merits that it offers. In particular, we should not be too quick to dismiss the *pragmatic* aspects of consequentialist reasoning. As Wolff (2006) notes, despite the unfavourable airing utilitarianism receives within moral philosophy today, it still offers unsurpassed insights when it comes to addressing the kinds of difficult decisions that those in public office need to make. Given the importance of consequences within policing, it seems only right that consequentialist reasoning should play a part in ethical policing.

The declining influence of *harm to others*

One example of consequentialist reasoning applied to policing contexts is John Stuart Mill's *harm to others* principle as it relates to conflicts in society. Police officers are routinely confronted with situations in which they are required to balance one person's rights against another's. In such scenarios it is not always immediately obvious who is in the right and who is in the wrong. Indeed, it might be the case that neither side is acting justly, or conversely, that neither side is at fault. As Delattre (2004) argues, police officers do not have luxurious time frames or resources to draw upon when settling such conflicts. The police operate in an immediate setting and are required to make instantaneous decisions over conflicting rights. While it is comforting for us to think of policing simplistically in terms of catching the bad guys, police officers are often dealing with the everyday conflicts that arise between human beings going about their business.

This challenge is recognised within John Stuart Mill's *harm to others* principle, which favours the unfettered freedom of individuals, providing they are not causing harm to others (Mill, 1859/1973). Mill's *harm to others* guide is representative of the kind of liberal individualism discussed in Chapter 2 that favours ethical neutrality as a governing tactic. It has provided police officers with a useful heuristic backdrop for dealing with conflicts, but increasingly it has come to be seen as a limited administrative response (Furedi, 2011) and thereby a problematic policing strategy.

There are good reasons why Mill's *harm to others* principle has been questioned. We recognise increasingly that what constitutes harm is open to interpretation, for example in terms of:

(1) the types of harm caused;
(2) the extent of the damage incurred by the victim; and,
(3) the extent to which the harm is readily observable to a third party.

Whereas police would previously have dealt almost exclusively with physical harm, whether against the person or their property, today's police officers are increasingly called upon to deal with incidents that are characterised by other forms of harm. For example, when dealing with domestic violence, officers need to be mindful not only of signs of physical abuse, but also of financial controlling and emotional and psychological damage. Similarly, whereas in previous times society may have been more tolerant of what might be perceived as low levels of violence, today we expect the police to take action across many more incidents. Over time, we have significantly lowered the threshold of what constitutes harm, or, put the other way, we have expanded 'the meaning of harm', as Furedi (2011, p.107) notes. At the same time, whereas harm was previously something that needed to be established objectively, increasingly today we take much more seriously subjective perceptions of harm.

Mill's *harm to others* principle is also questioned in relation to who or what should be included as *others*. For example, should it be restricted to the immediate target of the harm, or include as victims more widely those that have witnessed the harm, whether directly or mediated through news reports, social media and so on? Undoubtedly children growing up in a family environment in which violence is common are damaged even if they are not subjected to the violence personally. And when a teenager is mindlessly stabbed to death it causes considerable anxiety across communities, particularly for all young people and their parents, friends and families. Acts of violence have an impact not only directly on an intended target, but also indirectly on others, often in ways that could not be anticipated. This is recognised most explicitly within the definitions of hate crime.

Mill's *harm to others* principle is primarily a mechanism for limiting the interventions of authority in civil society. As we expand our understanding of what constitutes harm, we correspondingly increase the opportunities for those in authority to intervene in people's lives. However, the incorporation of human rights reasoning does more than this. The more we take seriously the question of human rights, the more we expand the roles of those in authority with an ever greater expectation that action should be taken. Indeed, we establish morally binding obligations on those in authority to proactively protect us from harm. The obligations imposed upon those in authority even go beyond protecting the rights of human beings alive today as we increasingly broaden the scope of who and what can be harmed. For example, from an ecological perspective we are encouraged to consider the harm caused by our actions against future generations, other species and natural environments (Benton, 1998, 2007, 2008; South, 1998; White, 2003, 2008, 2010, 2013; White and Graham, 2015; Wood, 2016b).

The more we expand the concept of harm at a societal level, the more likely it is that police officers are called upon to intervene in conflicts that take the form of competing rights. The *harm to others* principle loses its appeal the more the concept of harm is problematised. It ceases to offer a simplistic approach to responding to incidents because of the extent to which harm has become an increasingly complex notion. But more than this, human rights reasoning adopts a completely different approach to the pragmatic characteristics of Mill's *harm to others* principle. Human rights are not promoted because they offer the most practical way of resolving conflicts, but rather because they are seen to be the moral basis upon which conflicts should be resolved.

The ability to make informed, ethical judgements and decisions has increasingly become an expectation and requirement within police work. Human rights frame the actions and interventions of police officers in terms of notions such as proportionality. A police officer needs to consider whether he or she is justified in making an intervention or acting in a particular way; whether the action is proportionate and appropriate, and indeed necessary. Getting this right becomes more challenging and requires more thought, the more police are expected to intervene in more aspects of our lives. I suggest that it is important that policing retains a degree of the kind of pragmatism that is found within Mill's *harm to others* reasoning and this may well be provided by those aspects of human rights reasoning that focus on issues such as proportionality. The challenge, though, is making sure that the obligatory nature of human rights does not unduly diminish and limit the problem-solving requirements of good policing. Above all else, police officers are placed in difficult situations and they are called upon to deal with other people's problems, and people expect results.

The *dirty hands* doctrine

Police officers hold positions of public office and it is in this capacity that we consider ethical policing. We are not talking about the personal and private morality of each individual officer, but rather the ethical character with which they conduct themselves as police officers. As Bellamy (2007) argues, there is a long-established distinction within political philosophy between the private morality that guides an individual's activities and the public morality that informs public officials with responsibilities for people's safety, security and general well-being. This distinction is grounded, for example, most infamously in Machiavelli's (1981) *The Prince*, in which it is established that political leaders need to understand the nature of necessity as a prerequisite for the efficient rule of a nation. This perspective implies that it is one thing for an individual to internalise moral obligations through reasoning and self-reflection; however, it is altogether more challenging to establish appropriate moral obligations that are meaningful within the contexts of public office.

Simmonds (2002) refers to utilitarianism as a guide for 'those who exercise public power' (2002, p.20), rather than as a 'general moral philosophy' (2002, p.19). He also suggests that it is this kind of public guidance role that Jeremy Bentham had in mind when introducing utilitarianism at the end of the 18th century, rather than as a guide to 'private ethical reflection' (2002, p.23). So while utilitarianism might suffer as a general moral philosophy, it arguably retains an important role in public life. As Wolff (2006, p.19) says, 'although there are plenty of more appealing approaches to personal morality, we do not seem to have many candidate alternatives for public policy decision making'. Even within his critique of utilitarianism, Bernard Williams acknowledges a significant distinction between utilitarianism as a personal system of morality as opposed to one designed for public office: 'The fathers of utilitarianism thought of it principally as a system of social and political decision, as offering a criterion and basis of judgement for legislators and administrators' (Williams, 1973, p.135).

Bellamy (2007, p.513) refers to the dirty hands doctrine in this context and cites Sidney Axinn's argument that 'leaders who are so concerned with their own personal morality ... will not do what is necessary'. As Bellamy (2007, p.513) summarises, '[p]olitical leaders ... get their hands dirty by acting in ways normally considered immoral in the private world in order to secure the state and the common life it defends'.

The dirty hands doctrine promotes the idea that those in public office need to get their hands dirty in order to do what is expected of them. It articulates a realist perspective, one that is mistrustful of the kind of moral reasoning associated with Kant and Rawls. Indeed, from this realist perspective, Coady (2008) portrays human rights as potentially harmful to the extent that they lead us to assume that the hard work of politics is achieved through pronouncements and declarations of intended good deeds and nothing more.

Perhaps the most popular expression of the dirty hands doctrine within a policing context comes from the fictional *Dirty Harry* character, which has become a standard illustrative example of the ethical considerations confronting police (Klockars, 1980; Miller et al, 2006; Delattre, 2011). In the film *Dirty Harry*, the protagonist is confronted with a ticking-time-bomb scenario that leads him to torture a criminal, Scorpio, who has kidnapped a young girl and left her to suffocate in an enclosed space. This is one of a series of crimes Scorpio has committed to extort ransom money from the city authorities. Harry captures Scorpio but needs to uncover the whereabouts of the buried girl quickly if he is to save her life. Is Harry morally right to torture Scorpio? Clearly, from a human rights perspective the answer is no; indeed the peremptory character of human rights thinking (Simmonds, 2002) even precludes engagement with the question. However, from the dirty hands perspective the answer might be yes, if it can be determined that Harry did what was necessary in order to save a young girl's life.

We should note that justifying Harry's actions in this scenario would not imply that we support the routine use of torture. This is an extreme circumstance, which applies by definition to all ticking-time-bomb scenarios. They are extreme examples of instances that very few police officers will ever experience throughout their whole career. We are not talking about policing norms here. A more controversial question is whether or not in justifying Harry's actions we are saying that he acted morally. Steinhoff (2006) argues that there are times when it is morally appropriate for torture to take place, and he specifically supports Harry's torturing of Scorpio, seeing it as the morally right thing to do.

Steinhoff (2006) is writing from a position of wanting to reduce torture. He is not a supporter of torture. His concern is that simply prohibiting torture through a United Nations Declaration does little to stop its use in practice. Amnesty International (2006) argue that this is evidenced by the UK government's use in the early 1970s of *sensory deprivation* techniques against suspected Irish terrorists. While falling short of being defined as torture, these techniques amounted to the kinds of 'cruel, inhuman or degrading treatment or punishment' as established in the United Nations Convention Against Torture (UNCAT).[2] In the post-9/11 world (Strauss, 2003), the USA has increasingly resorted to claims of exceptionalism in justifying illiberal, counter-terror strategies, such as those carried out in Guantanamo Bay. There appears to be a growing move in different countries to adopt a kind of approach that Kleinig (2004) notes was implemented in Israel, where the law was modified to sanction torture in exceptional circumstances, and Steinhoff (2006) makes references to similar clauses in German legislation. In the UK there has been much debate around the legality and morality of using control orders against suspected terrorists (Kleinig, 2001). Steinhoff (2006) is following Henry Shue (1978), who had previously argued in a seminal paper that despite almost universal condemnation of torture, it was nonetheless on the rise. He says '[t]orture is indeed contrary to every relevant international law, including the laws of war. No other practice except slavery is so universally and unanimously condemned in law and human convention. Yet unlike slavery, which is still most definitely practiced but affects relatively few people, torture is widespread and growing' (Shue, 1978: 124). Perhaps the only aspect of Shue's (1978) statement above that would be challenged today is that slavery is likewise on the increase.

In order to reduce torture, Steinhoff (2006) argues that we first need to accept that simply getting everyone to agree in the abstract that torture is wrong does not prevent it from occurring. We therefore need to consider what the conditions are under which torture could be seen as legitimate, and from this how it should be administered. It might seem counterintuitive to approach the reduction of torture by starting with an argument that outlines the conditions under which torture would be acceptable but establishing the conditions under which it is morally preferable to torture than to not torture are such that we would still make torture illegal (Kleinig, 2005, 2007). Both Klockars (1980) and Kleinig (2005) approach ticking time bombs in this way. They show that it becomes virtually impossible to justify torture when we consider all of the factors that need to be established before it can take place. We need to know:

- that we have the right person;
- that he or she knows what we need to know;
- that information provided will be true;
- that we can act on it in a timely fashion to avert the impending catastrophe; and,
- that only torture will elicit the required information.

There are many more considerations and in real life we do not have the vantage point of an audience in a movie theatre. Dirty Harry, as those who have seen the film know, fails the test.

There are two particular arguments aimed at reducing torture that I wish to consider here. However, before doing so I want to make clear that my intention is primarily to illustrate through these arguments how consequential reasoning can be used to establish meaningful aspirations in place of morally binding obligations to guide ethical policing.

The first argument is provided by Alan Dershowitz. He approaches the increase in torture from a lawyer's perspective by suggesting the introduction of torture warrants as a way of curbing illicit torture. He uses the example of search warrants to show how this could work in practice, arguing that the introduction of search warrants dramatically reduced the number of illegal police searches and, perhaps more importantly, transformed the way police approached the question of searching people's properties. Dershowitz (2003) starts by accepting that in a particular instance there might be a morally justifiable case to be made for using torture. Assuming this to be the case, how should we proceed? He makes the case that it is much better insisting on justifications being made prior to torture happening, rather than after the event. While recognising that the instances in which a torture warrant might be deemed necessary are most likely to be subject to challenging time frames, he nonetheless believes that almost instant decisions could be taken to ensure a timely response to requests.

Secondly, he also suggests that it should be high-ranking judges who take the responsibility of assessing whether there are grounds for issuing a torture warrant. This is to ensure that such decisions would not be taken lightly. High-ranking judges hold prestigious and well-paid positions in society that they would not wish to jeopardise. Such individuals also hold expertise in legal matters and are used to resisting political expediency and protecting rights.

An alternative approach is provided by Steinhoff (2006), who counters both aspects of Dershowitz's (2003) arguments. For Steinhoff (2006) it should be police officers in the field who decide whether torture is morally justifiable and they need to make that decision themselves based upon their assessment of the situation. They are then accountable for their actions after the event and will be judged at this point as to whether they have acted legitimately or illegally. Steinhoff (2006) argues that the legitimacy of the state is called into question if it is deemed to sanction torture as a legitimate, legal tool. For Steinhoff (2006) it is important that we keep a clear distinction between the morality and legality of torture. He favours using the logic of civil disobedience to deal with torture. Civil disobedience is recognised as actions that are undertaken by a person in the full knowledge that what they are doing is illegal but where their motivation for breaking the law is premised upon a conviction that their action is morally superior to the law itself. An appeal to the civil disobedience character of their offence will be tested through a criminal trial. If successful, the judge will take this into account when sentencing. Of course, the seriousness of an offence is also taken into consideration and if a police officer's moral defence regarding the use of torture is unsuccessful, then they will definitely receive a lengthy custodial sentence given the severity with which torture is regarded. For Steinhoff (2006) this in itself is a weighty enough disincentive for an officer to use torture.

Steinhoff's (2006) views on this matter partly chime with what I am arguing regarding ethical policing. I agree that the state sanctioning of torture through the issuing of torture warrants is highly problematic. We know that torture is highly unreliable and if the state sanctions torture, then it also becomes morally responsible for ensuring that it becomes more reliable. This would require a whole infrastructure of state-sanctioned administration through government departments and police units focusing on the use of torture. There would need to be university departments created to develop knowledge and expertise in torture techniques. It would not be too long before we had a Professor of Waterboarding conducting research to support evidence-based torture practice. However, Steinhoff's (2006) approach is weakened by his support of Dirty Harry. I suggest that Harry is not the best example to draw upon in making a case for the dirty hands doctrine. It is made clear at the outset of the film that he is considered *dirty* well before he encounters Scorpio. Are we to assume that he has experienced more often than most ticking-time-bomb situations? Or is it more likely that he treats *all* situations with little or no respect for rights and just procedures? Away from the fictional drama of cinema, a Dirty Harry character in reality should have been dismissed from the police service, at the very least, long before he encountered Scorpio. This is precisely what concerns Dershowitz (2003) and explains his preference for taking this decision-making capacity away from officers.

It is important to stress that the dirty hands doctrine does not favour inherently dirty public officials who are always looking for opportunities to cut corners, bend rules and get away with unjust practices. It is not a charter for amoral or immoral leaders. Quite the opposite. What the dirty hands doctrine entails is hiring public officials who are highly principled, law-abiding, moral characters, who nonetheless take seriously their position as public officials such that they are willing to take moral responsibility to act in ways that will *on occasion* require them to make difficult decisions outside of the normal processes and procedures governing their roles.

Lesser evil ethics

The dirty hands perspective assumes that public officials should not have dirty hands all of the time, but rather they should be prepared to get their hands dirty when it is necessary to do so. The issue of necessity is critical here. It highlights the logic of *lesser evil* ethics (Ignatieff, 2004). Bellamy (2007) sees lesser evil ethics simply as a form of utilitarianism, one that applies the utility calculation to minimise pain rather than maximise happiness. There are many policing scenarios in which there are no positive outcomes possible and the police are therefore required to choose the course of action that produces the least worst outcome. An extreme view of lesser evil ethics is provided by what we refer to as Sophie's Choice (Kleinig, 2002). In William Styron's novel, *Sophie's Choice*, a Polish mother is presented on her arrival at Auschwitz with the option of saving one of her two children in the knowledge that the other will face certain death. If she does not choose, then both children die. Such a terrible choice has become synonymous within moral philosophy with any decision in which an unbearable consequence is inevitable.

In one sense, I suggest that the choice presented to Sophie is not a meaningful choice. The circumstances here are so barbaric and inhumane that it becomes meaningless to consider this as an ethical dilemma. Thankfully, police officers will probably never have to make such an impossible choice but if they do, judging them on this decision would only add to the inhumanity of the situation.

Police officers are more likely to face less extreme versions of lesser evil ethical scenarios. Indeed, they will frequently find themselves in situations where they are required to make a choice between options that are neither unambiguously good nor bad. Often, the choice will be between different bad options. A choice still needs to be made, even though we know that the choice will lead to bad consequences. Indeed, lesser evil ethics highlights that no matter how limited and difficult the choices presented to police officers are, it is necessary for a decision to be made.

Officers need to accept this responsibility. As Delattre (2011) suggests, indecision is not an option for police officers. It would be better, within reason, for officers to make a bad decision, providing it is made in good faith, rather than make no decision at all. Of course, bad decisions need to be answered and rectified as much as possible and it is assumed that officers and police institutions will learn and develop from the realisation that bad decisions have been made. This is the basic requirement of a learning organisation (Senge, 2010). Nonetheless, it is important for officers to recognise that if they are incapable of making decisions, then they are abdicating their responsibilities and leaving the fate of others to someone else or to chance. The choice confronting Sophie is a reminder that no matter how difficult the decision encountered by an officer will be, it is unlikely to be as demanding as the one she had to make. Police officers are required to make brave decisions and stand by them and there will be times when the lesser evil is the best that police officers can opt for.

The problematic nature of obligation with contexts of police ethics: consequences matter!

The central argument in this chapter is that the kind of principles and values discussed in the earlier part of the book are necessary for policing to be considered ethical, but at the same time there is a danger that they become too restrictive if and when they pay too little attention to the nature of police work. Ethical policing is not something that can be established in the abstract. Pagon (2004), for example, argues that although police ethics is generally understood as applied ethics, it is relatively underdeveloped, particularly with regard to its policing dimension. He suggests that police ethics is too often philosophical ethics illustrated with police examples without due consideration to the specificities of policing contexts. As Kleinig (2004) notes, for example, loyalty can be seen as both a virtue and a vice within policing contexts. Westmarland (2005, p.146) similarly considers how police culture in general informs police ethics, making reference to 'the "blue code" or "blue curtain" of silence'. She also notes elsewhere that policing is often characterised by the 'unscripted' and 'unpredictable' nature of police encounters (Westmarland, 2014, p.465).

We need to appreciate the need for pragmatism in policing with a focus on consequences, without undermining too much the insights from deontological perspectives and human rights reasoning. Obligations express reasoned commitments to act in particular ways without exceptions. This is what gives power, for example, to human rights. It is the morally binding obligations created by the existence of the rights that ensures principles and values established through human rights are taken seriously by those in authority. But what is the cost of developing obligations at the level of an individual's conscience to act in this way? Alternatively, if we use human rights to establish aspirations rather than obligations, as I suggested in Chapter 3, we clearly reduce the power of the rights to ensure that such matters are dealt with appropriately. So one question is: How do we ensure that aspirations are taken seriously as expectations, such that it would initiate investigation if they were not met? However, at the same time, we need to consider, in response to Alderson's (1998) call for principled policing, whether there is an opposite problem of policing becoming too principled. In other words, do police officers lose the capacity to deal with problems if we make them conform too tightly to non-consequential principles?

An emphasis in the procedural justice literature has been the need to focus on how the police conduct themselves rather than on policing outcomes. In moral terms, this reinforces the view that ethical policing is defined more by a deontological consideration of what we are obliged to do, than it is by the good consequences of what our actions achieve. However, as Steinhoff (2006) argues, in public office consequences matter. Kleinig (2002) likewise identifies operational pitfalls that arise from giving insufficient attention to consequences in policing and even John Rawls, while identifying his approach as deontological, acknowledges the inherent importance of consequences in moral thinking: 'All ethical doctrines worth our attention take consequences into account in judging rightness. One which did not would simply be irrational, crazy' (Rawls, 1971, p.26). Indeed, notwithstanding the conceptual clarity of presenting ethical approaches as being either deontological (and thereby non-consequentialist) or consequentialist (and thereby concerned with ends over the means), in practice, ethical reasoning will always contain consideration of both the intended ends and the proposed means of achieving them (Kleinig, 2019). An advocate of a highly principled approach will be prepared to compromise, if and when the consequences of not doing so become extreme, just as the most ardent consequentialist will be balanced in their reasoning to avoid a disproportionate disjuncture when considering the cost of utilising particular means to achieve specific beneficial ends. An example of the former is expressed by Rawls (1971, p.4) when he says 'an injustice is tolerable only when it is necessary to avoid an even greater injustice'. Here Rawls allows for a consequential qualification to his otherwise deontological approach. An example of the latter is provided by John Stuart Mill (1863/1973) when he says 'better to be Socrates dissatisfied than a fool satisfied'. In other words, for Mill the cost of happiness becomes too great if it is only achieved by embracing ignorance over the pursuit of truth. The main point here though is that the difference between deontological and consequential reasoning should be seen as a matter of emphasis.

It is in this vein that Wolff (2006) acknowledges the validity of certain criticisms of utilitarian reasoning. For example, utilitarian reasoning implies that one person might need to suffer in order to allow for another individual's gain. However, this point can be, and often is, exaggerated. While it is true that the consequential aspect of utilitarianism supports in the abstract the statement that *the ends justify the means*, in practice utilitarian thinkers do not support absolutely any means irrespective of how insignificant the gains are. The *ends* might well be given greater priority in utilitarian reasoning but not to the complete exclusion of considering the appropriateness of the means used to achieve these ends. It is an abstract caricature of utilitarianism to highlight the logical inconsistencies within this form of consequential reasoning without recognising how utilitarian reasoning is applied as a guide to public policy decision making.

Moral aspirations as opposed to morally binding obligations

At this point I turn to the work of Richard Brandt, who presents an alternative but equally comprehensive moral treatise to that provided by John Rawls. In a foreword to the 1998 edition of Brandt's (1979) *A Theory of the Good and the Right*, Peter Singer compares Brandt's efforts favourably against Rawls' (1971) great work. Singer (1998), a contemporary utilitarian, is particularly impressed by what he sees as the unique approach adopted by Brandt in engaging with long-standing moral questions.

First, Singer (1998, p.v) emphasises that Brandt does not take for granted the assumption that when we ask 'What ought I do?' we mean 'What ought I, morally, to do?' in a way that necessarily prioritises 'morality over all other practical considerations' (see also Singer, 1979, chapter 10). This is important for understanding ethical policing because it entails more than simply understanding what the right thing to do is, and then applying it to policing contexts. Moral values and principles are important but they need to be balanced appropriately against other considerations. When a police officer considers what should be done in a particular context, he or she needs to factor in many different variables. There will always be enduring moral considerations featuring prominently in their thought processes, but at times there might be matters of consequence that are of such significance that they impose themselves on the officer's reasoning. Importantly, the officer needs to be open to different considerations in ways that are simply not permissible from a strict deontological approach.

Secondly, Singer (1998) suggests that Brandt does not assume that the answer to 'What ought I do?' is necessarily the same as the answer to the different question of 'What system of morality should I support for adoption by my society?' (Singer, 1998, pp.v–vi). From the perspective of understanding ethical policing, this emphasises that it is not the role of the police officer to serve an ethical theory, but rather that moral arguments serve the police officer. Ethical policing needs to be purposeful and the purpose should be to serve the interests of society in line with the responsibilities a police officer has as a public official. It is not the purpose of ethical policing to promote a particular system of morality.

Brandt's work is further presented by Singer (1998) as an attempt to establish a rational understanding of morality, in a way that does not reject completely self-interest and desires as motivating factors for good and right actions. Singer (1998, p.vii) argues that Brandt 'does not follow Kant in holding that reason provides us with categorical imperatives, that is, imperatives that are binding on us irrespective of our desires'. Moral values are important components of ethical policing and it is right that they shape, constrain and empower the activities of police officers and the aims of police institutions. However, this becomes problematic if and when it creates morally binding obligations that prevent an open, thoughtful and critical mind from considering all aspects of a policing issue. Brandt (1979, p.197) makes a clear distinction here between 'the merely desirable for conduct, and the morally obligatory'. He says further '[i]t is one thing to know what rational persons would want everyone to do, or no one to do. It is another thing to know what rational persons would want everyone to be *required to do*, by conscience' (emphasis in original).

It is the binding nature of moral obligations and the peremptory quality of deontological reasoning that Brandt (1979) questions. I agree with Brandt (1979) that moral obligation is achieved at a cost, one which we normally ignore and fail to take account of. He says '[w]e may prefer that people should not do certain things but it is another question whether we want them … to be forbidden by conscience to do these things' (Brandt, 1979, p.198).

Imbuing moral obligations into our conscience in this way prevents us asking a whole range of questions that may be pertinent and of relevance in solving this or that policing problem. Ethical policing is not about compliance with specific moral obligations that bind us to a particular course of action. As Brandt (1979, p.198) says, 'consciences' can 'prevent people from doing … what rational people think they should be doing'. And he continues by arguing that in preventing people from acting in a 'morally wrong' way, we need to take account of 'the costs of having motivated them to in this way on account of conscience' (1979, p.199). Being bound by our conscience means that the ethical reasoning and decision making has already taken place before the police officer encounters a policing problem. The officer is thus not expected to think about the situation they encounter on arrival at the scene, beyond selecting the correct response from an arsenal of pre-loaded, morally binding solutions.

Brandt (1979) offers a different approach by seeing moral arguments in aspirational, rather than obligatory, terms. They should have considerable influence and need to be at the forefront of the officer's mind when making decisions, but not at the exclusion of all other considerations. Ethical policing requires officers to give due weight to moral considerations and even obliges them to be able to give reassurances that this has occurred. However, I use 'oblige' here in a more common spoken sense rather than in a strict deontological, morally binding sense. Moreover, I mean that they are obliged simply to demonstrate that they have taken into account appropriate moral considerations and to justify why they have not been acted upon, if and when this happens to be the case. Policing ceases to be ethical if treating moral arguments as aspirations is taken too lightly and simply used as an opportunity to act amorally. However, I suggest that policing also ceases to be ethical if police officers are incapable of considering a whole host of different factors, moral and non-moral, when formulating appropriate and proportionate responses.

One way of providing policing with a strong moral basis, while still retaining opportunities for consequential reasoning and due consideration of non-moral factors, is through particular aspects of human rights reasoning. Human rights can be both helpful and unhelpful in this respect, though. They are unhelpful, I suggest, when they are imposed as morally binding obligations that need to be imbued within the conscience of a police officer; however, they are helpful to the extent that they require police officers to question what is appropriate within a given situation, to ensure that a response is necessary and proportionate and to instil expectations that officers can justify their actions. Officers need to be accountable and morally responsible for their decisions and actions.[3] Importantly, these critical components of human rights reasoning offer police officers tools to replace John Stuart Mill's increasingly problematic *harm to others* approach.

Conclusion

This chapter has shifted the focus away from principles and the *deontological* approach to ethics by outlining the consequentialism of *utilitarian* approaches to ethical reasoning. The chapter argues that while human rights dominate the policy world of policing, utilitarian reasoning has greater purchase in the operational contexts of police practice. The attractiveness of utilitarian reasoning within policing is that good is derived from the results of actions, not by simply performing the actions in and of themselves. Utilitarianism is a form of consequentialism; ethical reasoning that emphasises the consequences of doing, or not doing, a particular action. Consequences clearly matter within policing, hence the durability of utilitarian reasoning within policing. However, utilitarianism has been rightly criticised because of its lack of moral content and the extent to which it arguably allows for the justification of immoral acts. The qualified defence of utilitarian reasoning provided in this chapter emphasises the adoption of an aspirational approach to rights, as opposed to seeing them as morally binding obligations in the way conceived by Kant. A distinction is also made here between individual and public morality. Consequentialism is a deeply embedded and necessary feature of public morality and this can be seen within ethical debates regarding means and ends, through the general literature on *dirty hands* in public office and the police-specific focus on *Dirty Harry*. In the next chapter, I consider how this kind of reasoning can be embedded within police practice.

Notes

[1]   I am indebted to Jean-Paul Brodeur for this reference following a comment he made at a CEPOL conference in Germany, September 2007.

[2]   The full title of UNCAT is the United Nations Convention against Torture and Other Cruel, Inhuman or Degrading Treatment or Punishment.

[3]   I have deliberately avoided using the mnemonic JAPAN here. Partly because I struggle to say mnemonic but more substantively because I want to avoid an over-simplification. I sometimes hear officers go through the mnemonic JAPAN letter by letter as if it is a checklist. The problem with this is that first it implies a chronological order that seems inappropriate, and secondly it implies that only these five concepts need to be considered. Responsibility is missing for me and I am sure there are other such words that capture what is required. It is difficult not to assume that the selection and ordering of terms is determined more by fitting the mnemonic than by finding the most appropriate expressions of what is required.

Suggested further reading

Bayley, D.H. (2002) 'Law Enforcement and the Rule of Law: Is There a Tradeoff?', *Criminology and Public Policy*, 2(1): 133–54

Kleinig, J. (2002) 'Rethinking Noble Cause Corruption', *International Journal of Police Science and Management*, 4(4): 287–314

Kleinig, J. (2019) *Ends and Means in Policing*. London: Taylor and Francis

Singer, P. (1979) *Practical Ethics*. Cambridge: Cambridge University Press. Chapters 9 and 10

Wolff, J. (2006) 'Making the World Safe for Utilitarianism', in Anthony O'Hear (ed) *Political Philosophy*. Cambridge: Cambridge University Press

6

Embedding ethics within
police practice

Introduction

In earlier chapters I have argued that principles play an important role in shaping ethical policing by providing enduring values that need to be given due weight when considering an appropriate course of action. However, I have also argued that principles can become unhelpful to police officers if and when they become morally binding obligations. Likewise, I have stressed the importance of consequences in ethical policing, but at the same time cautioned against too great a focus on the ends without due consideration of how appropriate and proportionate the means are. I continue with these lines of argument in this chapter by considering insights from an Aristotelian-inspired virtue ethics, and the contemporary influence this has upon ethical reasoning (Crisp and Slote, 1997). In particular, I will draw upon Anscombe's (1958) criticisms of what she sees as the shared legalistic morality of both deontology and utilitarianism. The renewed interest in virtue ethics is presented by Anscombe (1958) as a remedy to what she sees as diminished ethical thinking as a consequence of this legalistic characteristic of modern moral debate.

I use virtue ethics to re-emphasise a bottom-up approach (Marks and Sklansky, 2008) to understanding ethical policing. I argue that the focus on virtues fosters and supports ethical policing because of the extent to which it embodies ethical reasoning in moral agents, who are placed within professional contexts. Within professional contexts, virtue ethics are not to be established at the top of the organisation and cascaded down through the workforce, but are rather embedded within the ethical reasoning practised by officers across different policing contexts.

There are different challenges to putting ethical police into practice, however; one I wish to highlight is the need for senior officers, often under contrary external pressures, to trust front-line officers. Leaders and managers are by their very nature prone to take control of matters and impose their authority on situations. Policing is no exception. If policing needs to be ethical, police leaders will make sure that ethical it is, but this admirable quality is ultimately misplaced here. We need to take seriously the idea that *all* police officers are leaders, but this will only be realised in meaningful ways if *all* police officers are given the moral space to make decisions for themselves. If they are constantly told what to do, when and how to do it, then they will not develop the moral capacity required for ethical policing.

All of this implies the need for police discretion. This is central to the argument presented in the book. However, rather than revisiting police discretion directly, I use instead Aristotle's notion of practical wisdom (*phronēsis*) to express police discretion through the idea of reflective practice and ethical policing more generally. I consider the importance of reflective practice in terms of both the capacity of individual officers to make informed, ethical decisions and also the capacity of police organisations to embed, support, maintain and allow reflective practice to flourish. This also entails finding ways of garnering societal trust in policing, especially given the extent to which police officers are increasingly managed, scrutinised and evaluated (Chan, 2003). Likewise, the extent to which the law has become a more intrusive part of everyday matters is challenging. As Bingham (2011) argues, legal reasoning is at odds with discretion. In particular, he suggests that Dicey's notion of the rule of law was explicitly opposed to conferring 'discretionary decision-making powers on officials' (2011, p.48). Virtue ethics and reflective practice allow for a different approach to police discretion.

An officer's responsibilities within ethical policing

Ethical policing, as I present it, places greater emphasis on a police officer's capacity to make informed and appropriate decisions. It creates a greater expectation that police officers, as moral agents, should be required to make judgements as opposed to simply following a set of rules or laws, or imbibing morally binding obligations, or even worse, doing what they are told to do without question or consideration of what it is they are being asked to do. However, this is true only to the extent that ethical policing is premised upon an officer's ethical reasoning and his or her capacity to make informed decisions and judgements. As I have argued, this is not necessarily achieved through a code of ethics, which can easily and readily become little more than a compliance mechanism. If a police officer's decision to act or not act is predetermined by others, then the police role becomes subservient such that ethical considerations become redundant. Ethical policing is only given shape through dealing with the inherent ambiguities of human societies and it only becomes meaningful to the extent that police officers are required to make professional judgements.

This does not mean that following orders negates ethical policing. Police officers are expected to follow orders routinely and this is a central requirement of the role. However, at the same time, it is also enshrined within the idea of police that an officer needs to decide whether to follow an order or not, effectively to decide whether it is a *lawful* order, such that he or she can justify and take responsibility for the decision taken. This means that a police officer makes a professional judgement when deciding to follow a lawful order. This is established in England and Wales within the notion of the *office of constable*, which applies to all police officers 'irrespective of rank' and establishes that each officer is 'an independent legal official' with 'personal liability for their actions' (Police Federation, 2008, p.6). Justifications should not be based on the officer's own personal value system. When a police officer justifies his or her actions, it has to be done within the context of his or her role as a police officer and all that such a position of public office entails. Here Cohen's (1996) linking of discretion to objectivity is also important to note.

All of this implies that ethical policing requires high levels of trust. There needs to be trust established between police services and the communities they serve (Jackson et al, 2013), but also between chief officers and the various political officials with responsibilities towards police governance. This includes PCCs and the Home Secretary, but also organisations such as the Independent Office for Police Conduct (IOPC). Trust is a recurring theme when it comes to dealing with police complaints and, as I have argued elsewhere (Wood, 2012), there is a continuous call for ever greater levels of independence on the part of those investigating complaints against the police. Kempa (2007, p.113) likewise notes the recurring demands for 'an independent civilian component' to be at the heart of the police complaints system. Sklansky (2008) argues that attention also needs to be paid to how police officers are regarded within police organisations to generate more trust between police leaders and front-line officers. Trust is important within and across all of these contexts but is perhaps of greatest significance when considering the trust afforded front-line officers. The question is, do we trust the police enough to allow ethical policing?

Consider here the *ring of Gyges test*. The mythical ring of Gyges is drawn upon by Plato to discuss why individuals act judicially. In book 1 of *The Republic*, written some 2,500 years ago, Plato presents us with a discussion between Socrates and Thrasymachus concerning what it means to be just. The differences presented in the discussion between the two protagonists are illustrated later in book 2 by Glaucon, who recalls the story of the ring of Gyges (Plato, 1955, p.90; 2.359d).

The ring of Gyges allows its wearer to become invisible, which leads Glaucon to ask whether a just person would behave any differently from an unjust person given the opportunity of immunity from detection provided by the ring. Consider what would happen if we were to give police officers the ring of Gyges. It begs the question:

Do police perform duties in a just and fair manner because of an internalised sense of being a professional officer, or because of external constraints, provided by supervisors enforcing force policies, Home Office directives, legislation and other external bodies?

Let us assume that officers fall into one of three categories:

- Category A comprises officers who would continue to perform duties completely unaffected by the powers offered by the ring. This might be because they have internalised appropriate values, such as human rights principles, and have thereby imbibed morally binding obligations of the kind I have discussed in earlier chapters. It might also be because they have understood the long-term consequential merit in observing the rule of law in the short term along the lines discussed by Bayley (2002).
- Category B includes officers who would take advantage of the immunity offered by the ring of Gyges, but in relatively benign ways. The temptation, for example, to avoid certain processes and procedures in order to gather evidence that could lead to the conviction of a serious criminal would be understandable. These officers could be characterised as rule benders of the kind considered by Kleinig (2002), who are driven by a strong sense of justice, but frustrated by what they see as unnecessary and unhelpful procedural hurdles. If they are exhibiting ethical reasoning, it is a form of consequentialism, one that has given disproportionate emphasis to the ends over the means.
- Category C is reserved for those officers who would act corruptly by taking full advantage of the anonymity created by the ring of Gyges, committing serious crimes in the process, in order to benefit their own pocket and/or career progression. Such officers lack moral character and by implication it is difficult to see on what grounds their employment within the police could be justified.

The introduction of body-worn cameras brings a new dimension to the ring of Gyges test by adding a new layer of visibility to policing. Indeed this is itself on top of other technologies that make police work more candid than it has ever been, for example through CCTV, mobile devices, social media and so on (Goldsmith, 2010). Body-worn cameras no doubt have an impact on how police officers perform duties and research suggests that this impact is positive (Ariel et al, 2017; Braga et al, 2017).

There is an important point about supervision here. I suggest that it is preferable to have police officers who require minimal supervision. The more we rely on external constraints to modify and direct behaviour, the more we are reliant upon, and committed to, increasing levels of supervision. This is expensive and notwithstanding technical solutions also impractical (Reiner, 2010). Unnecessarily high levels of supervision diminish the extent to which officers internalise responsibility. Likewise, micro-management reinforces a climate of suspicion in which officers become good at giving accounts without necessarily being accountable (Ericson, 1995). A climate of mistrust creates a sense of us and them, in which officers become protective of one another and through a misplaced police loyalty (Kleinig, 2004) are more likely to help colleagues evade detection (Westmarland, 2005).

Aristotle's virtue ethics

So far in the book I have focused on the two major schools of ethical theory, the consequential reasoning of utilitarianism and the deontology of Kant and Rawls. However, as Crisp and Slote (1997) note, there emerged in the second half of the 20th century a renewed interest in virtue ethics as an alternative to both consequentialism and deontology.

Virtue ethics is most commonly associated with the Ancient Greek philosopher Aristotle (384–22 BC) and is derived from his use of the Greek term for virtue, aretē. Virtue-centred ethics is thus sometimes referred to as aretaic. Foot (1978) also considers the development of virtue ethics through the work of St Thomas Aquinas (1225–74) to be important. Although she sees Aquinas as largely following Aristotle, she nonetheless argues that Aquinas offers new insights and provides greater detail than Aristotle on some aspects of virtue ethics.

Aristotle's most familiar ethical arguments are presented in the Nicomachean Ethics.[1] I will outline key aspects of Aristotle's ethical reasoning to provide a flavour of virtue ethics before considering virtue ethics as it re-emerged as a significant influence on ethical thought towards the end of the 20th century and, in particular, as a challenge to deontology and consequentialism.

A key methodological aspect of Aristotle's ethics, and perhaps the best-known feature of his approach, is found within his 'famous doctrine of the golden mean' (Russell, 1985, p.185). Aristotle establishes the virtues as a balanced and appropriate behaviour between two vices, which are portrayed respectively as excessive or deficient variations. For example, courage is one of the virtues identified by Aristotle and it is seen as the golden mean falling between the excessive vice of rashness and the deficient vice of cowardice. The virtues are thus presented as human qualities that are balanced appropriately. Courage is a virtue and where this quality is lacking in a person, we say that person exhibits cowardice. On the other hand, if the courage is not bounded and balanced appropriately, it can become excessive, leading to rashness. Aristotle conceives of the virtues in this way and links them to the idea of human flourishing.

Hursthouse (1991) notes that virtue ethics is criticised on a number of fronts regarding a supposed lack of precision. Human flourishing, for example, is taken to be a rather vague concept. Likewise, it is not clear why certain traits are held to be virtues, while others are not, and it is suggested that there are inherent conflicts between the different virtues when applied in practice. Russell (1985) also questions whether it is appropriate to present all of the virtues as a mean in the way suggested by Aristotle. For example, he questions how meaningful it is to present truthfulness in this way. The implication in Russell's (1985) concern is that truthfulness is not as readily captured as a quality on a spectrum in the way that courage is.

Hursthouse (1991) does not deny any of these challenges but she argues that they are not unique to virtue ethics. Indeed, she argues that they are common in deontology and consequentialism alike. Echoing John Stuart Mill's comments on the impossibility of constructing a system of ethical reasoning that does not produce contradictions, Hursthouse (1991) simply counters by arguing that any conflicts, contradictions or vagaries in virtue ethics are of less significance than the equivalents are within deontology and consequentialism. Moreover, she stresses that within virtue ethics there is an explicit focus on the need for wisdom in the selection, application and balancing of the different virtues, much more so than is the case in the other major ethical theories. Fitzpatrick (2008, p.66) suggests in a similar vein that it is one thing to list Aristotle's virtues, but this does not tell us 'what they *mean* in any given context'. Hursthouse (1991) does not deny that there are difficult philosophical questions raised against virtue ethics, but she sees these as questions that apply to all ethical approaches and, moreover, that the approach taken in virtue approaches addresses these questions better than any other known approach.

Hursthouse's (1991) point is illustrated if we consider a response to Russell's (1985) view that truthfulness does not quite fit Aristotle's approach regarding other virtues. It seems to me that Russell's (1985) concern here is that truthfulness is more appropriately seen to be either present or absent. From this perspective, it does not make sense to think of lying as a deficiency in relation to truthfulness, in the way that cowardice is understood as a deficiency in relation to courage. Likewise, from Russell's (1985) implied reasoning, it is hard to comprehend what is meant by excessive truthfulness. However, understanding truthfulness as a mean in the way envisaged by Aristotle makes much more sense if we think about it in terms of how being truthful is put into practice. Hursthouse (1991) emphasises the importance of wisdom as a virtue not only in and of itself, but also in relation to the other virtues. The point she makes is that within virtue ethics, all conflicts and contradictions are resolved, not through introspective reasoning, but rather through experienced practice. As Williams (1972, p.56) puts it, the virtues represent 'dispositions to right action'. In other words, such conflicts are not rational problems that can be solved abstractly by theoreticians. They are rather practical challenges that stimulate the intuitive insights of practitioners developed over time through the experience of practice. Hursthouse (1991, p.224) notes that we have 'youthful mathematical geniuses, but rarely, if ever, youthful moral geniuses'. She argues this is recognised within virtue ethics and incorporated into its approach from the outset like no other ethical theory. There is from this perspective an art to being truthful. An honest person is someone who genuinely tries to capture the truthfulness of a situation. A deficient vice is committed if and when a person deliberately holds back information that distorts the truthfulness of an account. This is because they are less than honest. An excessive vice is committed by the person who relays all factual information without any reflection on what is appropriate and pertinent to a discussion. The overly zealous desire to contribute all kinds of truths to a situation can likewise distort the true picture and present false impressions. Truthfulness as a virtue is thus a mean between these vices in that it provides an honest disclosure of everything that is of relevance, but nothing more.

Another feature of Aristotle's ethical reasoning worthy of note here is its teleological character. Teleological reasoning establishes the purpose of a thing and derives notions of justice from an understanding of that purpose (see Miller, 2004a). *Tèlos* is the Greek word for purpose. Sandel (2010) illustrates this aspect of Aristotle's ethical reasoning with an example involving the just distribution of flutes. The question he poses is: *Who should the best flute go to?* In answering the question Sandel (2010) emphasises that for Aristotle there is a focus on just deserts; the idea that the right person should receive the best flute on merit, and that they should be deserving of this privilege. But how do we establish who this should be?

In a society such as ours it is most likely to be the person with the most money who gets the best flute. This is justified by some on the basis that the person with the most money is deserving of such a privileged status because it has been earned through hard work and/or the application of a superior intellect and/or some other superior quality that they have above others. It will of course be argued by some that wealth comes from good fortune, misappropriation and unequal opportunities, which are all morally indefensible. Therefore the rich and the wealthy are not deserving of the best flute, indeed distributing the best flute to the least privileged person could be seen as a way of redressing social and economic inequalities. Those that have enjoyed the fewest privileges are deemed more deserving from this perspective.

The point here is not to engage with the politics or economics of the question but rather to show that in both cases the just thing to do is determined by values that are incidental to flutes. The factors used to establish who deserves the best flute have nothing to do with the relative flute-playing abilities of this rich person or that poor person. Sandel (2010) shows that for Aristotle the person most deserving of the best flute is simply the person who is the best flute player. A utilitarian might also draw the same conclusion as Aristotle on this point, but as Sandel (2010) shows, it would be for different reasons. For the utilitarian, giving the best flute to the best flute player will produce the best music and this will create the greatest good for the greatest number. However, for Aristotle the reasons should relate to the purpose of flutes and this is what determines the just course of action; 'the best flutes should go to the best flute players because that's what flutes are *for* – to be played well'(Sandel, 2010, p.188, emphasis in original).

The importance of stressing this aspect of Aristotle's thinking becomes clearer when we consider what he sees as the purpose of politics: 'For Aristotle, the purpose of politics is not to set up a framework of rights that is neutral among ends. It is to form good citizens and to cultivate good character' (Sandel, 2010, p.193). Aristotle's understanding of the purpose of politics is thus different from that of both Kant and the utilitarian in two important ways: first, it establishes civic virtues above individual freedom as the primary purpose of politics; secondly, it does so not on consequentialist grounds, nor on the basis of a reasoned morality, but rather because this is the purpose of a human society and this is what human flourishing requires in order to meet its goal. As Sandel (2010) argues, from this Aristotelian perspective, the question of distributive justice is not related to resources, but rather primarily focused on positions of public office: 'Who should have the right to rule?' (Sandel, 2010, p.192).

The idea of ethical policing I am presenting is, in my view, deepened by this teleological perspective. Implicit within what I call ethical policing is a policing purpose, and while this is not easy to define in simple terms, it is shaped by the sensibilities of Aristotle and the view that 'the end of politics is the good life' (Sandel, 2010, p.195). I see the purpose of policing to be supporting the realisation of the good life by playing an integral role in the formation of 'good habits ... good character ... civic virtue' (Sandel, 2010, p.199). A key dimension of ethical policing is having such purpose.

The re-emergence of virtue ethics in the 20th century

Interest in Aristotle's approach to ethics waned significantly during the rise of liberal individualism and against the backdrop of the Enlightenment with its focus on rationality. However, a renewed interest in virtue ethics was initiated by an influential paper published by Mary Anscombe in 1958 (Crisp and Slote, 1997). Anscombe (1958) produced a scathing attack on both consequentialism and deontology, which she argued had in different ways corrupted ethical thinking. She sees consequentialism as a necessarily 'shallow philosophy' (Anscombe, 1958, p.37) to the extent that it applies a rather simplistic rational modelling of cost benefit analysis to complex questions of human behaviour and the characteristics of a just society. However, deontology is also challenged for moralising ethical considerations through abstract rational thought. She argues that in order to re-engage with ethics, we must first return to the virtue ethics of Aristotle before we can move forward and advance ethical thought.

Anscombe (1958) was particularly critical of the extent to which moral discussions had taken on a legalistic tone. She suggested that modern moral theorists had been influenced by a 'law conception of ethics' (Anscombe, 1958, p.30), which she argues came from the influence of Christianity from that time. As MacIntyre (1985, p.266) argues, Kantian deontology is in many respects a 'secularized version of Protestantism'. Although much of modern moral thought had been developed independent of any religious legislator, Anscombe (1958, p.38) nonetheless notes a significant connection between the two and argues the secular presentation of morality simply means that we are left with a 'divine-law conception of ethics' that has at the same time rejected 'the notion of a divine legislator'. Anscombe (1958) notes that this lack of an appropriate legislator is recognised as problematic within consequentialism and deontology, such that its advocates search for alternative surrogates to perform this function. However, she is more concerned to show that framing ethics in this legalistic way is the primary problem.

In many respects Anscombe (1958) is calling into question many of the ideas that had dominated ethical debate over the previous two centuries. She is dismissive of utilitarianism on the grounds that it has no way of avoiding potentially inhumane consequences, if and when these consequences achieve the greatest good for the greatest number. Here virtue ethics shares with deontology a concern that consequentialism more broadly lacks a sufficiently robust moral component. However, she focuses her critical attention more explicitly on the way morality comes to dominate ethical reasoning following the influence of Kant. Using the logic of virtue ethics, we might see consequentialism as an ethical theory that is lacking moral direction, while deontology is seen as an excessively moral ethical theory. Virtue ethics provides the golden mean from this perspective. An example of virtue ethics understood in this way is provided within Aristotle's concept of *phronēsis*. As Grint (2007) notes, the Aristotelian notion of *phronēsis* (practical wisdom) integrates the notions of *technē* (competence and skills) and *episteme* (specialist knowledge and understanding). It is meaningless from an Aristotelian perspective for someone to be seen as virtuous but incompetent. As Foot (1978) notes, good intentions rather than knowledge and competence demonstrate virtue, but ignorance and incompetence, whether intended or not, negate virtue. She says, while 'it is primarily by his intentions that a man's moral dispositions are judged', the negative corollary of this is that 'failures in performance rather than intention may show a lack of virtue' (Foot, 1978, p.165).

Williams (1985) shares with Anscombe (1958) a concern with what he sees as the undue and unhelpful influence of morality on ethical thinking. He sees morality as 'a particular variety of ethical thought', one which 'we would be better off without' (Williams, 1985, p.45). He illustrates his argument with reference to the way Kantian deontology transforms the way we think about obligation.

He contrasts its everyday use against the way it is transformed as moral obligation in deontology: 'There is an everyday notion of obligation, as one consideration among others, and it is ethically useful. Morality is distinguished by the special notion of obligation it uses, and by the significance it gives to it' (1985, p.45).

Williams (1985) acknowledges that this kind of moral reasoning has addressed social injustices and produced justice in the world. A moral obligation is, as I have suggested in previous chapters, a powerful ethical concept. Applied in the right place, at the right time, this can have a significant and positive impact against immoral acts. However, Williams (1985) remains concerned that there is a cost to the influence morality has over ethical reasoning, arising from an unduly elevated and misplaced emphasis on moral obligation within politics. He sees it as a philosophical error within what he calls the morality component of ethical thinking to assume that 'without its ultimately pure justice, there is no justice at all', and he sees such thinking as 'the most abstract expressions of a deeply rooted and still powerful misconception of life' (Williams, 1985, p.65).

The idea of a moral obligation is problematic for Anscombe (1958) too, and I suggest her arguments have resonance when considering ethical policing. Like Williams (1985), Anscombe (1958, p.34) also thinks that 'you can do ethics without' morality. She argues that adding the term 'moral' to other useful ethical terms offers little in the way of substance, it merely adds a psychological, 'compelling force' (1958, p.43). In this respect she argues that saying something is morally wrong goes further than saying something is unjust, but without actually adding any content to the argument. Similarly, Anscombe (1958, p.30) sees an 'indispensable' need for the 'ordinary' use of concepts such as '"should", "needs", "ought", "must"' within ethical thinking but questions the legalistic thinking of modern moral thinkers when these notions are treated in a 'special sense' to produce legally interpreted associations with terms such as, '"is obliged", or "is bound", or "is required to"'. Anscombe (1958) argues that it is much better to describe actions in more precise ways and without the added psychological force derived from the legalistic implications of deontology: 'It would be a great improvement if, instead of "morally wrong", one always named a genus such as "untruthful", "unchaste", "unjust"' (Anscombe, 1958, p.34).

For Anscombe (1958), the use of a term such as 'morally wrong' is an example of how Kant's morality has influenced ethical debate today by creating generalised abstractions, which she believes diminishes our approach to ethics. This concern is illustrated in a different context by MacIntyre (1966) when he contrasts the Ancient Greek use of the term 'duty' and the way it has come to be understood following Kant. For Aristotle, MacIntyre (1966) argues, a person's duty is intricately entwined with his or her duties, as farmer, architect or soldier. Here, the 'morality of role fulfilment' (MacIntyre, 1966, p.94) is a dominant feature of Aristotle's understanding of virtue, but from Kant onwards he suggests that this link is broken: 'It is when we detach a man from his roles, but still leave him with the concept of "duty," that the concept is necessarily transformed' (1966, p.93).

In place of virtue understood in terms of the specific contexts of what someone does, today we have morality framed in general terms. We no longer ask 'what it is to do one's duty as', in our case as a police officer, but rather as a person (MacIntyre, 1966, p.94).

MacIntyre (1966) notes that we still speak about the duties of a police officer in a way that echoes an Aristotelian understanding, but in the main we tend to speak more in terms of the duty a person has simply to be a good human being. Even within policing today, we are more likely to think of duty in terms of the general, abstracted duty of care that an officer has as a core aspect of all policing activities. Or duty is conceived in legalist terms in relation to upholding laws and/or human rights obligations. The important point for MacIntyre (1966) is that 'the link between duty and duties' (p.94) is broken, such that 'the pursuit of duty becomes a realm of its own' (p.86). Duty, like obligation, takes on a moral life of its own with a compelling power that is ultimately incomprehensible outside the social contexts in which a Kantian-inspired deontology dominates our ethical thinking.

The more we focus on duties, as opposed to the abstract notion of duty, the more nuanced we become in contemplating ethical policing. The different contexts within which various aspects of police work operate, as Miller et al (2006) suggest, are such that it becomes more appropriate to think about the different ethical qualities that we should emphasise according to each specific police role. This emphasis on role morality in policing stresses that ethical policing looks different within a neighbourhood policing context than it does within a criminal investigative team, just as covert police activities present very different ethical challenges to those experienced by a school liaison officer or a response officer policing a busy town centre on a Friday evening.

Context, particularism and the linking of ethics to a practice

The issue of context is important to note as an enduring challenge to the universal claims of modern ethical theory. MacIntyre (1985) argues that morality is always linked historically and culturally to specific times and places such that we have the morality of this society or of this culture but not morality in the abstract, unconnected to a specific time and place: 'Morality which is no particular society's morality is to be found nowhere' (MacIntyre, 1985, pp.265–6). This clearly supports objections raised against the universalism of Kant's deontology and the view 'that the nature of human reason is such that there are principles and concepts necessarily assented to by any rational being' 1985, p.266).

Dancy (2004) offers the perspective of particularism as a counter view to the prevailing dominance of universalism in Western ethical thought. He reserves special attention to the role principles play within universal ethical theories. Dancy's (2004) main line of argument is that morality does not require principles in order to function and therefore adding principles into the mix is only likely to complicate matters and make them worse: 'morality can get along perfectly well without principles … the imposition of principles on an area that doesn't need them is likely to lead to some sort of distortion' (Dancy, 2004, p.2). He also notes the particularist view that ethical judgements are most challenging in the nuances and specifics of different instances, and the extensive variability of each instance reduces universal principles to limited use: 'Principles deal in sameness, and there just aren't enough samenesses to go round' (2004, p.2).

Within policing contexts, Dancy's (2004) approach suggests that police officers could never be given sufficient guidance on how to act in all situations because there are simply too many possibilities to cover. Dancy (2004) sees universal ethical statements as being the result of things we know from past experience and as such pertain to instances that require little ethical attention. Universal values express the ethical norms that are widely accepted and understood. An officer is more likely to need help in unfamiliar situations and in circumstances that do not quite equate to the descriptions found within the universal statements. It is here that Dancy (2004) argues that ethics does not require principles, indeed principles can get in the way of ethical reasoning.

The emphasis on context helps to situate ethical reasoning. Indeed, as Crisp and Slote (1997, p.3) note, a key component of virtue ethics is that it focuses on 'moral agents and their lives, rather than on discrete actions'. This understanding of ethics has also influenced knowledge more generally. As Kotzee (2013) observes, the development of virtue epistemology places greater emphasis on the role the knower plays in establishing knowledge: it asks 'not so much what knowledge is', but rather 'what it is to be a good knower' (Kotzee, 2013, p.157). Indeed, Pritchard (2013) argues that from this perspective, we cannot speak of knowledge in the abstract because it is always only given meaning in specific contexts through cognitive agents. This 'cognitive agency' becomes the critical factor for Pritchard (2013, p.237), and for MacAllister (2012) it is this that draws out a significant normative dimension to epistemological questions. The link between knowing and ethics is developed through virtue epistemology, such that police knowledge becomes unintelligible without placing 'intellectual qualities and habits' centre stage (MacAllister, 2012, p.253). It is the use of the word *habits* here that more than anything else articulates the Aristotelian sense of virtue ethics. Ethical policing requires 'a sizeable majority of knowing police officers' (Wood et al, 2018), but implicit within the definition of a knowing police officer is the idea of a cognitive agent who is at the same time a moral agent. Virtue epistemology adds this Aristotelian teleological sense of purpose to cognitive activities in a way that embeds ethics within what we understand to be a knowing police officer. This is illustrated by Pritchard (2013, p.236) through the use of a 'continuum of cognitive agency', in which the purpose of epistemology is articulated through different stages, but where 'understanding', not 'knowledge', is presented as the ultimate aim. Wringe (2015, p.32) considers the educative lessons from this perspective, favouring 'transformative' learning over 'an additive conception of education'. Police learning, of the kind required for ethical policing, needs to foster such a transformative quality by ensuring that the moral purpose of policing is embedded within notions of police knowledge.

Virtue ethics thus situates ethical reasoning in the moral lives of real people rather than in the abstract philosophical ruminations of an ethical theorist. Understood in this way, ethics become embodied within moral agents, what Slote (1995) refers to as agent-based virtue ethics. This comprises anyone who thinks seriously about substantive life choices, and in the context of this book, it includes all police officers who take seriously the moral responsibility that their role as a public official entails. We thereby diminish the potential for ethics to be seen as abstract and unconnected from real life circumstances.

MacIntyre (1985) illustrates how ethical reasoning comes to be embodied in this way with an example of an initially reluctant seven-year-old chess player. MacIntyre (1985) shows that at first the child is motivated to play chess well through incentives that are external to the game of chess. The child is rewarded with candy when he or she performs well. These incentives work to motivate the child and over time the child begins to excel at chess. At this point the child takes great satisfaction from their achievements *as a chess player.*

MacIntyre (1985) uses this illustrative thought experiment to show how ethics is rooted within the specifics of what he defines as a practice, a definition which includes chess but would also include policing. First, to the extent that the child is initially motivated exclusively by incentives that are external to the game of chess, he or she has no compulsion not to cheat. Indeed, if he or she could guarantee getting away with cheating, then it would make sense to do so. This is because the child could achieve the objective of more candy more easily this way and is in no way committed to behaving otherwise. However, as the child becomes ever more competent at playing chess, his or her motivation becomes more than simply attaining candy. They are now inclined to take pleasure from playing chess well and the motivations here are internal to the game of chess itself. Now if the child wins by cheating, it will not satisfy his or her new objective, which can only be reached by winning within the rules of the game: 'if the child cheats, he or she will be defeating not me, but himself or herself' (MacIntyre, 1985, p.188).

If we apply this logic to policing as a practice we are presented with police officers who might have all sorts of incentives to perform their duties competently. Some of these incentives we can say are internal to the purpose of policing, to what defines policing as a practice. Other incentives will be external to policing as a practice and will be incidental to the purpose of policing. The external incentives could cover a wide range of different types of motivating factors. Some of them will be clearly counter to any meaningful articulation of a policing purpose. For example, if an officer is incentivised by financial gain beyond the parameters of a police officer's salary, or by other such personal advantages, then such an incentive can clearly be seen as not only external to the purpose of policing but also counter to it. An officer motivated in this way is a liability and a high-risk case of police corruption waiting to happen. He or she would fall under Category C in relation to the ring of Gyges test discussed earlier.

A different example could be the officer who is motivated by meeting targets set by a supervisor they want to impress. Here we have a situation that is much more akin to the seven-year-old chess player. The officer will be engaged with police practice in a positive way and, if we assume for the moment that the targets set by the supervisor articulate well the purpose of policing, in achieving the targets the officer will be doing good police work. However, because doing good police work is not the primary motivation for the officer, he or she will not be considered virtuous. As with the seven-year-old chess player, the motivation is such that it would be rational for the police officer to meet the targets however they could, irrespective of whether the means are legitimate or not, and assuming that any wrongdoing goes undetected. This officer would fall under Category B in the ring of Gyges test. In thinking how we get them from this position to Category A, MacIntyre's (1985) seven-year-old chess player illustration is insightful. Just as the chess player developed the internal motivation to play chess well *by playing chess well*, it is hoped that the police officer develops internal motivations to police well *by policing well*.

Bayley's (2002) use of consequential reasoning to get police officers to see the value of the rule of law in instrumental, consequential ways has the potential to develop into a genuine internally generated sense of satisfaction and pride in doing good police work within the parameters of the rule of law. Importantly, we can imagine a developing situation that mimics the example of the seven-year-old chess player for the officer motivated by meeting targets in a way that is not possible with the corrupt officer. The corrupt officer will not be able to achieve his or her external aims by doing policing well. Also, understanding the development of the officer motivated initially by targets tells us something important about the nature of officers within Category A of the ring of Gyges test. It should be noted that an officer who has an internal motivation to realise the purpose of policing is different from the officer whose actions are bound at the level of his or her conscience by morally binding obligations. There is an important difference here between the moral agent in virtue ethics terms, who is driven by the purpose of policing and thereby rooted in the practice of policing, and the moral agent understood through deontology, who is driven by universal values established in the abstract through rational thought. The former is deemed virtuous in Aristotelian terms as a police officer, whereas the latter is a moral person in Kantian terms, who just happens to be a police officer. Importantly, the Kantian approach does not tell us whether the person is a good police officer, only that they are a good person. In the Aristotelian sense, the person and their role as a police officer are entwined.

I see MacIntyre's (1985) use of a practice to illustrate virtue ethics in this way insightful when thinking about ethical policing. On the one hand, it shows how ethical thinking can be learnt, nurtured, developed and honed through practice within appropriate professional settings and social circumstances. It also highlights the merit of virtue ethics as it relates to professional practice as opposed to universal values regarding what it means to be good in the abstract. At the same time, it suggests that there are some individuals who should never be police officers. This latter point has implications for recruitment to ensure the right people are selected in the first place, but also in terms of dealing better with officers who fall short of expectations, even after being supported within the context of a learning organisation. This point is stressed by Delattre (2011, p.6):

> No one who does not already care about being a good person and doing what is right can have a serious ethical question. A person must have achieved a disposition to do the right thing in the right way at the right time for the right reasons before any moral perplexities can arise.

Understanding virtue as it relates to the will

Another way of thinking about the link between virtue ethics and practice is through Foot's (1978, p.165) observations that 'virtue belongs to the will'. Aristotle draws a distinction between intellectual and moral virtues (Anscombe, 1958). His notion of *phronēsis*, for example, is considered to be an intellectual virtue (Foot, 1978). However, as Foot (1978) argues, there are points where wisdom can be seen to have both intellectual and moral attributes. For example, wisdom is contrasted against cleverness, on the grounds that cleverness occurs irrespective of the virtue of its outcome, whereas wisdom implies only outcomes that can be categorised as just. Cleverness can be used for illicit gain in ways that are not possible within the definition of wisdom. So while both wisdom and cleverness demonstrate intellectual qualities, it is only wisdom that is linked to moral purpose.

It is here that Foot (1978) suggests the link between virtue and a person's will: 'it is the will that is good in a man of virtue' (Foot, 1978, p.165). She says that implicit within the notion of wisdom is a will to carry out virtuous acts, and that the virtuous person demonstrates the will to be wise. But virtues only exist because there are always temptations to do other than virtuous things: 'virtues are about what is difficult for men' (1978, p.169). In this respect, Foot (1978) sees will as a corrective endeavour, by which she means it is not something that is carried out in the abstract, but rather as a corrective to an imbalance. She illustrates her thinking here with various examples; industry is a virtue because it counters the temptation to be idle; the virtue of hope overcomes the temptation towards despair, and humility is a virtue 'only because men tend to think too well of themselves' (1978, p.170).

Courage, a virtue often associated with policing, exists because fear tempts us to run when we should stand firm. However, we need to recognise that this does not mean that officers should never run. Indeed, an officer who never turned away from danger would most probably be guilty of the vice of *rashness* at least some of the time. Courage is only exhibited if the officer stands when they *should* stand. This is a matter of judgement.

This is where the idea of practical wisdom becomes important in understanding ethical policing. The police officer is not necessarily educated in ethical theory, but rather experienced in making ethical decisions and judgements. The knowledge a police officer has contributes nothing towards ethical policing if it is not accompanied by a will to be a virtuous person, understood here not in a Kantian sense but rather in the Aristotelian linking of a person in context, for example as a police officer. If a police officer is not motivated by the purpose of policing, they cannot be seen as a virtuous person. Nor can they be seen as wise, no matter how clever they are. Indeed, given the opportunities available for a police officer to be corrupt, a clever police officer who lacks the will to be virtuous is probably more likely to be a corrupt police officer.

Police discretion and the idea of reflective police practice

I have deliberately avoided referring to police discretion because it has become such a politically contested term. There are numerous published arguments demonstrating the central importance of police discretion (Kleinig, 1996; Waddington, 1999; Neyroud and Beckley, 2001; Davis, 2002; Neyroud, 2003; Reiner, 2010). While I have not drawn out specific points from these texts, the importance of police discretion is implied throughout the discussions thus far in that I have continually emphasised the need for officers to be given the moral space to make informed judgements and decisions. To be clear on this point, this requires a high degree of discretion, understood as professional judgement (Davis, 2002) and contextualised by the various components of ethical policing I have developed through the various chapters. This is what gives police discretion its objectivity (Cohen, 1996). Importantly, discretion does not mean that police officers have the freedom to do as they please. Of course no serious supporter of police discretion would suggest they should, but this is implied whenever police discretion is attacked and reduced in practice.

The parameters of police discretion understood as professional judgement and decision making should be clearly bounded by consideration of appropriate principles and values, and due weight needs to be given to human rights; likewise consequences should be considered proportionately, and above all, decisions must be readily justified in meaningful and intelligible ways. As Dworkin (1978, p.31) notes, discretion 'is a relative concept'. The components of discretion just mentioned provide the parameters that form the ring in the doughnut analogy Dworkin (1978) uses to explain discretion as a bounded capacity to make professional decisions and judgements. Rather than revisiting debates about police discretion, my preference is to approach the substance of those debates through a virtue ethics lens and the idea of reflective practice developed by Donald Schön.

Schön's (1983) seminal publication has been highly influential in many professional areas, but until fairly recently it has been largely ignored within policing (Christopher, 2015). However, this is beginning to change and more attention is being given to reflective practice in policing contexts (Christopher, 2015; Wood and Williams, 2016; Lumsden and Goode, 2017; Wood et al, 2018; Wood, 2018) and criminal justice more widely (Armstrong et al, 2016). At the heart of Schön's (1983) account of reflective practice are ideas that chime with virtue ethics and virtue epistemology. They also reinforce a necessary level of police discretion. In relation to this book, and above all else, Schön's (1983) reflective practice is integral to understanding what I mean by ethical policing.

The first point to note about reflective practice is that Schön (1983) starts from a position that is deeply concerned with the lack of moral purpose in professional education (Wood and Williams, 2016). By moral purpose I mean an appropriate level of moral direction as opposed to an excessive form of moralism. Schön (1983) is also opposed to a technocratic application model of learning, where theory and practice are completely separated conceptually and in terms of a delivery model. Instead, he draws upon a range of educational philosophies that emphasise learning through doing (Dewey, 1904, 1916; Piaget, 1997), and in particular within professional contexts (Argyris and Schön, 1974, 1978). This imbues the idea of reflective practice with the kind of teleological sense of purpose at the heart of virtue ethics. Again, using the language of virtue ethics, we can see reflective practice as an ethical corrective (Foot, 1978) to the amorality of the professional education Schön (1983) is critiquing.

Building upon the idea of reflective practice as an ethical antidote against the overly technical, scientific application model of professional learning, Schön (1983) takes the idea that we can know through doing, and from this establishes that we can also reflect in action (Wood and

Williams, 2016). The next step in Schön's (1983) thinking is to situate knowing and reflecting within the specifics of professional contexts, such that we move from *knowing-in-action* and *reflecting-in-action* to the notions of *knowing-in-practice* and *reflecting-in-practice* (Schön, 1983, pp.59–61). This is an important step because it adds a layer of context that is all important in understanding the moral space within which police officers are reflecting. It provides a platform for understanding the extent to which Schön's (1983) thinking already at this point establishes the reflective practitioner as a moral agent with the capacity to make informed, discretionary decisions. To emphasise the point here, the reflective practitioner necessitates police discretion because without it there is simply not the required level of moral space for an officer to be reflective in a meaningful way.

The move from knowing and reflecting in action to knowing and reflecting in practice captures the first level of Schön's (1983) idea of reflective practice. The second level comes from the environment of the practice in which reflective practitioners are operating. MacIntyre's (1985) use of a practice to illustrate virtue ethics is insightful here. MacIntyre (1985, p.187) provides a fairly lengthy and detailed description of what he means by a practice, but of most importance for us here is simply the assumption that reflective practitioners are dependent upon, and only given meaning through, the existence of a practice. If we do not understand policing as a practice, then police officers cannot be reflective practitioners because they are denied the existence of a practice within which to reflect.

There is a mutually reinforcing relationship here between the practice and the reflective practitioners. The practice has to be a learning organisation and supportive of reflective practice in order to ensure reflective practitioners have sufficient moral space to be able to make discretionary decisions. At the same time though, reflective practitioners need to be aware of a practice's frames, which reflect the purpose of a practice and the social contexts within which it exists. Kinsella (2007) argues that such awareness is important in developing the critically reflective capacity of practitioners. The point about this relationship is that both the practitioner and the practice are continually improved through this reciprocal bond. If the relationship is broken, then the practitioner can become stuck in a repetitive routine of doing things that were perhaps once reflective, but are now customary, and the practice ceases to be transformative and simply cements existing practice as orthodoxy. Important in this aspect of Schön's (1983) thinking is the idea of organisational justice (Sklansky, 2008).

The third level of Schön's (1983) idea of reflective practice concerns how a practice and its practitioners are viewed within and across society, and the level of self-awareness that practitioners demonstrate in relation to how they are perceived in society. This is an added level of complexity but as I have argued in this book, ethical policing needs to be seen as such within society for it to have meaning. It is not enough to have thoughtful police officers operating in supportive police organisations for ethical policing, or reflective practice, to be established. There needs to be a corresponding level of societal support and recognition granting police officers the moral space to make ethical decisions, and an appropriate level of trust in police organisations to be able to ensure that the moral responsibility afforded to police officers is not abused. This reinforces the idea of police discretion as a burden requiring professional judgement and corresponding actions, rather than as a freedom to act with impunity.

A final consideration on reflective practice as it relates to police discretion and virtue ethics is that reflection goes beyond rationality understood narrowly as abstract, technical, scientific reasoning. Reflective practice is more aligned to the reasoning found within virtue ethics and virtue epistemology than it is to the rationalities of both deontology and consequentialism.

Worthy of note here is the influence of female contributors, beyond those just cited, to virtue ethics (Wolf, 1982) and moral reasoning more generally (Midgley, 1972, 1979; Murdoch, 1985; Warnock, 1966). Slote (1995) draws upon Gilligan (1982) and Noddings (1984) to note a distinction made between male and female approaches to moral discourse. For example, he refers to Gilligan's (1982) argument that 'men tend to conceive morality in terms of rights, justice, and autonomy, whereas women more frequently think of the moral in terms of caring, responsibility, and interrelations with others' (Slote, 1995, p.256). Likewise, he notes that within Noddings (1984) there is a focus on 'particularistic caring' (Slote, 1995, p.256) and the idea that morality is measured through such acts. By this he means that a caring person is someone who cares for this or that person, as opposed to someone who promotes the virtue of caring as a societal value. This presents a different approach to moral reasoning, one that fits much better within a virtue ethics approach, as opposed to the moral theorising associated with Kant and Rawls. Baier (1994) also acknowledges, with qualifications, a difference in the approach taken by women philosophers towards moral questions. She notes, echoing Gilligan (1982), that the various female moral philosophers are providing 'a different voice from the standard moral philosopher's voice'

(Baier, 1994, p.263). While at pains not to draw rash generalisations, Baier (1994) notes that despite making significant contributions to ethical reasoning, women do not appear to have much inclination towards developing moral theory. She sees this not as a deficiency in women, but rather as an indication that moral theory is not as essential or important as moral reasoning.

Conclusion

Throughout this book, while it has been necessary to engage with different moral theories, I have attempted to consistently argue that ethical policing is not reliant upon any particular moral theory. In this respect, along with Baier (1994), I do not see the lack of moral theorising as a deficiency in the contributions made by female moral philosophers but rather a strength. I see virtue ethics as a more welcoming home for different ethical voices, a place where different ethical values, such as caring and compassion, can come to the fore. These seem to me to be highly appropriate values for ethical policing.

The emphasis within virtue ethics on both embodying ethical reasoning within the moral agent, and the situating of moral decisions in particular moments, requires ethical reasoning to be less constrained by methodological rules and norms. This is not to dismiss completely the value of methodological default positions, but it is imperative that we understand them as useful devices that can become un-useful at times. The competence exhibited within ethical reasoning is primarily a measure of the agent's ability to discern on such matters: 'Competence requires knowledge of the default, if there is one. But it also requires an understanding of the sorts of condition that can overturn the default contribution, either by annulling it or reversing it' (Dancy, 2004, p.191).

This brings us back to the link between virtue ethics and virtue epistemology. Feyerabend's (1975) attack on scientific method, what Kidd (2013, p.413) refers to as a challenge to 'the "myth" of methodological monism' (2013, p.413), favours a kind of *epistemic pluralism*. Feyerabend (1975, 2001, 2011) has continually challenged the privileging of institutionalised science over other forms of knowing and in doing so has followed in the footsteps of Michael Polanyi. Polanyi (1946, 1958) challenged the idea that there was a mechanistic inevitability of knowledge advancing through the application of scientific method. Instead, he emphasised the personal contribution made towards knowledge acquisition. This stresses the importance of the cognitive, moral agent. It also draws attention to the idea Polanyi

(1966) developed in a later publication, namely that the understanding we have of things we know only tacitly, becomes more intelligible through related actions. This latter understanding also influenced Schön's (1983) thinking and the idea of reflective practice.

I see the contribution of virtue ethics to policing in this light. It emphasises that ethical policing is found in the actions of police officers operating in policing circumstances, not in force policies or a code of police ethics. Policies and codes can play a supportive role but at the same time they can become unhelpful and counterproductive if they discourage ethical reasoning. Virtue ethics emphasises experience and judgement, discretion and reflective practice in ways that foster ethical policing.

Note
[1] https://socialsciences.mcmaster.ca/econ/ugcm/3ll3/aristotle/Ethics.pdf

Suggested further reading

Crisp, R. and Slote, M. (eds) (1997) *Virtue Ethics*. Oxford: Oxford University Press. Introduction

Delattre, E.J. (2004) 'Justice, Safety and the Limits to the Tolerable', in P. Villiers and R. Adlam (eds) *Policing a Safe, Just and Tolerant Society: An International Model for Policing*. Winchester: Waterside Press, pp.24–35

Schön, D. (1983) *The Reflective Practitioner: How Professionals Think in Action*. New York: Basic Books

Concluding remarks

Given the topic, I do not feel that a conclusion is appropriate. The book deals with issues that have remained unresolved for centuries so I do not expect to resolve them here. I have consciously avoided an approach to police ethics that seeks to get the philosophy bit out of the way as quickly as possible. My intention has been to slow things down, to take more time over the philosophical points and recognise that so much more needs to be done. So I will simply summarise the different ideas that I have covered in the book before suggesting ideas for future developments.

Hopefully the development of the journey from ethical neutrality, through principled policing, deontology, justice as fairness, consequentialism and virtue ethics is seen as one that progresses and constructs an increasingly nuanced understanding of ethical policing. Each chapter has sought to build on the previous one to establish an understanding of ethical policing that takes different elements from each ethical perspective considered, with a focus throughout on the role that moral philosophy can play in enhancing our understanding of policing. This is particularly significant in thinking about ethical policing. The approach I am advocating is one that embeds moral reasoning within police practice, as opposed to an applied model that either interprets policing through ethical theories, or illustrates ethical theories with policing examples. My aim is primarily for our understanding of policing to be deepened through philosophical enquiry, although this can also develop our understanding of philosophical questions more broadly.

This is a good time to be asking questions about the purpose of policing and there are clearly ideas out there that require further exploration. This is evidenced, for example, in Professor Jennifer Brown's collection generated through the engagement with Lord Stevens' Independent Commission into the Future of Policing (Brown, 2014). The Independent Police Commission (IPC) was established at the invitation of the then shadow Home Secretary Yvette Cooper and was promoted at the time as the basis of a future Labour government's manifesto for policing. The failure of the Labour Party to gain office in the 2015 UK general election was therefore somewhat of a setback for the IPC but the edited collection nonetheless contains thought-provoking ideas regarding the future of policing (Innes, 2014; Loader, 2014; Millie, 2014). The project may have been stalled by the election result but this should not stop the creative thinking that was inspired by the process.

Waddington's (2013) point about the imbalance in how we currently think about police ethics is also a central theme. He argues that there is too much of a punitive approach that focuses on police wrongdoing at the expense of an ethical engagement with good police practice. I have argued in the book that we need to rebalance the focus more towards promoting ethical policing, as opposed to challenging unethical policing. The latter is no doubt important and is always likely to attract attention. Nonetheless, we need more engagement on understanding what ethical policing is, and more energy spent on exploring ways of embedding it in police practice. Above all else, we need to ensure that we do not make the mistake of thinking that the negation of unethical policing produces ethical policing.

Throughout the chapters I have sought to introduce different ethical ideas that I feel are the most insightful for understanding ethical policing. In Chapter 2 I argued that the idea of ethical neutrality and the influence of liberal individualism had lost its purchase in 21st-century policing. The classical liberal position simply fails to address a contemporary need to focus on victims and issues of vulnerability. The move to incorporate principles and values that are representative of a more caring society has slowly transformed policing. Advocates of principled policing might argue that there is still so much more to do, but the extent to which policing has moved away from a position of ethical neutrality is significant. I broadly welcome this development, while noting that value-led policing has its own problems. Nonetheless, the move away from ethical neutrality is in my view an inevitability within a society that trivialises liberal concerns and replaces them with democratic sensibilities (Wood, 2016a).

In Chapter 3 I considered this development by looking specifically at the role human rights play within policing. Human rights are powerful tools but in terms of thinking about ethical policing there are a number of interrelated factors that need to be considered. First, we cannot ignore the extent to which human rights are philosophically much weaker than suggested by the political and legal status they hold. Secondly, human rights promote international law and we are currently witnessing a reassertion of national will across the globe. Human rights have always existed in tension with nation states and this is intensifying in the face of concerns about international crime and terrorism. Thirdly, the universal claim of human rights is challenged on the basis that it represents Western, Enlightenment, male-dominated ideas of what it means to be human and thereby ignores other, non-Western, feminist and ecological perspectives. Fourthly, human rights are powerful tools in theory but still require willing enforcers to make them powerful in practice. Fifthly, and perhaps of most immediate and direct relevance to policing, human rights are expressed in both legal and moral terms. I argue that it is the moral component of human rights that is of most importance in understanding ethical policing but there is a tendency in policing to focus on a narrow, legal interpretation of human rights.

I considered these challenges further in Chapter 4 by outlining Rawlsian ideas of justice as fairness and the idea of police legitimacy fostered within the procedural justice literature. Rawls advances a Kantian-inspired deontological perspective and while I raise some concerns with this approach in policing contexts, I nonetheless see merit in the liberal democratic setting advocated by Rawls. I argue that legitimate political institutions are a necessity for ethical policing to be realised and, conversely, that ethical policing is not possible in authoritarian regimes. This is because ethical policing requires a sufficient degree of moral space for it to be realised. Rawls emphasises the need for the moral legitimacy of our political institutions and I include policing within this frame. At the same time, policing requires a high level of consensual legitimacy and this is provided within the procedural justice research. Consensual legitimacy is measured, captured and promoted through the procedural justice literature much better than it could be done through moral philosophy. However, it is important to stress that procedural justice research does not address the moral legitimacy of the police, which does require philosophical enquiry.

I also argued that against the deontological focus of Rawls, it is important not to lose sight of the importance of consequences in policing. This was the focus of Chapter 5. I argued that the morally binding obligations of a deontological approach become impractical in public life. Here I emphasised the insights that come from consequential reasoning, which is largely recognised to be a flawed ethical theory at the level of individual morality, but nonetheless still has merit as an approach to ethical reasoning within positions of public office. This was illustrated with references to dirty hands and Dirty Harry. I also revisited the merits of Mill's utilitarian use of the *harm to others* principle. Again, recognising that it fails to meet the expectations of contemporary society, its utility as a device for making difficult decisions for those in public office was noted. In particular, this includes rethinking aspects of ethical neutrality and the strategy of minimising police interventions in society. I argued that this is where the moral language of human rights is perhaps of most use and concepts such as proportionality, necessity, appropriateness and so on provide a more acceptable way of balancing police interventions in society than Mill's *harm to others* principle.

Chapter 6 draws upon the insights from Aristotelian virtue ethics, which has grown in influence from the late 20th century onwards to challenge the dominance of deontology and utilitarianism. There is an emphasis in virtue ethics on context but in a way that is different from consequential reasoning. Virtue ethics is much more concerned with the characteristics of the moral agents who embody ethical thinking and enact ethical decisions and judgements within professional practice. Moral agency understood from an Aristotelian perspective differs from a Kantian understanding as MacIntyre (1985) argues through the linking of virtues to practice, a link that does not exist in deontology.

This leads to the challenges in establishing all three dimensions of Schön's (1983) notion of reflective practice within policing. First there is the challenge of embedding ethical reasoning within police practice, such that police officers develop a confidence in their own professional capacity to make a difference. Secondly, reflective police practitioners need to be supported and provided with the opportunities to be reflective in meaningful ways. Thirdly, at a societal level we need much greater understanding of policing as a socially reflexive practice. Elsewhere, I have argued that we need something in policing akin to university hospitals (Wood, 2018). The creation of university police stations is required in my view to ensure that the moral space required for ethical policing to flourish is given a sufficiently meaningful institutional setting that is readily visible and open for the public to see. Ethical policing is brave policing. All of this requires police discretion, with an emphasis on experience, but rather than arguing for police discretion in the abstract, I suggest focusing on justifying and establishing practices that necessitate discretion in a way that stresses the link between police discretion and police objectivity (Cohen, 1996). This approach to developing ethical policing also follows the practice-based understanding of police reform advocated by Dick et al (2014).

Looking forward

Beyond the customary summation of the key points raised in the book I also want to take this opportunity to promote further the idea that philosophy has a role to play in advancing our understanding of policing. It is my view that we need a branch of the ever-growing community of policing pracademics[1] to focus on philosophical dimensions of policing to accompany the empirical research in procedural justice and evidence-based practice, building upon and complementing the rich history of the sociological research into police work. I have always been struck by Professor Sherman's (2011) arguments lamenting the lack of randomised control trials in policing in comparison to other areas of public life. This is changing and the Society of Evidence Based Policing (SEBP) has played, and is playing, a role in the development of evidence-based policing. Perhaps we need something akin to the SEBP to champion the case for the philosophy of policing. In Mike Cunningham, we have a philosopher at the helm of the College of Policing, and there are plenty of philosophically minded academics and practitioners in policing across universities and police services.

There are also significant developments happening in policing in England and Wales at the moment, not least with the introduction of the Policing Education Qualifications Framework (PEQF). We should note that there was an explosion of philosophical creativity in the UK centred on education in the late 1960s and early 1970s that coincided with the professional development of teachers, as the practice of teaching went through a similar process to what is happening in policing today. It is telling that one the leading policing academics over the past 30 years, Professor John Kleinig, whose philosophical contribution to policing remains in my view unsurpassed, was a visiting scholar at the Institute of Education in London in 1975. Although coming towards the tail end of that dynamic period for the philosophy of education, this was a vibrant time and place to be philosophising and it would appear to have made a lasting impression on Professor Kleinig, judging by his philosophical insights into policing. Could we replicate in policing a similarly dynamic philosophical development to that which occurred in education? At the very least, those inclined towards philosophical enquiry should not allow the opportunities to delve deeper into policing to simply pass us by. The introduction and development of the PEQF, and likewise the interest in police knowledge generated by evidenced-based policing, provide the perfect backdrop for philosophical enquiry. The procedural justice literature alone is constantly addressing issues such as legitimacy, obligation, trust and so on, which demand an accompanying philosophical treatment.

As a final comment I want to stress that I see all of the issues just discussed in terms of a journey towards ethical policing. I hope this book has gone some way to encouraging a greater number of philosophical contributions along these lines. Although only in the early stages of the journey, there is already much to build upon, and while the road ahead may indeed be a bumpy one, there is, I believe, momentum in our favour. Above all else, there is a professional will to take policing down this road that is stronger than perhaps it has ever been. The timing feels right.

Note

[1] The term 'pracademic' is increasingly used to refer to individuals who are engaged in both academic and professional practice simultaneously. I am using the term in its widest possible sense to include this definition but also all academics who engage sincerely with police practice and practitioners who are genuinely engaged with academic aspects of their professional practice.

References

Alderson, J. (1998) *Principled Policing: Protecting the Public with Integrity.* Winchester: Waterside Press

Alison, L. (2008) 'Introduction', in L. Alison and J. Crego (eds) *Policing Critical Incidents: Leadership and Critical Incident Management.* Cullompton: Willan, pp.1–17

Amnesty International (2006) *UK Human Rights: A Broken Promise.* AI Index: EUR 45/004/2006

Anscombe, G.E.M. (1958) 'Modern Moral Philosophy', *Philosophy*, 33(124): 1–19 [page references to reproduction in R. Crisp and M. Slote (eds) (1997) *Virtue Ethics.* Oxford: Oxford University Press, pp.26–44]

Ariel, B., Sutherland, A., Henstock, D., Young, J., Drover, P., Sykes, J., Megicks, S. and Henderson, R. (2017) '"Contagious Accountability": A Global Multisite Randomized Controlled Trial on the Effect of Police Body-Worn Cameras on Citizens' Complaints Against the Police', *Criminal Justice and Behaviour*, 44(2): 293–316

Argyris, C. and Schön, D. (1974) *Theory in Practice: Increasing Professional Effectiveness.* San Francisco, CA: Jossey Bass

Argyris, C. and Schön, D. (1978) *Organisational Learning: A Theory of Action Perspective.* Reading, MA: Addison Wesley

Armstrong, S., Blaustein, J. and Henry, A. (eds) (2016) *Reflexivity and Criminal Justice: Intersections of Policy, Practice and Research.* London: Palgrave Macmillan

Audit Commission (1993) *Helping with Enquiries: Tackling Crime Effectively.* London: HMSO

Ayer, A.J. (1936) [1990] *Language, Truth and Logic.* London: Penguin

Bacon, M. (2014) 'Police Culture and the New Policing Context', in J. Brown (ed) *The Future of Policing.* London: Routledge, pp.103–19

Baier, A. (1994) 'What Do Women Want in a Moral Theory?', in *Moral Prejudices: Essays on Ethics.* Cambridge, MA: Harvard University Press [page references to R. Crisp and M. Slote (eds) (1997) *Virtue Ethics.* Oxford: Oxford University Press, pp.263–77]

Banton, M. (1964) *The Policeman in the Community.* London: Tavistock

Bayley, D.H. (2002) 'Law Enforcement and the Rule of Law: Is There a Tradeoff?', *Criminology and Public Policy*, 2(1): 133–54

Bayley, D.H. and Shearing, C.D. (2001) *The New Structure of Policing: Description, Conceptualization, and Research Agenda.* Washington, DC: National Institute of Justice

Beardsmore, R.W. (1969) *Moral Reasoning*. London: Routledge and Kegan Paul

Beck, U. (1992) *Risk Society: Towards a New Modernity*. New Delhi: Sage

Bellamy, A. (2007) 'Dirty Hands and Lesser Evils in the War on Terror', *British Journal of Politics and International Relations*, 9: 509–26

Bellamy, R. (2000) *Rethinking Liberalism*. London: Pinter

Bentham, J. (1843) 'Anarchical Fantasies', in *The Collected Works of Jeremy Bentham. Volume 2*. Edited by J. Bowring. Edinburgh: William Tait

Benton, T. (1998) 'Rights and Justice on a Shared Planet: More Rights or New Relations?', *Theoretical Criminology*, 2(2): 149–75

Benton, T. (2007) 'Ecology, Community and Justice: The Meaning of Green', in P. Beirne and N. South (eds) *Issues in Green Criminology*. Cullompton: Willan, pp.3–31

Benton, T. (2008) 'Environmental Values and Human Purposes', *Environmental Values*, 17(2): 201–20

Berlin I. (1958) 'Two Concepts of Liberty', in I. Berlin (1990) *Four Essays on Liberty*. Oxford: Oxford University Press, pp.118–72

Bingham, T. (2011) *The Rule of Law*. London: Penguin

Bittner, E. (1970) *The Functions of the Police in Modern Society*. Rockville, MD: National Institute of Mental Health, Center for Studies of Crime and Delinquency

Blau, J. and Esparza, L.E. (2016) *Human Rights: A Primer*. 2nd edition. London: Routledge

Bottoms, A. and Tankebe, J. (2012) 'Beyond Procedural Justice: A Dialogic Approach to Legitimacy in Criminal Justice', *Journal of Criminal Law & Criminology*, 102(1): 119–70

Boyd, R. (2004) *Uncivil Society: The Perils of Pluralism and the Making of Modern Liberalism*. Lanham, MD: Lexington

Bradford, B. (2014) 'Policing and Social Identity: Procedural Justice, Inclusion and Cooperation Between Police and Public, *Policing and Society*, 24(1): 22–43

Bradley, A.W., Ewing, K.D. and Knight, C.J.S. (2014) *Constitutional and Administrative Law*. Harlow: Pearson

Braga, A., Coldren, J.R., Sousa, W., Rodriguez, D. and Alper, O. (2017) *The Benefits of Body-Worn Cameras: New Findings from a Randomized Controlled Trial at the Las Vegas Metropolitan Police Department*, Washington, DC: US Department of Justice, National Institute of Justice

Brandt, Richard B. (1979) *A Theory of the Good and the Right*. Amherst, NY: Prometheus Books [page reference to 1998 edition]

Brogden, M. and Ellison, G. (2013) *Policing in an Age of Austerity: A Postcolonial Perspective*. Abingdon: Routledge

Brown, J.M. (ed) (2014) *The Future of Policing*. London: Routledge

Bullock, K. and Johnson, P. (2012) 'The Impact of the Human Rights Act 1998 on Policing in England and Wales', *British Journal of Criminology*, 52(3): 630–50

Burke, E. (1790) *Reflections on the Revolution in France*. London: James Dodsley

Carlile, Lord (2011) *Sixth Report of the Independent Reviewer pursuant to section 14(3) of the Prevention of Terrorism Act 2005*, submitted by Lord Carlile of Berriew QC. London: The Stationery Office

Chan, J. (2003) *Fair Cop: Learning the Art of Policing*. Toronto: University of Toronto Press

Christopher, S. (2015) 'The Police Service Can Be a Critical Reflective Practice ... If It Wants', *Policing. A Journal of Policy and Practice*, 9(4): 326–39

Coady, C.A.J. (2008) *Messy Morality: The Challenge of Politics*. Oxford: Oxford University Press

Cockcroft, T. (2013) *Police Culture: Themes and Concepts*. London: Routledge

Cohen, H. (1996) 'Police Discretion and Police Objectivity', in J. Kleinig (ed) *Handled with Discretion: Ethical Issues in Police Decision Making*. London: Rowman and Littlefield, pp.91–106

College of Policing (2014) *Code of Ethics: Principles and Standards of Professional Behaviour for the Police Profession of England and Wales*. Available online at: https://www.college.police.uk/What-we-do/Ethics/Documents/Code_of_Ethics.pdf, accessed 23/01/2018

Crank, J., Flaherty, D. and Giacomazzi, A. (2007) 'The Noble Cause: An Empirical Assessment', *Journal of Criminal Justice*, 35: 103–16

Crisp, R. and Slote, M. (eds) (1997) *Virtue Ethics*. Oxford: Oxford University Press

Dancy, J. (2004) *Ethics Without Principles*. Oxford: Oxford University Press

Davis, H. (2016) *Human Rights Law*. 4th edition. Oxford: Oxford University Press

Davis, M. (2002) *Profession, Code, and Ethics: Towards a Morally Useful Theory of Today's Professions*. Aldershot: Ashgate

Delattre, E.J. (2004) 'Justice, Safety and the Limits to the Tolerable', in P. Villiers and R. Adlam (eds) *Policing a Safe, Just and Tolerant Society: An International Model for Policing*. Winchester: Waterside Press, pp.24–35

Delattre, E.J. (2011) *Character and Cops: Ethics and Policing*. 6th edition. Lanham, MD: Rowman & Littlefield

Den Boer, M. (2010) 'Towards a Governance Model of Police Cooperation in Europe: The Twist Between Networks and Bureaucracies', in F. Lemieux (ed) *International Police Cooperation: Emerging Issues, Theory and Practice*, Cullompton: Willan Publishing, pp.42–61

Dershowitz, A.M. (2002) *Why Terrorism Works: Understanding the Threat, Responding to the Challenge*. New Haven, CT: Yale University Press

Dershowitz, A. (2003) 'The Torture Warrant: A Response to Professor Strauss', *New York Law School Law Review*, 48(1&2): 275–94

Dershowitz, A. (2006) 'Should We Fight Terror with Torture?', *The Independent*, 3 July

Devlin, P. (1965) *The Enforcement of Morals*. Oxford: Oxford University Press

Dewey, J. (1904) 'The Relation of Theory to Practice in Education', *Third Yearbook of the National Society for the Scientific Study of Education*. Chicago, IL: University of Chicago Press, pp.9–30

Dewey, J. (1916) *Democracy and Education*. New York: Macmillan

Dick, P., Silvestri, M. and Westmarland, L. (2014) 'Women Police: Potential and Possibilities for Police Reform', in J. Brown (ed) *The Future of Policing*. London: Routledge, pp.134–48

Disley, E., Irving, B., Hughes, W. and Patruni, B. (2012) *Evaluation of the Implementation of the Europol Council Decision and of Europol's Activities*. Prepared for the Europol Management Board by RAND Europe. Cambridge: the RAND Corporation

Dworkin, R. (1978) *Taking Rights Seriously*. Cambridge, MA: Harvard University Press

Dworkin, R. (1986) *Law's Empire*. Oxford: Hart Publishing

Dryzek, J.S. and Dunleavy, P. (2009) *Theories of the Democratic State*. Basingstoke: Palgrave Macmillan

Eatwell, R. and Goodwin, M. (2018) *National Populism: The Revolt Against Liberal Democracy*. London: Penguin Random House UK

Edwards, C. (2005) *Changing Policing Theories for 21st Century Societies*. 2nd edition. Annandale, NSW: The Federation Press

Ericson, R.V. (1995) 'The News Media and Accountability in Criminal Justice', in P.C. Stenning (ed) *Accountability for Criminal Justice*. Toronto: Toronto University Press, pp.135–61

Etzioni, A. (1993) *The Spirit of Community: The Reinvention of American Society*. New York: Touchstone

Ewing, K.D. (2010) *Bonfire of the Liberties: New Labour, Human Rights, and the Rule of Law*. Oxford: Oxford University Press

Feyerabend, P. (1975) *Against Method: Outline of an Anarchistic Theory of Knowledge*. London: New Left Books

Feyerabend, P. (2001) *Conquest of Abundance: A Tale of Abstraction versus the Richness of Being*. Edited by B. Terpstra. Chicago, IL: Chicago University Press

Feyerabend, P. (2011) *The Tyranny of Science*. Edited by E. Oberheim. Cambridge: Polity

Fitzpatrick, T. (2008) *Applied Ethics & Social Problems: Moral Questions of Birth, Society and Death*. Bristol: Policy Press

Flanagan, Sir R. (2008) *The Review of Policing. Final Report*. London: Home Office

Fleming, J. (2015) 'Experience and Evidence: The Learning of Leadership', in J. Fleming (ed) *Police Leadership: Rising to the Top*. Oxford: Oxford University Press, pp.1–16

Fleming, J. (2018) 'How Do the Police Respond to Evidence Based Policing?', in R.A.W. Rhodes (ed) *Narrative Policy Analysis: Cases in Decentred Policy*. Basingstoke: Palgrave Macmillan, pp.221–39

Fleming, J. and Rhodes, R.A.W. (2018) 'Can Experience Be Evidence? Craft Knowledge and Evidence-Based Policing', *Policy & Politics*, 46(1): 3–26

Follesdal, A. (2014) 'Kant, Human Rights and Courts' in A. Follesdal and R. Maliks (eds) *Kantian Theory and Human Rights*. London: Routledge, pp.193–202

Foot, P. (1978) 'Virtues and Vices', in *Virtues and Vices and Other Essays in Moral Philosophy*. Oxford: Blackwell [page references to reproduction in R. Crisp and M. Slote (eds) (1997) *Virtue Ethics*. Oxford: Oxford University Press, pp.163–77]

Furedi, F. (2011) *On Tolerance: A Defence of Moral Independence*. London: Continuum

Gearty, C. (2006) *Can Human Rights Survive?*, Cambridge: Cambridge University Press

Giddens, A. (1991) *Modernity and Self-Identity: Self and Society in the Late Modern Age*. Cambridge: Cambridge University Press

Gilligan, C. (1982) *In a Different Voice: Psychological Theory and Women's Development*. Cambridge, MA: Harvard University Press

Goldsmith, A. (2010) 'Policing's New Visibility', *The British Journal of Criminology*, 50(5): 914–34

Goldstein, H. (1990) *Problem-Oriented Policing*. New York/London: McGraw-Hill

Gray, J. (1995) *Liberalism*. 2nd edition. Buckingham: Open University Press

Gray, J. (2000) *Two Faces of Liberalism*. Cambridge: Polity

Green, L. (2008) 'Positivism and the Inseparability of Law and Morals', *New York University Law Review*, 83: 1035–58

Grint, K. (2007) 'Learning to Lead: Can Aristotle Help Us Find the Road to Wisdom?', *Leadership* 3(2): 231–46

Haggard, P. (1993) *Police Ethics*. Lewiston, NY: The Edwin Mellen Press

Haldane, J. (2017) 'MacIntyre Against Morality', *First Things*. May. Available online: https://www.firstthings.com/article/2017/05/macintyre-against-morality, accessed 23/01/2019

Hart, H.L.A. (1957) 'Positivism and the Separation of Law and Morals', *Harvard Law Review*, 71: 593

Held, D. (1984) 'Central Perspectives on the Modern State' in G. McLennan, D. Held and S. Hall (eds) *The Idea of the Modern State*, Milton Keynes: Open University Press

Held, D. (2006) *Models of Democracy*. 3rd edition. Cambridge: Polity

Hill, C. (1999) 'Toleration in Seventeenth-Century England: Theory and Practice', in S. Mendus (ed) *The Politics of Toleration*. Edinburgh: Edinburgh University Press, pp.27–44

Hinsch, W. (2010) 'Justice, Legitimacy, and Constitutional Rights', *Critical Review of International Social and Political Philosophy*, 13(1): 39–54

Hobbes, T. (1651/2002) *Leviathan*. Edited by A.P. Martinich (2002) Peterborough, Ontario: Broadview Press

Holdaway, S. (1983) *Inside the British Police*. Oxford: Blackwell

Holgersson, S. and Gottschalk, P. (2008) 'Police Officers' Professional Knowledge', *Police Practice and Research. An International Journal*, 9(5): 365–78

Hopkins Burke, R. (ed) (2004) *Hard Cop, Soft Cop: Dilemmas and Debates in Contemporary Policing*. Cullompton: Willan

Hopkins Burke, R. and Morrill, R. (2004) 'Human Rights v. Community Rights: The Case of the Anti-Social Behaviour Order' in R. Hopkins Burke (ed) *Hard Cop, Soft Cop: Dilemmas and Debates in Contemporary Policing*. Cullompton: Willan, pp.226–41

Horne, A. and Berman, G. (2011) *Control Orders and the Prevention of Terrorism Act 2005*. Standard Note: SN/HA/3438. London: House of Commons Library

House of Lords (2008) *Europol: Coordinating the Fight Against Serious and Organised Crime*. European Union Committee. 29th Report of Session 2007–08. London: The Stationery Office

Hughes, G. (1998) *Understanding Crime Prevention: Social Control, Risk and Late Modernity*. Buckingham: Open University Press

Hughes, J. (2013) 'Theory of Professional Standards and Ethical Policing', in A. MacVean, P. Spindler, and C. Solf (eds) *Handbook of Policing, Ethics and Professional Standards*. Abingdon: Routledge, pp.7–16

Hursthouse, R. (1991) 'Virtue Theory and Abortion', *Philosophy and Public Affairs*, 20: 223–46 [page references to reproduction in R. Crisp and M. Slote (eds) (1997) *Virtue Ethics*. Oxford: Oxford University Press, pp.217–38]

Ignatieff, M. (2001) *Human Rights as Politics and Idolatry*. Princeton, NJ: Princeton University Press

Ignatieff, M. (2004) *The Lesser Evil: Political Ethics in an Age of Terror*. Toronto: Penguin Canada

Innes, M. (2014) 'Reinventing the Office of Constable: Progressive Policing in an Age of Austerity', in J. Brown (ed) *The Future of Policing*. London: Routledge, pp.64–78

Ip, J. (2013) 'Sunset Clauses and Counterterrorism Legislation', *Public Law* 74

Jackson, J. (2018) 'Norms, Normativity and the Legitimacy of Legal Authorities: International Perspectives', *Annual Review of Law and Social Science*, 14: 145–65

Jackson, J. and Bradford, B. (2019) *Blurring the Distinction Between Empirical and Normative Legitimacy? A Commentary on 'Police Legitimacy and Citizen Cooperation in China'*. LSE Law, Society and Economy Working Papers 4/2019, 26

Jackson, J., Asif, M., Bradford, B. and Zakar, M.Z. (2014) 'Corruption and Police Legitimacy in Lahore, Pakistan', *British Journal of Criminology*, 54: 1067–88

Jackson, J., Bradford, B., Stanko, B. and Hohl, K. (2013) *Just Authority? Trust in the Police in England and Wales*. London: Routledge

Johnston, D. (1994) *The Idea of Liberal Theory: A Critique and Reconstruction*. Princeton: Princeton University Press

Johnston, L. (1992) *The Rebirth of Private Policing*. London: Routledge

Johnston L. (1999) 'Private Policing: Uniformity and Diversity', in R. Mawby (ed) *Policing Across the World*. London: UCL Press

Johnston, L. (2000) *Policing Britain: Risk, Security and Governance*. Harlow: Longman

Jones, T. and Newburn, T. (1998) *Private Security and Public Policing*. Oxford: Clarendon Press

Jones, T. and Newburn T. (2002) 'The Transformation of Policing? Understanding Current Trends in Policing Systems', *British Journal of Criminology*, 42: 129–46

Joyce, P. (2011) 'Police Reform: From Police Authorities to Police and Crime Commissioners', *Safer Communities*, 10(4): 5–13

Kant, I. (1788/1909) *Critique of Practical Reason*. Translated by T. Kingsmill Abbott. London: Longmans, Green [republished by Dover in 2004]

Kempa, M. (2007) 'Tracing the Diffusion of Policing Governance Models from the British Isles and Back Again: Some Directions for Democratic Reform in Troubled Times', *Police Practice and Research. An International Journal*, 8(2): 107–23

Kempa, M., Stenning, P. and Wood, J. (2004) 'Policing Communal Spaces. A Reconfiguration of the "Mass Private Property" Hypothesis', *British Journal of Criminology*, 44(4): 562–81

Kidd, I.J. (2013) 'Feyerabend on Science and Education', *Journal of Philosophy of Education*, 47(3): 407–22

Kinsella, E.A. (2007) 'Embodied Reflections and the Epistemology of Reflective Practice', *Journal of Philosophy of Education*, 41(3): 395–409

Kleinig, J. (1996) *The Ethics of Policing*. Cambridge: Cambridge University Press

Kleinig, J. (1999) 'Human Dignity and Human Rights: An Emerging Concern in Police Practice', in G.W. Lynch (ed) *Human Dignity and the Police: Ethics and Integrity in Police Work*. Springfield, IL: Charles C. Thomas Publisher Ltd

Kleinig, J. (2001) 'National Security and Police Interrogation: Some Ethical Considerations', in S. Einstein and M. Amir (eds) *Policing, Security and Democracy: Special Aspects of 'Democratic Policing'*. Huntsville: Office of International Criminal Justice

Kleinig, J. (2002) 'Rethinking Noble Cause Corruption', *International Journal of Police Science and Management*, 4(4): 287–314

Kleinig, J. (2004) 'The Problematic Virtue of Loyalty', in P. Villiers and R. Adlam (eds) *Policing a Safe, Just and Tolerant Society: An International Model*. Winchester: Waterside Press, pp.78–87

Kleinig, J. (2005) 'Ticking Bombs and Torture Warrants', *Deakin Law Review*, 10(2): 614–27

Kleinig, J. (2007) 'Torture and Political Morality', in I. Primoratz (ed) *Politics and Morality*. Chippenham: Anthony Rowe, pp.209–27

Kleinig, J. (2019) *Ends and Means in Policing*. London: Taylor and Francis

Klockars, C.B. (1980) 'The Dirty Harry Problem', *The Annals of the American Academy of Political and Social Science*, 452: 33–47

Kotzee, B. (2013) 'Introduction: Education, Social Epistemology and Virtue Epistemology', *Journal of Philosophy of Education*, 47(2): 157–67

Liebling, A. (2004) *Prisons and Their Moral Performance: A Study of Values, Quality and Prison Life*. Oxford: Oxford University Press

Lister, S. (2013) 'The New Politics of the Police: Police and Crime Commissioners and the "Operational Independence" of the Police', *Policing: A Journal of Policy and Practice*, 7(3): 239–47

Loader, I. (2014) 'Why Do the Police Matter? Beyond the Myth of Crime Fighting', in J. Brown (ed) *The Future of Policing*. London: Routledge, pp.40–51

Loader, I. and Mulcahy, A. (2003) *Policing and the Conditions of England: Memory, Politics and Culture*. Oxford: Oxford University Press

Locke, J. (1690/1952) *The Second Treatise of Government*. Edited and Introduced by T.P. Peardon. New York: The Library of Liberal Arts

Loftus, B. (2009) *Police Culture in a Changing World*. Oxford: Oxford University Press

Lumsden, K. and Goode, J. (2017) 'Public Criminology, Reflexivity and the Enterprise University: Experiences of Research, Knowledge Transfer Work and Co-option with Police Forces'. *Theoretical Criminology*, 22(2): 243–57

Lustgarten, L. (1986) *The Governance of Police*. London: Sweet & Maxwell

MacAllister, J. (2012) 'Virtue Epistemology and the Philosophy of Education', *Journal of Philosophy of Education*, 46(2): 251–70

Machiavelli, N. (1981) *The Prince*. Harmondsworth: Penguin

MacIntyre, A. (1966) *A Short History of Ethics*. New York: Macmillan

MacIntyre, A. (1985) *After Virtue*. 2nd edition. London: Duckworth

MacIntyre, A. (1999) 'Toleration and the Goods of Conflict', in S. Mendus (ed) *The Politics of Toleration*. Edinburgh: Edinburgh University Press, pp.133–55

MacIntyre, A. (2004) 'Social Structures and Their Threat to Moral Agency', in P. Villiers and R. Adlam (eds) *Policing a Safe, Just and Tolerant Society: An International Model for Policing*. Winchester: Waterside Press, pp.36–54

MacVean, A. and Neyroud, P. (2012) *Police Ethics and Values*. London: Sage

MacVean, A. and Spindler, P. (2015) 'Principled and Ethical Policing: Some Considerations for Police Leaders', in J. Fleming (ed) *Police Leadership: Rising to the Top*. Oxford: Oxford University Press, pp.110–28

MacVean, A., Spindler, P. and Solf, C. (eds) (2013) *Handbook of Policing, Ethics and Professional Standards*. Abingdon: Routledge

Manning, P.K. (1977) *Police Work: The Social Organization of Policing*. 2nd edition. Prospect Heights, IL: Waveland Press

Manning, P.K. (2010) *Democratic Policing in a Changing World*. Boulder, CO: Paradigm Publishers

Marks, M. and Sklansky, D. (2008) 'Voices from Below: Unions and Participatory Arrangements in the Police Workplace', *Police Practice and Research. An International Journal*, 9(2): 85–94

Marshall, G. (1978) 'Police Accountability Revisited', in D. Butler and A. Halsey (eds) *Policy and Politics*. London: Macmillan, pp.51–65

Martinich, A.P. (2005) *Hobbes*. London: Routledge

Marx, G.T. (1988) *Undercover: Police Surveillance in America*. Berkeley, CA: University of California Press

McKinnon, C. (2006) *Toleration: A Critical Introduction*. London: Routledge

Mendus, S. (1988) 'Introduction', in S. Mendus (ed) *Justifying Toleration. Conceptual and Historical Perspectives*. Cambridge: Cambridge University Press, pp.1–19

Mendus, S. (1999) 'Introduction', in S. Mendus (ed) *The Politics of Toleration*. Edinburgh: Edinburgh University Press, pp.1–12

Midgley, M. (1972) 'Is "Moral" a Dirty Word?', *Philosophy* 47(181): 206–28

Midgley, M. (1979) 'The All-Female Number', *Philosophy* 54(210): 552–4

Mill, J.S. (1859/1973) *On Liberty*, in *The Utilitarians*. New York: Anchor Press, pp.473–60

Mill, J.S. (1863/1973) *Utilitarianism*. Reproduced in *The Utilitarians*. New York: Anchor Press, pp.399–472

Miller, S. (2004a) 'Moral Rights and the Institution of the Police', in T. Campbell and S. Miller (eds) *Human Rights and the Moral Responsibilities of Corporate and Public Sector Organisations*. Dordrecht: Kluwer, pp.167–88

Miller, S. (2004b) 'Combatting Noble Cause Corruption', in P. Villiers and R. Adlam (eds) *Policing a Safe, Just and Tolerant Society: An International Model for Policing*. Winchester: Waterside Press, pp.122–33

Miller, S., Blackler, J. and Alexandra, A. (2006) *Police Ethics*. 2nd edition. Crows Nest: Allen & Unwin

Millie, A. (2014) 'What Are the Police For? Rethinking Policing Post-austerity', in J. Brown (ed) *The Future of Policing*, London: Routledge, pp.52–63

Mitchell, R. and Huey, L. (eds) (2018) *Evidence Based Policing: An Introduction*. Bristol: Policy Press

Montefiore, A. (1958) *A Modern Introduction to Moral Philosophy*. London: Routledge & Kegan Paul

Montesquieu (Baron de), Charles de Secondat (1914 [1752]) *The Spirit of Laws*. Translated by Thomas Nugent, revised by J.V. Prichard. Based on a public domain edition published in 1914 by G. Bell & Sons, Rendered into HTML and text by Jon Roland of the Constitution Society. See especially, Book XXVI: 'Of Laws in Relation to the Order of Things Which They Determine', §24. Available online: http://www.constitution.org/cm/sol.txt, accessed 29/09/07

Morrell, K. and Bradford, B. (2019) *Policing and Public Management. Governance, Vices and Virtues*. London: Routledge

Mulhall, S. and Swift, A. (1996) *Liberals and Communitarians*. 2nd edition. Oxford: Blackwell

Murdoch, I. (1985) *The Sovereignty of Good*. London: Routledge

Müller, J.-W. (2016) *What Is Populism?*, Philadelphia, PA: University of Pennsylvania Press

Muir, W. (1977) *Police: Streetcorner Politicians*. Chicago, IL: The University of Chicago Press

Newburn, T. (1999) *Understanding and Preventing Police Corruption: Lessons from the Literature*. London: Home Office Policing and Reducing Crime Unit

Newburn, T. (2012) 'Police and Crime Commissioner: The Americanization of Policing or a Very British Reform?', *International Journal of Law, Crime and Justice*, 40: 31–46

Neyroud, P.W. (2003) 'Policing and Ethics', in T. Newburn (ed) *Handbook of Policing*. Cullompton, Devon: Willan, pp.578–602

Neyroud, P.W. (2006) 'Ethics in Policing: Performance and the Personalisation of Accountability in British Policing and Criminal Justice', *Legal Ethics*, 9(1): 16–34

Neyroud, P.W. and Beckley, A. (2001) *Policing, Ethics and Human Rights*. Cullompton: Willan

Neyroud, P. and Weisburd, D. (2014) 'Transforming the Police Through Science: The Challenge of Ownership', *Policing. A Journal of Policy and Practice*, 8(4): 287–93

Noddings, N. (1984) *Caring: A Feminine Approach to Ethics and Moral Education*. Berkeley, CA: University of California Press

Nowell-Smith, P.H. (1954) *Ethics*. London: Pelican

Nozick, R. (1974) *Anarchy, State and Utopia*. Oxford: Blackwell

Oakeshott, M. (1991) *Rationalism in Politics and Other Essays*. Indianapolis, IN: Liberty Fund

O'Hear, A. (1988) 'Academic Freedom and the University', in M. Tight (ed) *Academic Freedom and Responsibility*. Milton Keynes: SRHE/ Open University Press, pp.6–16

Ophuls, W. (1977) *Ecology and the Politics of Scarcity*. San Francisco, CA: W.H. Freeman

Padfield, N. (2010) *Criminal Law*. 7th edition. Oxford: Oxford University Press

Pagon, M. (2004) 'Ethics, Education and Integrity', in Peter Villiers and R. Adlam (eds) *Policing a Safe, Just and Tolerant Society: An International Model*. Winchester: Waterside Press

Paine, T. (1791) *Rights of Man*. London: A.S. Jordan

Patten, C. (1999) *A New Beginning: Policing in Northern Ireland*. The Report of the Independent Commission on Policing for Northern Ireland (Patten Report). London: HMSO

Piaget, J. (1977) *The Development of Thought: Equilibration of Cognitive Structures*. Oxford: Basil Blackwell

Plato (1955) *The Republic*. Translated with an introduction by Desmond Lee. London: Penguin

Polanyi, M. (1946) *Science, Faith, and Society*. Oxford: Oxford University Press

Polanyi, M. (1958) *Personal Knowledge: Towards a Post-Critical Philosophy*. Chicago, IL: University of Chicago Press

Polanyi, M. (1966) *The Tacit Dimension*. London: Routledge

Police Federation (2008) *The Office of Constable: The Bedrock of Modern Day British Policing*. Leatherhead: Police Federation of England and Wales

Pritchard, D. (2013) 'Epistemic Virtue and the Epistemology of Education', *Journal of Philosophy of Education*, 47(2): 236–47

Punch, M. (1985) *Conduct Unbecoming: The Social Construction of Police Deviance and Control*, London: Tavistock

Punch, M. (2003) 'Rotten Orchards: "Pestilence", Police Misconduct and System Failure', *Policing and Society*, 13(2): 171–96

Punch, M. (2007) *Zero Tolerance Policing*. Bristol: Policy Press

Punch, M. (2009) *Police Corruption: Deviancy, Accountability and Reform in Policing*. Cullompton: Willan

Ratcliffe, J. (2016) *Intelligence-led Policing*. 2nd edition. London: Routledge

Rawls, J. (1971) *A Theory of Justice*. Cambridge, MA: Belknap

Rawls, J. (1993) *Political Liberalism*. New York: Columbia University Press

Rawls, J. (2000) *Lectures on the History of Moral Philosophy*. Edited by B. Herman. Cambridge, MA: Harvard University Press

Raz, J. (1988) 'Autonomy, Toleration, and the Harm Principle', in S. Mendus (ed) *Justifying Toleration: Conceptual and Historical Perspectives*. Cambridge: Cambridge University Press, pp.155–75

Reiner, R. (2010) *The Politics of the Police*. 4th edition. Oxford: Oxford University Press

Reiner, R. (2013) 'Who Governs? Democracy, Plutocracy, Science and Prophecy in Policing', *Criminology and Criminal Justice*, 13(2): 161–80

Reiner, R. (2015) 'Utopia in One Institution? Can Policing Be Democratic in an Unjust Society?' Presented at *Policing and Democracy in the 21st Century*, The International Criminological Research Unit, Liverpool University, 17 September 2015

Rescher, N. (1993) *Pluralism: Against the Demand for Consensus*. Oxford: Clarendon Press

Rogers, C. (2013) 'The Commissioner Cometh: The Challenge for Democratic Policing in England and Wales', *International Journal of Law, Crime and Justice*, 41: 132–43

Rogers, C. (2016) *Plural Policing, Theory, Practice and Principles*. Bristol: Policy Press

Rowe, M. (2002) 'Policing Diversity: Themes and Concerns from the Recent British Experience', *Police Quarterly*, 5(4): 424–46

Russell, B. (1985) *A History of Western Philosophy*. London: Holiday House

Ryan, A. (1988) 'A More Tolerant Hobbes?', in S. Mendus (ed) *Justifying Toleration: Conceptual and Historical Perspectives*. Cambridge: Cambridge University Press, pp.37–60

Sampford, C. (2005) 'Reconceiving the Rule of Law for a Globalizing World', in S. Zifcak (ed) *Globalization and the Rule of Law*. London: Routledge, 9–31

Sampson, F. (2012) 'Hail to the Chief? How Far Does the Introduction of Elected Police Commissioners Herald a US-Style Politicization of Policing for the UK?', *Policing: A Journal of Policy and Practice*, 6(1): 4–15

Sandel, M. (1982) *Liberalism and the Limits of Justice*. Cambridge: Cambridge University Press

Sandel, M. (2010) *Justice. What's The Right Thing To Do?* London: Penguin

Scanlon, T.M. (2003) *The Difficulty of Tolerance: Essays in Political Philosophy*. Cambridge: Cambridge University Press

Schön, D. (1983) *The Reflective Practitioner: How Professionals Think in Action*. New York: Basic Books [page references to Avebury, Ashgate 1991 edition]

Sen, A. (2009) *The Idea of Justice*. London: Penguin

Senge, P.M. (2010) *The Fifth Discipline: The Art and Practice of the Learning Organization*. 3rd edition. London: Penguin Random House

Shearing, C. and Johnston, L. (2003) *Governing Security: Explorations of Policing and Justice*. London: Routledge

Sherman, L.W. (ed) (1974) *Police Corruption: A Sociological Perspective*. New York: Anchor

Sherman, L.W. (1998) 'Evidence Based Policing', *Ideas in American Policing*, July. Washington, DC: The Police Foundation

Sherman, L.W. (2011) *Professional Policing and Liberal Democracy*. The 2011 Benjamin Franklin Medal Lecture, Royal Society for the Encouragement of Arts, Manufactures and Commerce (RSA), London, 1 November.

Shue, H. (1978) 'Torture', *Philosophy and Public Affairs*, 7(2): 124–43

Simmonds, N.E. (2002) *Central Issues in Jurisprudence: Justice, Law and Rights*. London: Sweet & Maxwell

Simmons, A.J. (1979) *Moral Principles and Political Obligations*. Princeton, NJ: Princeton University Press

Simmons, A.J. (2001) *Justification and Legitimacy: Essays on Rights and Obligations*. Cambridge: Cambridge University Press

Singer, P. (1979) *Practical Ethics*. Cambridge: Cambridge University Press

Singer, P. (1998) 'Foreword' to R.B. Brandt *A Theory of the Good and the Right*. Amherst, NY: Prometheus Books

Skinns, L. (2011) *Police Custody: Governance, Legitimacy and Reform in the Criminal Justice Process*. London: Routledge

Sklansky, D.A. (2008) *Democracy and the Police*. Stanford, CA: Stanford University Press

Skolnick, J.H. (1966) *Justice Without Trial: Law Enforcement in Democratic Society*. New York: John Wiley & Sons

Slote, M. (1995) 'Agent-Based Virtue Ethics', *Midwest Studies in Philosophy*, 20: 83–101 [page references to reprint in R. Crisp and M. Slote (eds) (1997) *Virtue Ethics*. Oxford: Oxford University Press, pp.239–62]

Smart, J.J.C. and Williams, B. (1973) *Utilitarianism: For and Against*. Cambridge: Cambridge University Press

South, N. (1998) 'A Green Field for Criminology? A Proposal for a Perspective', *Theoretical Criminology*, 2(2): 211–33

Steinhoff, U. (2006) 'Torture – The Case for Dirty Harry and against Alan Dershowitz', *Journal of Applied Philosophy*, 23(3): 337–53

Stenning, P.C. (1989) 'Private Police and Public Police: Toward a Redefinition of the Police Role', in *Future Issues in Policing: Symposium Proceedings*, D.J. Loree (ed), Minister of Supply & Services Canada, Ottawa, pp.169–92

Stenning, P.C. (2011) *Governance of the Police: Independence, Accountability and Interference.* Ray Whitrod Memorial Lecture. 6 October 2011 at Flinders University, Adelaide. Available online at: http://www.justice.net.au/attachments/056_GovernanceOfPoliceWhitrodMemorialLecture2011.pdf, accessed 29/08/13

Stone, M. (2014) *Civil Liberties and Human Rights.* 10th edition. Oxford: Oxford University Press

Strauss, M. (2003) 'Torture', *New York Law School Law Review*, 48(1&2): 201–74

Sun, I.Y., Li, L., Wu, Y. and Hu, R. (2018) 'Police Legitimacy and Citizen Cooperation in China: Testing an Alternative Model, *Asian Journal of Criminology*, 13(4): 275–91

Sunshine, J. and Tyler, T.R. (2003) 'The Role of Procedural Justice and Legitimacy in Shaping Public Support for Policing', *Law and Society Review*, 37(3): 555–89

Tankebe, J. (2013) 'Viewing Things Differently: The Dimensions of Public Perceptions of Police Legitimacy', *Criminology*, 51: 103–35

Taylor, C. (1989) *Sources of the Self: The Making of the Modern Identity.* Cambridge: Cambridge University Press

Tralau, J. (ed) (2011) *Thomas Hobbes and Carl Schmitt: The Politics of Order and Myth.* London: Routledge

Turner, L. (2014) 'PCCs, Neo-liberal Hegemony and Democratic Policing', *Safer Communities*, 13(1): 13–21

Tyler, T. (1990) *Why People Obey the Law.* New Haven, CT: Yale University Press

Tyler, T. (2003) 'Procedural Justice, Legitimacy, and the Effective Rule of Law', *Crime and Justice*, 30: 283–357

Tyler, T.R. (2009) 'Legitimacy and Criminal Justice: The Benefits of Self-regulation', *Ohio State Journal of Criminal Law*, 7: 307–59

Tyler T.R. and Jackson J. (2014) 'Popular Legitimacy and the Exercise of Legal Authority: Motivating Compliance, Cooperation and Engagement', *Psychology, Public Policy and Law*, 20: 78–95

Uglow, S. (1988) *Policing Liberal Society.* Oxford: Oxford University Press

Uleman, J.K. (2010) *An Introduction to Kant's Moral Philosophy.* Cambridge: Cambridge University Press

Villiers, P. and Adlam, R. (2004) *Policing a Safe, Just and Tolerant Society: An International Model for Policing.* Winchester: Waterside Press

Waddington, P.A.J. (1999) *Policing Citizens.* London: UCL Press

Waddington, P.A.J. (2013) 'Introduction', in P.A.J. Waddington, J. Kleinig and M. Wright (eds) *Professional Police Practice. Scenarios and Dilemmas*. Oxford: Oxford University Press, pp.3–24

Waddington, P.A.J., Williams, K., Wright, M. and Newburn, T. (2017) *How People Judge Policing*. Oxford: Oxford University Press

Wakefield, A. (2003) *Selling Security: The Private Policing of Public Space*. Cullompton: Willan

Walker, N. (2000) *Policing in a Changing Constitutional Order*. London: Sweet & Maxwell

Walzer, M. (1983) *Spheres of Justice: A Defence of Pluralism and Equality*. New York: Basic Books

Warnock, M. (1966) *Ethics Since 1900*. 2nd edition. Oxford: Oxford University Press

Weinstein, D. (2011) *Utilitarianism and the New Liberalism*. Cambridge: Cambridge University Press

Weisburd, D. and Neyroud, P. (2013) 'Police Science: Toward a New Paradigm', *Australasian Policing*, 5(2): 13

Westley, W.A. (1970) *Violence and the Police: A Sociological Study of Law, Custom, and Morality*. Cambridge, MA: MIT Press

Westmarland, L. (2005) 'Police Ethics and Integrity: Breaking the Blue Code of Silence', *Policing and Society*, 15(2): 145–65

Westmarland, L. (2014) 'Ethics and Policing', in J. Brown (ed) *The Future of Policing*, London: Routledge, pp.463–75

Westmarland, L. and Rowe, M. (2018) 'Police Ethics and Integrity: Can a New Code Overturn the Blue Code?', *Policing and Society*, 28(7): 854–70

White, R. (2003) 'Environmental Issues and the Criminological Imagination', *Theoretical Criminology*, 7(4): 483–506

White, R. (2008) *Crimes Against Nature: Environmental Criminology and Ecological Justice*. Cullompton: Willan

White, R. (ed) (2010) *Global Environmental Harm: Criminological Perspectives*. Cullompton: Willan

White, R. (2013) 'The Conceptual Contours of Green Criminology', in R. Walters, D. Westerhuisand, and T. Wyatt (eds) *Emerging Issues in Green Criminology: Exploring Power, Justice and Harm*. Basingstoke: Palgrave Macmillan, pp.17–33

White, R. and Graham, H. (2015) 'Greening Justice: Examining the Interfaces of Criminal, Social and Ecological Justice', *British Journal of Criminology*, 55 (5): 845–65

Wilkinson, P. (2011) *Terrorism versus Democracy: The Liberal State Response*. 3rd edition. London: Routledge

Williams, B. (1972) *Morality*. Cambridge: Cambridge University Press. Canto edition 1993

Williams, B. (1973) 'A Critique of Utilitarianism' in J.J.C. Smart and B. Williams, *Utilitarianism: For and Against*. Cambridge: Cambridge University Press, pp.75–155

Williams, B. (1985) 'Morality, the Peculiar Institution', in *Ethics and the Limits of Philosophy*. London: Fontana [page number references to R. Crisp and M. Slote (eds) (1997) *Virtue Ethics*. Oxford: Oxford University Press, pp.45–65]

Williams, B. (1999) 'Tolerating the Intolerable', in S. Mendus (ed) *The Politics of Toleration*. Edinburgh: Edinburgh University Press, pp.65–76

Wilson, J.Q. and Kelling, G.E. (1982) 'Broken Windows: The Police and Neighborhood Safety', *Atlantic Monthly*, March

Winsor, T. (2012) *Independent Review of Police Officer and Staff Remuneration and Conditions Final Report* – Volume 1, March, Cm 8325-I. London: The Stationery Office

Wirrer, R. (2006) 'The Translation of Ethical Standards Into Practice', *Police Research and Management*, 6(3): 71–82

Wolf, S. (1982) 'Moral Saints', *Journal of Philosophy*, 79: 419–39

Wolff, J. (2006) 'Making the World Safe for Utilitarianism', in A. O'Hear (ed) *Political Philosophy*. Cambridge: Cambridge University Press, pp.1–22

Wollstonecraft, M. (1790) *A Vindication of the Rights of Men, in a Letter to the Right Honourable Edmund Burke*. London: Joseph Johnson

Wollstonecraft, M. (1792) *A Vindication of the Rights of Woman with Strictures on Moral and Political Subjects*. London: Joseph Johnson

Wood, D.A. (2012) 'Police Complaints in the United Kingdom', in D. MacAlister (ed) *Police Involved Deaths: The Need for Reform*. Vancouver: British Columbia Civil Liberties Association, pp.73–99

Wood, D.A. (2016a) 'The Importance of Liberal Values within Policing: Police and Crime Commissioners, Police Independence and the Spectre of Illiberal Democracy', *Policing and Society: An International Journal of Research and Policy*, 26(2): 148–64

Wood, D.A. (2016b) 'Can the Individual Survive the Greening of Criminology?', in M. Hall, T. Wyatt, N. South, A. Nurse, G. Potter and J. Maher (eds) *Greening Criminology in the 21st Century: Contemporary Debates and Future Directions in the Study of Environmental Harm*, Abingdon: Routledge, pp.42–58

Wood, D.A. (2018) 'Embedding Learning and Assessment Within Police Practice: The Opportunities and Challenges Arising from the Introduction of the PEQF in England and Wales', *Policing: A Journal of Policy and Practice*, https://doi.org/10.1093/police/pay087

Wood, D.A. and Bryant, R.P. (2015) 'Researching Police Professionalism' in M. Brunger, S. Tong and D. Martin (eds) *Introduction to Policing Research: Taking Lessons from Practice*. Abingdon: Routledge, pp.87–99

Wood, D.A. and Williams, E. (2016) 'The Politics of Establishing Reflexivity as a Core Component of Good Policing', in S. Armstrong, J. Blaustein and A. Henry (eds) *Reflexivity and Criminal Justice: Intersections of Policy, Practice and Research*. London: Palgrave Macmillan, pp.215–36

Wood, D.A., Cockcroft, T., Tong, S. and Bryant, R. (2018) 'The Importance of Context and Cognitive Agency in Developing Police Knowledge: Going Beyond the Police Science Discourse', *The Police Journal: Theory, Practice and Principles*, 91(2): 173–87

Wood, J.D. and Dupont, B. (eds) (2006) *Democracy, Society and the Governance of Security*. Cambridge: Cambridge University Press

Wright, A. (2002) *Policing: An Introduction to Concepts and Practice*. Cullompton: Willan

Wringe, C. (2015) 'Beyond Useful Knowledge: Developing the Subjective Self', *Journal of Philosophy of Education*, 49(1): 32–44

Zakaria, F. (2004) *The Future of Freedom: Illiberal Democracy at Home and Abroad*. London: W.W. Norton & Company

Zifcak, S. (2005) 'Globalizing the Rule of Law: Rethinking Values and Reforming Institutions', in S. Zifcak (ed) *Globalization and the Rule of Law*. London: Routledge, pp.32–64

Index

A

absolutism 69–70
academic law 59
accountability 55, 87, 88, 107
    see also consent, policing by
Adlam, R. 57
Alderson, J. 3, 4, 8, 13, 27, 29, 30–1,
        34, 38, 40, 42, 43, 44, 47, 58, 110
Alison, L. 84–5
ambiguity in morality 36
American Convention on Human
        Rights (1978) 53
Amnesty International 105
amorality 3, 42–3, 86
analytic statements 23
Anscombe, M. 117, 125, 126, 127, 133
Antisocial Behaviour Orders (ASBOs)
        55
apartheid 41
applied ethics 111, 141
Aquinas, St Thomas 50, 121
Aristotle 15, 77, 117, 118, 121–5, 128,
        132, 133, 134, 144
aspirational versus obligatory principles
        44, 71, 110, 111–14
attitudinal approaches to legitimacy 16,
        76, 79
authoritarian societies 79–80, 85–7
authority
    and ethical neutrality 36–7
    government 52
    harm to others principle 102
    and human rights 53, 54, 58
    and justice 46–7
    and legitimacy 76
    national sovereignty 61, 67
    order maintenance 67
    practice versus conceptualisation
        68
    procedural justice 78
    questioning of 87
    trusting junior officers 117–18
    see also legitimacy

B

Bacon, M. 1
bad laws 15
'bads,' distribution of 47
Baier, A. 137–8
balance of probabilities proof standard
        63
balancing of obligations, good policing
        involves 22, 24, 100, 144
Bayley, D.H. 100, 120, 132
Beardsmore, R.W. 7, 8, 46
Beck, U. 47
Beckley, A. 53, 57, 134
Bellamy, R. 38, 40, 103, 104, 108
benevolent dictatorship 33, 86
Bentham, J. 10, 50, 61, 97, 103
Berlin, I. 29
Berman, G. 63, 64
best practice 20
beyond reasonable doubt proof standard
        63
Bill of Rights (1688) 57–8
Bingham, T. 118
Bittner, E. 73
Blau, J. 53
blue code/blue curtain of silence 111
body cameras 121
Bottoms, A. 6, 16, 74, 77
bottom-up approaches 77, 117
Boyd, R. 31, 34, 47
Bradford, B. 6, 16, 74, 76, 77, 78
Bradley, A.W. 58
Brandt, R.B. 10, 44, 68, 74, 111–12,
        113
Brexit 63, 84
Brown, J. 141
Bullock, K. 57, 58
bureaucracy 54
Burke, E. 52

autonomy, individual 32–3, 34
Axinn, S. 104
Ayer, A.J. 23

C

calling, police work as a   1, 17
cameras   121
caring   137
Carlile of Berriew QC, Lord   63, 64
categorical imperative   81, 112
CCTV   121
chaos   33, 34, 47, 73, 95, 96
Charter of the Forest (1217)   51
child sex abuse cases   38–9
Christopher, S.   135
civic values   15
civic virtue   125
civil disobedience   107
civil law   55, 63
civil rights   21
civilian input into police   119
climate change   84
   see also ecological challenges
Coady, C.A.J.   50, 60, 68–70, 71, 86,
   104
Code of Ethics (College of Policing, 2014)
   14, 24
codes of ethics   4, 13–14, 23–5, 49,
   118, 139
coercion   96
cognitive agency   130
Cohen, H.   119, 134, 144
collective will of the police   45
College of Policing   4, 14, 24, 145
Committee on Standards in Public Life
   2
communitarianism   55, 92
community policing, as oxymoronic
   term   22, 36
community responsiveness   55
community rights   55
competence   18, 126
competitive authoritarianism   86
complaints   119
compliance   18, 25, 43, 49, 54, 79,
   118
compulsion   87
conflict, inevitability of   33, 36
conflict avoidance   34
conflict resolution   37
conflicts of interest   39
conscience   44, 68, 113

consensual legitimacy   20, 67, 75–9, 84,
   85, 86, 93, 143
consensus   22, 33, 34, 35, 36
consent, policing by   21–2, 54, 55, 56,
   69, 75–9, 84
consequential ethical reasoning   95–115
   contradictions in   122
   defined   10
   dirty hands doctrine   103–8
   harm to others principle   100–3
   and human rights   53, 58
   lesser evil ethics   83, 108–9
   noble cause corruption   98–100
   pragmatic aspects of   100
   principles   44
   ring of Gyges test   120
   and utilitarianism   96–8
   utilitarianism   96–8
   and virtue ethics   121–2, 125, 126,
      132
constitutions   87, 96
contested practice, policing as   4
context   16, 128–33
control orders   63–4, 105
corruption
   ethical policing is more than the
      absence of   5, 13, 17, 42
   identifying unethical behaviours   42
   and immorality   41
   motivations for   131
   noble cause corruption   41, 97,
      98–100
   ring of Gyges test   120, 131, 132
   and will   134
counter-terrorism   64–5, 66, 105
courage   122, 134
covert methods   7
Crank, J.   98
criminal justice system   67–8, 91–2
Crisp, R.   117, 121, 125, 129
critical friends   2–4
cultural context   128–9
culture, police   111, 121
Cunningham, M.   145

D

Dancy, J.   10, 129, 138
data integrity   6

Davis, H. 62, 134
decision-making processes
  bad decisions 109
  building moral capacity for 118
  discretion 134–5
  giving *all* police officers moral space
    118
  and human rights 57, 68, 80, 84
  indecision not an option 109
  lesser evil ethics 83, 108–9
  moral obligations as aspirational
    113
  open and transparent 25
  pragmatic aspects of 102–3
  speed of 84–5, 101, 106
  when asked to do something immoral
    82–3
decriminalisation 45
Delattre, E.J. 1, 4, 26, 34, 57, 84, 95,
    97, 100–1, 104, 109, 133
democracy
  history of 33, 38, 50–2
  and human rights 62
  illiberal democracy 85
  and justice 46
  Police and Crime Commissioners
    (PCCs) 55
  policing by consent 56–7, 76
  rights-based thinking 50–1
  social democracy 86
  see also liberal democracies
democratic accountability 55
democratic policing 43
Den Boer, M. 61
deontological ethics
  and Christianity 126
  and consequential reasoning 95
  contradictions in 122
  and duty 128
  harm to others principle 100
  human rights 53, 58, 68
  legitimacy 81, 143
  and moral agency 132
  moral obligations 43–7, 111, 112,
    113
  universalism 129
  utilitarianism 97, 98
  and virtue ethics 121–2, 125

Dershowitz, A.M. 50, 60, 65, 106,
    107, 108
deservedness 124
Devlin, Lord 45
Dicey, A.V. 118
Dick, P. 144
dictatorship 33, 36, 46, 51, 85
dirty hands doctrine 103–8, 115, 143
Dirty Harry scenarios 97, 104, 106,
    108, 115, 143
'dirty' situations of police work 95
discretion, police 25, 99, 118, 119,
    134–8, 144
discrimination 44, 67
disinterestedness 36, 47, 48
Disley, E. 65, 66
distributive justice 47, 77, 125
domestic violence 101, 102
Dryzek, J.S. 86
due process 75
Dunleavy, P. 86
duties, positional 14, 16, 49, 59, 70,
    82, 128
duty, notions of 43–7, 51, 58, 128
duty of care 7, 54, 128
Dworkin, R. 61, 135

E
ecological challenges 21, 84, 85, 102,
    143
elitism 84
emotional harm 101
emotive theory of ethics 23
empathy 36
empirical statements 23
empiricism 6, 20, 74–5, 76, 77, 78, 81
end justifies the means 97–8, 111
Enlightenment 51–2, 60, 73, 125, 142
environmental rights 21
epistemic pluralism 138
equality 52, 87, 89
Esparza, L.E. 53
ethical codes *see* codes of ethics
ethical dilemmas 64, 109
ethical neutrality 29–48, 142, 143
  and liberalism 29
  limitations of 38–41
  as misnomer 38

ethical neutrality (continued)
   versus moral absolutism   69–70
   policing historically associated with
      3–4
Etzioni, A.   67–8
EU policing   65–6
European Convention on Human Rights
   (ECHR)   49, 53, 58, 62
European Court of Human Rights   53
Europol   65–6
everyday occurrences, ethical policing in
   26, 56, 96, 99, 101
evidence-based practice   6–7, 20, 145
Ewing, K.D.   63
exceptional individuals, police as   1
exceptionalism   105
existence of police, debating   21
experience, practical   78, 123, 134, 136,
   144
extreme circumstances   14, 36, 52,
   80–1, 99, 105
extremism   68

F
fairness   16, 53, 67, 75, 91
   see also justice as fairness
female philosophers' approaches to moral
   discourse   137
feminist philosophy   52, 143
Feyerabend, P.   2, 138
fire brigade policing   39
Fitzpatrick, T.   122
Fleming, J.   1
following orders   58, 118–19
Foot, P.   121, 126, 133, 135
freedom of choice   44
freedom of speech   58
freedoms generally see liberty
French Revolution   52, 61
fundamentalism   68
Furedi, F.   32, 101
future generations   102

G
Gearty, C.   50, 53, 60, 62, 73
Giddens, A.   47
Gilligan, C.   137
globalisation   53, 59–60

Godwin, W.   97
golden mean doctrine   122, 126
Goldstein, H.   39
good life   125
Gottschalk, P.   18
government
   authority of   87
   fragmentation of   59–60, 67
   and human rights   64
   national sovereignty   60, 61–6, 67,
      73
   rights-based thinking   51–2
   state crimes   52
   see also authority; democracy; liberal
      democracies
Gray, J.   29, 33, 34, 35, 36, 44, 51, 60,
   67, 68, 73
Green, L.   44–5
Grint, K.   126
Guantanamo Bay   105

H
Haggard, P.   58
Haldane, J.   46
harm to others principle   37, 83, 100–3,
   113, 143
Hart, H.L.A.   44, 45, 50
Hart-Devlin dispute   45
hate crime   102
Held, D.   34, 46, 61
hierarchical structures   58
history of police   3–4, 20–1
Hobbes, T.   32, 33, 46, 51, 66, 73, 85
Holgersson, S.   18
Home Secretaries   64, 119, 141
homosexuality   45
Hopkins Burke, R.   22, 38, 55
Horne, A.   63, 64
Hughes, G.   67
Hughes, J.   16, 17
human dignity   15, 51, 58, 62, 82
human flourishing   122, 125
human rights   9, 49–72, 142–3
   aspirational versus obligatory
      principles   71, 110
   breaches of   55–6, 63–5
   challenges of embedding in policing
      54–7

consensual legitimacy 84
and counter-terrorism 63–5
and the decline of political realism 68
dirty hands doctrine 104
do not necessarily achieve their aims 66–70
and ethical neutrality 35
harm to others principle 102
history of 50–4
as independent values 79
institutionalisation of 15, 49, 53–7, 60, 62, 67
international universalism of 60, 61–6, 142
legalistic perceptions of 49–50, 54, 59, 70, 143
means and ends discourse 98
as modern dominant expression of morality 53, 62
moral component 54
and moral obligations 110, 113
moralism 68–9
as parents of law 50
and PCCs 55
peremptory norms 44
and police legitimacy 21, 92
as potential moral basis for policing 57–60
as a relationship 70
second order to safety and security 67
in times of crisis/emergency 55–6, 64, 65
Human Rights Act (HRA, 1998) 40, 49, 53, 57, 58, 59
Hursthouse, R. 8, 122–3

I
idealisation of policing 19
see also perfectionism
Ignatieff, M. 50, 53, 60, 62, 73, 83, 108
illegal acts 107
see also rule-bending
illiberal democracy 85, 86
immorality 14–15, 41–3, 80, 81, 86, 104, 127

impartiality 30, 36, 37, 47
imposition, ethics felt as an 58, 69
Independent Commission into the Future of Policing 141
independent complaints investigations 119
Independent Office for Police Conduct (IOPC) 119
Independent Police Commission 141
individualism 38, 51, 61, 62, 76, 84, 92, 142
see also liberal individualism
inequality 38, 89, 124
intelligence-led policing 7, 39
intention 82, 126
intergovernmental policing 65–6
interventions, government 37
intuition 40, 62, 123
Ip, J. 64–5

J
Jackson, J. 42, 74, 76, 77, 78
JAPAN 115n3
Johnson, P. 57, 58
Johnston, A. 64, 84
Joint Committee on Human Rights (JCHR) 63
Joint Investigative Teams (JITs) 66
journey, ethical policing as a 19, 25, 145–6
judicial oversight 63
just deserts 124
just society 88–9
JUSTICE 63
justice as fairness 9, 43, 46, 74, 81, 88–92, 95, 143

K
Kant, I. 4, 43–7, 51, 58, 71, 81, 88, 98, 104, 112, 114, 125, 126, 128, 129, 132, 134, 137, 143
Kempa, M. 119
Kidd, I.J. 138
Kinsella, E.A. 136
Kleinig, J. 3, 4, 10, 24, 41, 58, 96, 97, 98, 99–100, 105, 106, 108, 110, 111, 120, 121, 134, 145

Klockars, C.B.   95, 97, 104, 106
knowing-in-practice   136
knowledge and cognitive agency
     129–30, 138
Kotzee, B.   129

L
law enforcement, policing is more than
     21
lawful orders   119
law-morals relationship   44–5, 49, 54
Lawrence, Stephen   3
learning organisations   3, 25, 109, 133,
     136
least worst outcomes   108
legal obligations, versus moral obligations
     14, 59
legal positivism   44–5
legal principles/conventions   21
legitimacy
     attitudinal approaches to legitimacy
          16, 76, 79
     and authority   76
     consensual legitimacy   20, 67, 75–9,
          84, 85, 86, 93, 143
     and corruption   42
     democratic authority   74
     and human rights   57
     and the law   21
     liberal democracies   21, 79–87
     moral legitimacy   78, 83–5, 93, 143
     normative approaches   20
     perceptions of   16, 76
     philosophical accounts of   74–5
     and power relations   15
     procedural justice   9, 20, 21, 74–9,
          90–1, 93, 143
     public compliance   75
     state legitimacy and torture   107
lesser evil ethics   83, 108–9
Leviathan (Hobbes)   46, 85
liberal, definition of term   29
liberal democracies
     and the contested nature of policing
          20–2
     and human rights   53, 56
     and justice   46–7, 143
     and legitimacy   79–87

and the moral space of policing   96
and peace   67
policing by consent   76
political context for policing
     21–2
rights-based thinking   51
liberal individualism   31–7, 38, 47, 55,
     101, 125, 142
liberal policing   29–48
     see also ethical neutrality
liberalism   31–7, 84, 85, 142
liberty   29, 32, 58, 65, 76, 86, 89,
     101
Liberty   63
Liebling, A.   15
lies   44, 123
live and let live   36
Locke, J.   51, 88
logical positivism   23
London riots, 2011   66
loyalty   83, 111, 121
Lustgarten, L.   21, 59

M
MacAllister, J.   130
Machiavelli, N,   103
MacIntyre, A.   4, 8, 9, 13, 32, 35, 36,
     43, 47, 55, 59, 60, 70, 74, 80, 82,
     83, 125–6, 128–9, 130–1, 132,
     136
Macpherson Report   35
MacVean, A.   2, 16
Magna Carta   50, 52, 57–8
majoritarian mechanisms   22, 54, 56
Manning, P.K.   9, 43, 57, 87
Marks, M.   117
Marshall, G.   21
Martinich, A.P.   33
Marx, G.T.   6, 30
maximum security society   30
May, Theresa   66
meaningful statements   23
means and ends discourse   97–8, 111
Mendus, S.   32
Metropolitan Police   21, 76
Midgley, M.   137
Mill, J.S.   32, 37, 86, 92, 95, 97, 100–3,
     111, 113, 122, 124, 143

Miller, S.   4, 5, 34, 40, 98, 104, 128
minor offences   99
miscarriages of justice   92, 98
mistaken morality   100
mistakes in judgement   25
modus vivendi   35
Montefiore, A.   41
Montesquieu, (Baron de) C.   99
moral, definition of   41
moral agency
    going beyond intention   82
    and human rights   59, 70
    liberal democracies   80, 81–2
    linking of ethics to practice   130
    normative approaches   20
    police officers as moral agents   4,
        13, 118
    and the reflective practitioner   136
    and virtue ethics   129, 130, 132
moral communities   15–16
moral legitimacy   78, 83–5, 93, 143
moral obligations
    beyond legal/positional duty   59
    consequential ethical reasoning   98,
        109–14
    cost of   113, 127
    deontological ethics   43–7, 127
    and following orders   58
    at the heart of good policing   14–18
    human rights   51, 53, 58
    versus moral aspirations   109–14
    morally binding obligations   58, 71,
        102, 106, 110, 111–14, 118, 120,
        132, 143
moral performance   15–16
moral philosophy
    amorality versus immorality   41–3
    and human rights   62
    and legitimacy   74–5
    not necessarily abstract   23
    and perception of legitimacy   76
    and police legitimacy   74–5
    and policing   22–4
    rights-based thinking   50, 51
    role of reasoning   7
    seen as less objective than the law
        59
    use of 'right' and 'good'   97

moral reasoning, importance of   6–8,
    22
moral rights, protection of   40, 96
moral space   79, 80, 118, 143, 144
moralism   50, 60, 68–70, 71, 86, 135
'morally wrong,' use of term   127–8
Morrell, K.   74
Morrill, R.   22, 55
motivations for moral actions   131–2,
    134
Mulhall, S.   55, 92
Murdoch, I.   137

N
National Decision Model (NDM)   24,
    25
national sovereignty   60, 61–6, 67, 73
natural law   50, 51, 60
Nazi Germany   14, 31, 41, 52, 60, 66,
    82
necessity   57, 103, 104, 108, 144
Newburn, T.   3, 76
Neyroud, P.   2, 53, 57, 58, 134
Nicomachean Ethics (Aristotle)   121–2
9/11   60, 63, 65, 105
noble cause corruption   41, 97,
    98–100
Noddings, N.   137
non-consequential ethical reasoning
    9–10, 44, 110
normative approaches   19–20, 46, 77–8,
    130
Northern Ireland   37
Nowell-Smith, P.H.   24

O
Oakeshott, M.   38
objectivity   8, 119, 134
obligation, moral *see* moral obligations
office of constable   119
O'Hear, A.   2
On Liberty (Mill, 1859)   32, 86
operational realities of police work
    95–115
order maintenance   66–7, 96
orders, following   58, 118–19
ordinary citizens, police as   1
organisational justice   19, 136–7

outcomes and principles 44, 110
over-formalisation 99
over-principled policing 110

P
Padfield, N. 59
Pagon, M. 109–10
Paine, T. 52
particularism 10, 128–33, 137
peaceful coexistence 33, 34, 35, 38
Peasants' Revolt 51
Peelian policing 55, 76
peremptory norms 44
perfectionism 5, 10, 25
personal liability for actions 119
phronēsis (practical wisdom) 118, 126, 133–4
Plato 46, 77, 85, 119–20
pluralism, moral 33–4
pluralistic nature of humanity 35
Polanyi, M. 138
Police and Crime Commissioners (PCCs) 55, 66, 76, 119
Police Federation 119
police reform 19, 144
Policing Education Qualifications Framework (PEQF) 145
Policing Liberal Society (Uglow, 1988) 29, 31, 35, 37
popular will, police conforming to 54, 56, 57, 79
populism 85
positional duties 14, 16, 49, 59, 70, 82, 128
positive law 50, 61
power relations
    authoritarian societies 85
    and legitimacy 15, 46
    liberal individualism 34
    moralism 70
    redressing imbalances in 48
pracademics 145
practical wisdom (*phronēsis*) 118, 126, 133–4
practice, ethics in 95–115, 117–39, 141
practice, policing as a 136
pragmatic policing 95–115

Prevention of Terrorism Act (2005) 63
Prince, The (Machiavelli, 1981) 103
principled policing 29–48, 49, 56, 58, 84, 86, 110, 129, 142
Principled Policing (Alderson, 1998) 29, 34, 40
prisons 15
Pritchard, D. 130
privacy 30, 76, 84
private realm 38, 45, 46, 103
privilege 34, 46, 89, 124
proactive policing 38, 39, 48
problem-oriented policing 39
procedural justice
    imperfect procedural justice 91–2
    liberal democracies 81, 86
    literature 6
    need for philosophy 145
    police conduct 110
    and police legitimacy 9, 20, 21, 74–9, 90–1, 93, 143
    policing as moral performance 16
    Rawls' ethics 43, 91
professional learning 135–6, 145
    see also training of police
professional standards 16–18
professionalisation of policing 75
progressive thinking 40
proportionality 57, 64, 71, 102–3, 134–5, 144
public office 103, 125
public principles 44–6
Punch, M. 3, 39, 42
punitive approaches to unethical policing 3, 17, 142
purpose of policing 112, 125, 141

R
race relations 35
racial ideologies 34, 41
racial profiling 44
randomised control trials 145
Ratcliffe, J. 39
rationality
    human rights 62, 68
    and moral obligations 113
    and morality 7

peremptory norms 44
procedural justice 89, 91
versus reasonableness 71
and reflective practice 137
science 73
and the veil of ignorance 90
and virtue ethics 125
Rawls, J. 9, 32, 43, 46, 47, 73–4, 75,
    81, 87–92, 93, 104, 110–11, 112,
    137, 143
realities of police work 95–115
reasonable doubt 99
reasonable suspicion 63
recruitment of police officers 133
redistributive justice 47
reflective practice 6, 10, 18–19, 71,
    118, 134–9, 144
Reiner, R. 4, 13, 21, 30, 34, 36, 55,
    57, 59, 73, 76, 87, 121, 134
religion 36, 53, 62, 68, 125–6
Republic, The (Plato) 46, 85, 119–20
Rescher, N. 22, 35
resilience 1
resistance to police as an institution
    21
restraint 39
reward systems 17
right to rule 78
rights-based thinking 49–72
ring of Gyges test 119–21, 131, 132
riots, London 2011 66
role morality 128
Rotherham abuse scandal 3
Rousseau, J.-J. 88
Rowe, M. 42
Royal Ulster Constabulary (RUC) 37
rule of law 21, 100, 118
rule-bending 97–8, 99, 100, 103–8,
    120
Russell, B. 122, 123
Russia 31
Ryan, A. 32

S

Sampford, C. 61
Sandel, M. 15, 47, 124, 125
Saudi Arabia 62
Savile, Jimmy 38

Scanlon, T.M. 49–50
Schmitt, C. 66
Schön, D. 10, 18–19, 135, 139, 144
science 2, 6, 24, 73, 74, 76, 135, 138,
    145
search warrants 106
security 47, 63–4, 67
selectivity 46
self-preservation 82–3
self-sacrifice 83
Sen, A. 47, 50, 52, 60, 71, 73, 75
Senge, P.M. 3, 25, 109
senior police officers 117–18
sense of justice 100
Sherman, L.W. 3, 145
Shue, H. 60, 105
Sidgwick, H. 97
Simmonds, N.E. 44, 97, 103
Simmons, A.J. 8, 9, 14, 16, 75, 76
Singer, P. 112
Skinns, L. 75
Sklansky, D.A. 19, 117, 119, 136
slavery 15, 60, 90, 105
Slote, M. 117, 121, 125, 129, 130,
    137
Smith, J. 64
social contract 88, 90
social democracy 86
social justice 53
social rights 21
socialism 53
Society of Evidence Based Policing
    (SEBP) 145
society's understandings of policing 19,
    137
socio-legal reasoning 21
Sophie's Choice 108–9
Spencer, H. 97
Spindler, P. 2, 38–9
St Thomas Aquinas 50, 121
standards of proof 63
state actors, police as 16
state crimes 52, 67
Steinhoff, U. 105, 107, 110
Stenning, P.C. 59
Stevens Commission 141
Stone, M. 57–8, 59, 70
Styron, W. 108

Sun, I.Y. 78
sunset clauses 65
supervision of police officers 121
Swift, A. 55, 92

T

Tankebe, J. 6, 16, 74, 77, 78
technology 24, 121
teleological reasoning 123–5, 130
terrorism 7, 26, 36, 56, 60, 63–5
Theory of Justice, A (Rawls, 1971) 74
Theory of the Good and the Right, A
    (Brandt, 1979) 112
ticking time bombs 97, 104–5, 106,
    108
tolerance 48
toleration 32, 76
torture 60, 98, 104, 105–7
training of police 57, 130, 132
Tralau, J. 47, 50, 66, 73
transformative learning 130
transnational issues 60, 63, 64, 65
transparency 25, 46, 84
Treaty of Lisbon 65, 66
Treaty of Westphalia 61
trivialisation 46
trust 78, 117–18, 119, 121
truthfulness 122, 123
Tyler, T. 6, 16, 74, 75, 77, 90

U

Uglow, S. 8, 13, 27, 29, 30, 31, 35, 37,
    39, 40, 42, 43, 47
Uleman, J.K. 81
unethical behaviours, identifying 42
unethical duties 14, 17
unethical policing, ethical policing is
    more than the absence of 5,
    142
United Nations 52, 58, 105
United Nations Convention Against
    Torture (UNCAT) 105
Universal Declaration of Human Rights
    (UDHR) 49, 52, 53, 58, 62
universal ethical statements 129
university police stations 144
unprincipled policing 41–2, 45
USA 60, 63, 65, 77, 105

utilitarianism 10, 90, 96–100, 103–15,
    124, 126, 143

V

value judgements 38
values, explicit articulation of 48
veil of ignorance 89–90
victims
    harm to others principle 101–2
    indirect 102
    victims as offenders 37
vigilante groups 68, 100
Villiers, P. 57
violence 96, 102
virtue ethics 6, 10, 117–39, 144
vulnerable, protection of the 7, 33, 38,
    40, 47, 54

W

Waddington, P.A.J. 1, 3, 4, 6, 7, 17, 18,
    21, 22, 34, 36, 59, 74, 76, 77, 78,
    87, 134, 142
Walker, N. 21, 87
Warnock, M. 23, 137
wealth distribution 47, 67, 124
Western-centric thinking 60, 73, 142
Westmarland, L. 42, 111, 121
will, and virtue ethics 133–4
Williams, B. 19, 32, 104, 123, 126, 127
Winsor Report 18
Wirrer, R. 58
wisdom 122–3, 133
    see also phronēsis (practical wisdom)
witnesses 101–2
Wolf, S. 137
Wolfenden Report 45
Wolff, J. 10, 40, 100, 103–4, 111
Wollstonecraft, M. 52
Wood, D.A. 7, 19, 22, 38, 47, 55, 76,
    84, 85, 86, 102, 119, 129–30,
    135, 142
Wright, A. 4, 13, 20
Wringe, C. 130

Z

Zakaria, F. 85
zero-tolerance policing 39
Zifcak, S. 61